IRAN

Since the Islamic revolutionary movement overthrew the "Peacock Throne" (the Shah) in 1979, the Islamic Republic has maintained its credibility and the loyalty of the people of Iran. It has survived an extremely destructive war with Iraq, isolation from the West and the rest of the Middle East except Syria, and the death of Ayatollah Khomeini.

This book explores the social transformation of Iran in this period stressing the importance of political culture and ideology. It argues that the systematic building of a legitimate Islamic political culture is the key to the success of the regime.

The authors of this book address specific aspects of Iran's political culture within a general theoretical framework laid out in the introduction. There is discussion of a wide range of topics ranging from the relationship of the individual to society to "Westoxication", from Shi'ism to the Islamization of film culture.

This book will be used by students and scholars of the Middle East, of politics and political sociology and by those involved in the study of revolutions.

IRAN

Political Culture in the Islamic Republic

Edited by

Samih K. Farsoun and Mehrdad Mashayekhi

London and New York

First published 1992
by Routledge
11 New Fetter Lane, London EC4P 4EE

Simultaneously published in the USA and Canada
by Routledge
a division of Routledge, Chapman and Hall, Inc.
29 West 35th Street, New York, NY 10001

Typeset in Palatino by Witwell Ltd, Southport
Printed and bound in Great Britain by
T.J. Press (Padstow) Ltd, Padstow, Cornwall

British Library Cataloguing in Publication Data
A catalogue record for this book is available from the British
Library

0–415–03142–7

Library of Congress Cataloging in Publication Data
Iran: political culture in the Islamic Republic/edited by Samih
K. Farsoun and Mehrdad Mashayekhi.
p. cm.
Includes bibliographical references and index.
ISBN 0–415–03142–7
1. Iran-Politics and government-1979- 2. Political culture-
-Iran. I. Farsoun, Samih K. II. Mashayekhi, Mehrdad.
DS318.825.I65   1992
955.05′4-dc20
91-36455
CIP

CONTENTS

v

TABLES

FOREWORD: IRAN AND THE PRISM OF POLITICAL CULTURE

Mansour Farhang

The birth of the Islamic Republic and its evolution over the past thirteen years seem to support the view that revolutions, like earthquakes, come as a surprise and defy prediction in the course of their development. This is not meant to imply that we are unable to understand the forces that produce and shape revolutionary change. Studies of modern revolutions have yielded plenty of information and insights about their origins and inner dynamics. What remains beyond reach is a theory of revolution that could penetrate the phenomenon across time and cultures. To be sure, modern social revolutions show significant similarities in their inception and unfolding, but they possess such unique qualities and historical particularities that no single theoretical perspective can be applied to them all. Moreover, the literature on each modern revolution contains diverse and often contradictory notions of how they happened and why they evolved as they did. The American and French (let alone the Russian and Chinese) revolutions are still the subject of contending theoretical claims. This record is unlikely to be improved by scholarly work on the Iranian Revolution. The extreme complexity of the phenomenon makes it unrealistic to expect otherwise.

The diverse and elusive cultural context of modern revolutionary change seems to be an insurmountable obstacle to attempts at theory building. For, in the process of revolutionary transformation, people often find themselves in new and unexpected situations, but individuals or groups do not always respond to the challenges of the new situation in uniform ways. There is a mediating or intervening mechanism, a prism through which possibilities are seen and refracted. As

Barrington Moore, Jr has explained:

> The intervening variable, which it is convenient to call culture, screens out certain parts of the objective situation and emphasizes other parts. There are limits to the amount of variations in perception and human behavior that can come from this source. Still the residue of truth in the cultural explanation is that what looks like an opportunity or a temptation to one group of people will not necessarily seem so to another group with a different historical experience and living in a different form of society.[1]

The need to focus on the prism of culture in the study of the Iranian Revolution is particularly acute because it is the first modern revolution whose idiom of discourse is exclusively derived from native sources and whose moral claims are advanced in confrontation with the ideological and political currents of the contemporary world. Political Culture is a dynamic and evolving force; it is the product of both the collective history of a society and the life histories of its members; it provides the subjective orientation to politics and shapes the individuals' perception of who they are and how they differ from others. Cultural norms have a direct and habitual impact on how people evaluate their social world. Political power is so sensitive to cultural bearings that cultural variations play a decisive role in determining the political development of the society.

The paradigms of "modernization" and "dependency" (the two schools of thought that informed the study of the Third World in the 1960s and 1970s) cannot adequately explain either the causes or the consequences of the Iranian Revolution. These analytic categories, when used in a reductionist manner, tend to disregard or minimize the role of religion and political culture in the affairs of society. The Western academic literature on Iran before the fall of the Pahlavi monarchy shows an embarrassing lack of attention to Shi'ism as a religion or a cultural system. In this regard most Iranian intellectuals were equally negligent. The view of secularism, as an inevitable and irreversible process, was so much a part of the liberal and leftist perspective that few partisan observers saw the need to question it. The Iranian Revolution was a watershed event in illustrating that comprehension of political/cultural particularities is indispensable for a coherent understanding of political behavior and social change. This is especially so in societies where exercise of power is not sufficiently institutionalized. As James Manor has explained:

> The political dramas that are being enacted and the imaginings that occur in the Third World are often concerned with more than just political authority and economic development. They often entail attempts to shape, define, create or suppress civil society and popular reactions thereto. They can also entail deep, complex cultural conflicts, encounters between world-views and sets of values, to inspire illusions or devotion, and to transform reality. In other words, the scope of politics in Third World settings is usually broader than in the West, and our modes of analysis must accommodate themselves to that reality more effectively than the familiar paradigms have done.[2]

Political culture is not an all-explanatory concept; it only provides a setting for enquiry. Thus the application of the approach to the study of politics should not minimize the importance of learning how material forces and social institutions influence the course of a political movement or the priorities of its leaders and followers. The concept of political culture may defy the idea of searching for a comprehensive theory, but it promises to enhance our understanding of what is actually happening in the society.

It is important to bear in mind that political culture refers to what people believe to be the case in a given situation, not what is actually the case. Attitudes toward power, authority and the role of the self in the social order are among the important attributes of political culture. In Iran, where an uninterrupted history of despotism has made its mark on the national consciousness, people tend to perceive the political world more with emotion, fatalism and distrust than with ideological or interest-oriented considerations. The beliefs and values of the country's educated and Westernized élite differ in important ways from those of the populace, but when it comes to political behavior, significant characteristics are shared across social classes. In the 1979 Revolution there were no compelling structural–material reasons for the Islamists' hegemonic control of the Iranian state and society. The emphasis is on the term *hegemonic*, because given the socio-historical causes of the Iranian Revolution it was unavoidable that the active clergy were going to play a principal role in the new regime. It was the failure of the alternative political formations to seize the space between the clergy's firm position of leadership and their potential to gain monopoly control that resulted in the ascendancy of the Islamists. The destructive behavior of the secularists served the religious forces well. Yet, the Islamists were not alone in their preference for exclusive rule. Most of the organized groups of the period had similar potential.

Perception of politics as a zero-sum game is what most Iranians, regardless of ideology or class origin, have in common. Centuries of invasion from without and oppression from within have conditioned the Iranians to see politics as an interplay between peril and refuge from peril. Iran's Islamic rulers maintain that the only way to cure this malady is to restore a set of former conditions associated with the seventh century dominion of Prophet Mohammad and Imam Ali (the founder of Shi'ism and the fourth successor to the Prophet). This atavistic view compels the Iranian theocrats to stress behavior modification in the domain of social morality as a central aspect of their effort to obtain a quick return to an imagined glorious past.

The dictates of puritanical atavism are largely confined to defining standards of acceptability pertaining to such matters as courtship and socio-sexual mores, dress code, public entertainment and popular art. In these religio-cultural spheres the governing authorities reject the distinction between the personal and the political. Secularists are assumed to have seditious attitudes toward Islam and, consequently, even their appearance as participants in dissident activity could subject them to accusations of "acting against God" and "corrupting the earth." What is interesting about the Islamization of social life is that while the state is busy imposing rules and standards, many Iranians find ways of carrying out their favorite activities behind closed doors. Centuries of subjugation to despotism has taught Iranians the skill to surmount governmental interference in their private lives. The Islamic vice squads have encouraged social cynicism rather than the emergence of a new public morality. Iranians who have long displayed a gift for adjusting to officially sanctioned restrictions usually manage to circumvent the will of authorities.

The Islamic Republic has produced an entirely new political élite, but the structure of power remains as autocratic as it was before the revolution. While Ayatollah Khomeini was alive, his decisions, like those of the Shah, were presented *ex cathedral* and beyond challenge. The exaltation of Khomeini as the sole source of authority for an entire political system was virtually identical with the flattery exacted on behalf of the Shah by his élite. The Shah was routinely described by the Iranian mass media as His Imperial Majesty, the Shah of Shahs, the Light of the Aryans, the Founder of a New Civilization and the Great Commander of the Armed Forces. And Ayatollah Khomeini was referred to as the *Imam-e-Ommat*, the Founder and Leader of the Islamic Republic, the Hope of the World's Oppressed and the Commander of the Faithful. This astonishing continuity in the public extolment of the two men, in spite of their vast differences in thought and personality, is a telling commentary on Iranian political life. Only a culture-based analysis can provide some clue as to why a traditional religious populist man and a secular modernist monarch, as uncontested leaders of their country, chose to project themselves as they did, and why the general public seemed to see the continuity as normal.

Similarly, the Islamists have shown no more interest in building a civil society than their monarchist predecessors. Neither have they done anything to establish a functional or institutional distinction between the state and the regime. They have simply maintained the pre-revolutionary practice of organizing and using the state as an instrument of the regime. Another inherited practice by the revolutionary officials is their intolerance toward the formation of independent professional associations, civic groups or trade unions. As in the past, all such organizations are controlled by the state and their leaders are closely tied to the security or executive agencies of government.

Exaggeration is a common trait in all politicians, but the leaders of some countries engage in it more than others. The Islamic authorities in Iran certainly fall into this category. For example, in their zeal to claim that Islam possesses perfect knowledge of all human endeavor, Iran's clerical spokesmen have, over the past thirteen years, repeatedly maintained that Islam has its own distinct answers to the economic problems facing the country. In actuality, however, the pre-revolutionary capitalist system, weakened by additional defects and inequities, has remained in place, and the economic performance of the Islamic Republic has been extremely poor. Declining real income, falling standard of living, massive unemployment, shrinking oil revenues, worsening distribution of wealth and income, increasing migration to the cities, underproduction, inefficient utilization of both industrial and agricultural capacity, and rapid population growth plague the Iranian Republic. The ruling clerics' original popular base, the urban poor and lower middle class, has suffered most from the deteriorating economic situation. Based on the Iranian experience, Islam may be a cultural and legal alternative to liberalism and socialism but it has virtually nothing to say about the practical organization of economic life in the contemporary world. Since Khomeini's death the government has tried to abandon his rhetorical call for an Islamic economics in favor of some concrete policy options and programmes. President Rafsanjani clearly wants a mixed economy managed by technocrats, preferably Western-trained. Mr Rafsanjani is aware that progress in this direction requires normalization of the country's foreign relations. This necessary task, however, has to be pursued with extreme caution because, after thirteen years of justifying immense material and human sacrifices in the name of exporting the revolution, the Islamic Republic cannot afford to appear to be rushing toward conventional diplomacy and international accommodation.

In spite of its repressive rule and massive failure in the economic realm, the Islamic Republic may yet become a catalyst for a progressive change in the Iranian political culture. For the revolutionary transformation of the society has significantly bridged, from a socio-cultural perspective, the gap between the political élite and the masses. This is a positive development in Iran, despite the unappealing character of the leadership. The revolution has also succeeded in ending overt foreign interference in the internal affairs of the country, a process that had gone on for more than a century. These achievements contribute to Iran's political maturity. Moreover, the revolution has made Iranians far more conscious of secularism, pluralism and popular sovereignty. The experience of theocracy has meant systematic negation of such ideas and arrangements, and as such, has given a new value to what is absent. Ordinary Iranians might not express their longings in these terms, but their aspiration for a less regimented life seems evident, as does their growing hostility to manipulation of the symbols of Islam for repressive purposes.

The immensely popular revolution of 1979 did not change the politics of fragmentation, exclusion, and imposition in Iranian society. Nearly all political elements on the scene, whether by action or inaction, contributed to the failure. Thus for the third time in this century (once in the Constitutional Revolution of 1906–11, and again in the Mossadeq era of 1951–53) Iranians, after a successful struggle against despotism, failed to rise above their entrenched political culture and ended up with a new form of repressive regime. The irony, as well as the challenge, of the situation appears when one considers the fact that the ideology of the new order has deep roots in the popular religious culture of the country. It may be a blessing that Iranians can no longer hold the intruding "other" responsible for what has happened to their homeland. This is a priceless lesson for a people who habitually blame foreigners for their own flaws and failings.

NOTES

1 Barrington Moore, Jr, *Social Origins of Dictatorship and Democracy* (Beacon Press, Boston, 1966), p. 485.
2 James Manor, *Rethinking Third World Politics* (Longman Publishers, New York, 1991), pp. 4–5.

1

INTRODUCTION
Iran's political culture

Samih K. Farsoun and Mehrdad Mashayekhi

Contrary to the expectations of experts, the Islamic Revolution of Iran persisted, its government stabilized and its hold on Iranian society consolidated in spite of the many and powerful challenges it had faced since it came to power in 1979. The Islamic Republic survived a devastating and immensely costly eight-year war with Iraq, a crippling economic and arms embargo imposed by the West, a campaign of assassinations of its leadership by internal enemies as well as political opposition from varied opponents. The political, social and economic turmoil in the Islamic Republic, caused by internal opposition of the Mojahedeen, the liberals and the left as well as the ethnic minorities, was only surpassed by the active efforts of the external enemies to destabilize and destroy the Islamic regime. Iran was isolated without allies in Western Europe or the Middle East except for Syria. Perhaps only the Cold War saved the Islamic Republic from a potential direct Western/American assault or war. Instead, the United States, Western Europe, Kuwait and Saudi Arabia, and the Soviet Union aided Iraq's war effort against Iran. The final military impasse between Iraq and Iran before the ceasefire in August 1988 was possible partly because the United States supplied Iraq with crucial military intelligence.

All the above challenges as well as the death of its founder and charismatic leader, Ayatollah Rouhollah Khomeini, not only failed to destabilize the Islamic Republic and topple its leadership but also failed to alienate the vast support of the proponents of the Islamic Revolution. Despite the fact of the great human and material losses during the war, the severe repression of all opposition groups, and the extensive author-

1

itarian character of the state, the Islamic Republic nevertheless managed to develop a wide social base, legitimacy and loyalty among broad segments of the Iranian people. How was that possible? In other words, how did the Islamic Republic manage to renew and reproduce mass mobilization, destroy the former Shah's political and social order and establish a distinctive new order? This book attempts to answer the above questions. Its focus is on one neglected aspect, the consensus-building efforts by the Islamic regime pursued to win the hearts and minds of the Iranian people, the basis for the success of such efforts and the nature/character of this new Iranian consensus. Consensus-building efforts involve the creation of a legitimate "political culture."

Political culture is the "system of empirical beliefs, expressive symbols, and values which define the situation in which political action takes place."[1] This book is a collection of studies by a group of social scientists which addresses important aspects of the political culture of post-revolutionary Iran. Specifically, the ideological, organizational and cultural dimensions of Shi'i Islam are analyzed as related instances of the Islamic political culture which re-emerged in the 1960s in a modern mantle as a political culture of opposition to the Shah's regime and which became dominant, perhaps hegemonic, in the Islamic Republic after the revolution. The importance of focusing on the question of political culture in Iran is in large part related to the highly charged ideological character of the clerical theocracy of the Islamic Republic and its overcentralized and monopolistic state. Political, military, ideological, cultural, religious and economic institutions (new or restructured) are all employed to consolidate and reproduce Islamic (clerical) hegemony.

In the early 1980s, a new wave of books designed to explain the revolution were published. Some dissected the political economy of modern Iran.[2] The best of them, however, attempted to examine the political and cultural evolution of Iran between the two revolutions (the Constitutional Revolution of 1905–09 and the Islamic Revolution of 1978–9),[3] to assess the religious culture and its role in the revolution,[4] and, finally, to determine the economic bases of the revolution.[5] By the mid 1980s new studies which addressed the nature of post-revolutionary Iran were published. Most were descriptive[6] and lacked a guiding thesis or an explanatory theorem. Even the more sophisticated analyses of post-revolutionary Iran which presented a multi-dimensional analysis focused too much on the role of prominent personalities.[7] One study, *The Government of God*,[8] did make use of sociological theories of social change to explain the dynamics of Iran.[9] Others, anchored in respective social science disciplines, emphasized varied viewpoints.[10] Finally, another genre stressed the cultural dimension of Iran.[11]

Neglected or insufficiently addressed in the literature is a significant dimension which, we believe, is responsible for both the victory of the Islamic movement and the staying power of the Islamic Republic. This is the dimension of ideology and political culture. It is our contention that an Islamic ideology, and more broadly political culture, anchored in the wider Islamic culture, was central to the victory of the Islamic movement not only against the Shah's regime but also over its coalition allies – the liberal–nationalists, the socialists, the communists and Islamic liberals and socialists – in the opposition. Certain recent studies of Iran approached the study of the political culture of the Islamic Republic as an historical process originating in the rise of Islam in the seventh century, or in the emergence of Shi'i Islam as the official religion of the country in the sixteenth century.[12] They are quite useful prologues to the more focused analyses in this book of the political culture of the Islamic Republic in post-revolutionary Iran, especially its investigations into the conscious renewal process of Islamic political culture by the clergy.

A combination of social, political, and organizational-mobilizational factors collectively favored the rise of the Islamic revolutionaries and in turn allowed them to forge ahead. Not only did the Islamicists emerge as the leaders of the opposition to the Shah but also the Islamic movement set the parameters of the common discourse of opposition. This common discourse was composed of four major related concepts shared by all opposition groups to the Shah.

The four principal concepts of this discourse which underlie the ideology and political culture of the Islamic movement and the Islamic Republic are the following. First is nationalism, a strong and overarching preoccupation with the question of national independence exemplified by anti-imperialism and anti-foreign intervention. Second, populism, an ideological belief in the common people as the subject of history and social change. Third, social justice, a mobilizational ideology to redress the grievance and give economic security to the vast numbers of people who had been dispossessed and disenfranchised by the Shah's regime. Fourth is the 1960s-based Third Worldist strategy of revolutionary violence to achieve liberation, independence, change, and social justice for and by the masses. The above elements of political cultural discourse informed and set the parameters of political dynamics of revolutionary and post-revolutionary Iran. These elements echoed and resonated in differing emphases among the contending allies in opposition to the Shah's regime. Interestingly, these very same elements, perhaps in addition to the emergent issues of human rights and democracy, again in differing emphases and ordering, continue to inform the ideology of most opponents of the Islamic Republic. The tacit and at times active alliance of the opposition groups who overthrew the Shah's regime disintegrated, shortly after the revolution succeeded, into a vicious and lethal power struggle which ended in the consolidation of Islamic hegemony.

In post-revolutionary Iran, the Islamic Republic fused Shi'i culture and politics into a single integrated political culture which it set out systematically to institutionalize. The overcentralized, monopolistic and ideological nature of the state in the Islamic Republic forces every oppositional movement to be similarly and simultaneously political–cultural in nature. Thus the highly charged cultural nature of the Islamic Republic conditions its rivals to wage their challenge in strong ideological–cultural terms as well. The struggle for the hearts and minds of the Iranian people has been and continues to be waged through the promotion of contending visions which structure the parameters of political discourse and of political, social and cultural struggle. This book, then, is a study of the political culture of the Islamic Republic.

SOCIAL FORMATION AND POLITICAL CULTURE

A constructive point of departure for analyzing most Third World social formations, including Iran, is to view them as the articulation of various modes of production, produced largely as a result of penetration of foreign capital into pre-capitalist relations. The outcome is often societies of transitional nature,

characterized by a coexistence of different types of socioeconomic relations, sometimes referred to as "combined and
uneven development."[13] Contrary to an economistic reading of
the concept, this articulation is not and should not be limited to
economic relations; rather, it also includes political, social and
cultural relations and institutions; or in short, a combination of
"all stages of civilization." This approach is capable of avoiding
simplistic assumptions and erroneous implications of both the
modernization and dependency schools of thought. The former
has maintained an over-optimistic view of the "modernization"
process in the Third World by assuming a universalistic and
linear transition from traditional to modern society, similar to
the historical transition of today's advanced capitalist societies
of Western Europe and North America. The logical policy
recommendation of this discourse would be an extension and
acceleration of all-sided penetration of the Third World by the
advanced industrialized capitalist nations.

The Third Worldist discourse, that of the dependency school,
often has reverted to an opposite pessimistic interpretation by
concluding that the economic development of the "periphery" is
inversely related to its contacts with the advanced economies.
Perpetuation of the present relations, accordingly, only is
capable of generating the "development of underdevelopment"
or by other accounts "dependent development." Further, this
discourse manifests a strong economistic tendency by attribut-
ing a dependant nature (the metropolis–satellite relation) to all
social, political, and cultural relations prevailing in the "periphery" due to the effect of capitalist penetration from outside.
The policy implication of this perspective is "delinking" from
the world system and the pursuit of an "autarkic" path of
socioeconomic development.

Neither of these theoretical frameworks were equipped to
deal adequately with the complexities of Iranian society, the
revolution of 1978–9, and the post-revolutionary transformations, especially in the realm of political culture. The
modernization theorists were totally perplexed by the
emergence of the Islamic Republic of Iran, due, in part, to the
presence of a high level of "modernization" indicators in pre-
revolutionary Iran. Nor could they explain the rise and consolidation of an Islamic political culture with its "irrational" and
"anachronistic" values instead of a secular political culture

characterized by pluralism, rationality, innovation, public opinion, etc.

While the dependency discourse had no difficulty explaining the anti-Western and independence seeking feature of the Iranian Revolution, its abstract and universalistic reasoning prevented the *dependentistas* from coming to grips with the particularities of Iranian social transformation. Why, for example, did the Shi'ite clergy lead the revolutionary movement instead of the working class or secular intelligentsia? Furthermore, given the fact that since the nineteenth century, Iranian society was integrated into the world capitalist market and expectedly should have been dependent in its entirety, how could an Islamic movement representing centuries-old indigenous religious values, institutions, and relations overwhelm the modern state and come to power? Answers to these questions were not forthcoming. And this is where both the modernization and dependency discourses converge.

It is our contention that these and some other shortcomings can be evaded by resorting to the theoretical framework organized around the notion of the articulation of modes of production (including the "superstructural" relations of culture, politics, ideology, etc.) Perhaps the most salient aspect of this approach, as relates to our discussion of political culture, is its conceptualization of transitional Third World social formations as entities with "dislocated" instances, i.e., noncorrespondence between and within all economic, political, and cultural–ideological relations.[14] Thus, not only does one observe a combination of various economic forms, but also the coexistence of various social and political institutions, discourses, and cultures, from the most modern to the traditional, in one society. Abdol-Karim Soroush, a leading Islamic thinker, has recently argued that Iranian society is characterized by *three* coexisting cultures, namely *farhang-e melli* (national culture), *farhang-e dini* (religious culture), and *farhang-e gharbi* (Western culture).[15] Obviously, these diverse relations are represented by various social classes and categories who have vested interests in preserving those institutions and cultures. The dynamics governing the interaction among these social groups primarily stems from the reproductive requirements of the emerging modern (metropolitan) classes who promote socioeconomic modernization in conflict with the resistance of some other social groups who are either totally or partially against the imposed social changes sought by the metropolis and its internal support classes. This conflict is social, political, and cultural–ideological at the same time. Based on this perspective, the study of political cultures is "the historical account of their emergence, a critical analysis of the political and economic forces they represent, a study of their internal character and a rigorous critique or negation of their logic and effect."[16]

PRECONDITIONS OF THE ISLAMIC REVOLUTION

Under Shah Mohammad Reza Pahlavi, particularly during the 1960s and 1970s, Iran exhibited many contradictions and dislocations typically associated with combined and uneven development. The developmentalist strategy of the Shah, organized around the *de facto* alliance of the state, foreign capital, and domestic comprador bourgeoisie, accelerated capitalist economic development and "Westernization" of the culture. The uneven and contradictory nature of this process is evident in many areas of society and in increasing income inequality (the Gini coefficient of inequality grew from 0.4552 in 1959–60 to 0.4945 in 1973–4). In the rural areas, the Shah's land reform program effectively undermined the traditional organization of agricultural production without substituting it with a coherent, modern and rational strategy. The increasing migration of landless peasants to cities and their settlement in surrounding slums testify to the technocratic rationale behind the land reform. The increasing concentration of political, commercial, recreational, and educational facilities in Tehran and other big urban centers, and the open door economic policies promoting foreign investment are examples of the Shah's policies. The open door policy resulted in the bankruptcy of small scale domestic producers and traders of the bazaar. Its results are most evident in the ratio of exports to imports which declined from 30 per cent in 1950 to only 5 per cent in 1975.

The regime adopted authoritarian policies against all its opposition including the clergy. Beginning in the early 1960s, the state, concerned by Islamic militancy, made encroachments on the clergy's traditional financial, social, cultural, and administrative prerogatives. In the words of one scholar studying this period:

> Future shock was considered virtuous, the goal of rational modernization, to be pressed forward ruthlessly by means of science, technology, planning and despotic authority. No element of tradition, no personal desire, no aesthetic value, no religious qualm, no philosophical hesitancy was to stand in the way.[17]

The Shah had correctly understood that his developmentalist strategy stood no chances of success without a concomitant policy of cultural modernization. Various institutions particularly education, mass media, leisure, and state bureaucracy along with a number of legal reforms in spheres such as the family, economy, and religion were all employed to instill a new world view among the populace and a new social order in the country. Justification of these policies required an ideology; this had already taken shape under his father, Reza Shah (1925–41).

Pahlavi's official ideology was formed out of a loose combination of selective aspects of Western cultural values and ethos (increasingly American), and a romantic view of the ancient, pre-Islamic Persian civilization. None, however, had much relevance to the everyday life of the people. The ideology's function was to remind people of the desirability of the monarchy and of Western presence in Iran. The celebration of 2,500 years of monarchy in 1971 underscored this point. This Pahlavi ideology and the related cultural policies appealed only to a minority, predominantly among the comprador bourgeoisie, landed classes, and military and bureaucratic elites. However, the growing new middle class expressed tacit support only for specific aspects of the cultural modernization process, especially its cornerstone: the secularization tendency. Although the progress of secularization was most evident in state institutions, it failed to encompass the political culture of the society at large or advance the institutions of civil society. As a result Iranian political culture during the period of the monarchy remained fragmented and incoherent.

The Pahlavi regime's failure to create a unified secular political culture was primarily caused by its separation of secularization from democratization. Thus, it failed to expand its social base of support among the new middle strata, the intelligentsia, and the working class, the very social groups whose participation and support would be vital to any serious attempt toward modernization. By excluding these social groups from political participation, the regime undermined the formation of the institutions of civil society, exacerbated the already present crisis of legitimacy and practically drove them toward dissident social political movements and political cultures. All in all, by the mid-1970s, one could identify four political cultures in Pahlavi Iran. The first was a disorganized and weak official monarchist political culture which claimed legitimacy on the basis of a continuous 2,500 years of monarchy. It was at odds with all the essentials of a secular, democratic political culture which stressed freedom of speech, freedom of association, universal suffrage, cultural tolerance, respect for human rights and compromise.

Various dissident social groups sought alternative ideologies to express their frustration. They included the Islamicists, led by the clergy. The Islamic political culture derived its legitimacy from thirteen centuries of Shi'i history and tradition with its affinity for political protest and oppositional values. In fact, since the seventh century, the Shi'i branch of Islam has been a political–ideological instrument in the formation of a distinctly Irano-Islamic national identity. Another was dormant, and yet potentially credible; this was the liberal–nationalistic political culture, deriving its legitimacy from notions of constitutionalism and national independence. This political culture consolidated itself mainly during the movement for nationalization of the Iranian oil industry (1951–3), and was led by the National Front and the then prime minister, Dr Mohammad Mossadeq. Finally a small, but highly militant socialist political movement, deriving its legitimacy from its support of economic justice for the deprived, its anti-imperialist struggles, and its action-orientedness emerged vibrant in the 1960s and articulated a socialist political culture. Since its inception around the turn of the century, students, the secular intelligentsia, sections of the working class, and some ethnic minorities have been the social base of this political tradition.

The Iranian masses, unhappy with the Pahlavi regime and its ideology, responded to Islamic appeals. Here, the pivotal question is what prevented the alternative contenders for power – i.e., the liberal nationalists and the socialists – from succeeding against the Islamicists, and from advancing their ideology and their secular political culture?

During the formative years of the revolution in the 1970s both the liberal–nationalist and the socialist political groups had experienced a phase of decline and consequently were not in a position to attract the popular masses. Contrary to the 1940s and early 1950s when the communist Tudeh Party and the liberal National Front constituted the two dominant political groups, the era after the 1953 coup witnessed a different reality. This new reality allowed the surge of religious opposition. To begin with, the Shah's secret police and military apparatus practically annihilated these organized secular political groups.

Other factors also played a role. In the case of the liberal–nationalists, the structural transformations of the Iranian economy resulting from increased integration into the world market undermined the economic position of the domestic or national bourgeoisie – a principal social base for liberal nationalism in Iran. Thus, by the early 1960s, a more conservative second National Front emerged. However, it lacked the charismatic and inspiring leadership of Dr Mossadeq and lacked a coherent political ideology and agenda. Indeed, the disillusioned radical faction of the Front often sought refuge or involvement either in the Islamic Freedom Movement or the socialist oriented circles typically affiliated with the Tehran University student organizations. Thus, the more conservative mainstream of the Nationalist Front had little appeal to the increasingly radicalized youth of the 1970s, the urban poor, or the industrial working class.

In the case of the secular socialist movement in the post-1953 coup era, it practically had to rebuild itself anew and had great difficulty institutionalizing itself under the persistent repression of the Shah's regime. However, a new generation of activists, inspired by the Third Worldist ideology of armed struggle, developed, in response, a totally underground and secretive mode of political activity. This mode of political organizing and activity in the context of severe Pahlavi repression significantly narrowed the socialist movement's appeal and social base. It remained largely restricted to secular intelligentsia and thus was in no position to construct a popular ideology nor institutionalize a political culture that could challenge the Shah's regime or compete with the historically rooted Islamic political culture. Furthermore, the secular socialist discourse emphasizing the Third Worldist "dependency problematic" in Iran, a problematic defining the central dilemma as the confrontation of Western influence, had strong affinities with the Islamicist's concern for *Gharbzadegi* (Westoxication).

Ironically, the political discourse of the socialists and liberal-nationalists was not greatly different from the Islamicists in so far as all defined Iran's dilemma as dependency on the West/US with all its economic, political and cultural implications. It is this common discourse that facilitated cooperation and unity between the socialists, the liberal–nationalists and the rising Islamic movement. Cooperation between these opposition movements took the form of a populist pact against the Shah. By 1978, when the revolutionary moment arrived, the secular socialist and liberal–nationalist political cultures were confined to limited segments of the population – students, intellectuals, some ethnic minorities and some strata of the new middle class. The Islamic opposition, on the other hand, based on the bazaaris, the traditional middle strata, the urban poor and the clergy, had been gaining momentum and surged significantly to the lead.

The conditions responsible for Islamic resurgence in Iran are varied and complex. Suffice it here to point out a few factors relevant especially during the Shah's reign. Foremost among these is what Michael Fischer argued: "What has produced the Islamic form of the revolution was not Islamic revivalism so much as the repression of other modes of political discourse."[18] Fred Halliday confirms this point also. He states that "one negative factor played its part in giving prominence to Islam as an ideology of opposition, namely, the destruction by the Shah and his father of the *secular* opposition forces that had mobilized protest movements in earlier decades."[19] Thus, the only real locus of social protest against the Shah became the religious institutions. Their mobilizing role in the absence or marginal status of secular opposition explains in large part the Iranian revolution's religious idiom, leadership, forms of organization and proclaimed goals.

This unique twentieth-century revolution was carried out principally by political–cultural confrontation, not by armed conflict, against a regime which did not enjoy a cultural–ideological hegemony. The revolution was all the more remarkable in that the regime had not been weakened by external confrontation. The rapid and uneven economic development brought together in opposition a coalition of bazaar merchants, the clergy, and the urban poor. These, in addition to the important segments of the students, the intelligentsia, the middle and the working classes confronted a politically isolated and weak monarchy whose ideology was incoherent and whose army was demoralized. The opposition congealed suddenly and spontaneously in 1978–9 and spread largely through religious networks by clergy based in practically every neighborhood in the city and every locality in the countryside. The clergy directed the revolutionary struggle throughout the land. To the slogans of freedom and independence from foreign (US) domination, the clergy added "Islamic Republic." In short, the Islamic clergy provided the political leadership of the revolution, the dominant discourse of opposition and the principles for an alternative society. An Islamic political culture, long in the making, finally came to define the terms of revolt and the character of the future society.

RECONSTRUCTION OF THE ISLAMIC
POLITICAL CULTURE

Since the early 1950s there were sporadic attempts to incorporate modern political and social concepts into the Islamic Canon. This was a reaction to the emergence of secular political discourses (Marxism, liberalism, nationalism) as well as a growing Western influence in Iran after the 1953 *coup d'état*. After the death of Ayatollah Boroujerdi, the conservative "source of emulation" in 1961, conditions became more ripe for this purpose. A group of reformist and politically-minded Shi'i scholars and clergymen, led by Morteza Motahhari and including Mohammad Beheshti, Morteza Jazayeri, Mahmud Taleqani, took the opportunity to introduce their reformist arguments in accordance with the changing Iranian conditions. Their arguments were presented as a series of public lectures sponsored by the Monthly Religious Society between 1960 and 1963 in Tehran. In 1961, a volume of essays entitled *An Inquiry into the Principle of Marja'iyat* was published which included many speeches presented to the Monthly Lectures.

Some of the major issues discussed in this path-breaking book include government in Islam, the need for the clergy's independent financial organization, viewing Islam as a total way of life, the need for attracting and guiding youth, and the necessity of acting collectively as a community.[20] The essay by Allameh Tabataba'i, in particular, regarding *velayat* (loyalty to the rule of the Imams) develops a political philosophy for the need of political rule by a Muslim jurisprudent (*faqih*).

A third significant attempt to formulate a more politico-ideological and interventionist interpretation of Islam is the publication of three volumes of the book *Maktab-e Tashayyo'* by a number of politically minded Islamic thinkers between 1959 and 1965 who were willing to respond to the necessity of the "revival of religious thought" by establishing a formidable Islamic propaganda institution. Another major development is the founding of *Husseiniyeh-e Ershad*, a religious institution in Tehran (1965–73) that organized public lectures, focusing on the concerns of the educated youth. Instrumental in its immense popularity was Dr Ali Shar'iati, an Islamic critical sociologist with Third Worldist and anti-imperialist views who regularly lectured there. He presented old religious issues in the new light of a social scientific framework. Shar'iati posed fundamental questions to the radicalized youth of the time: how can we secure our national identity? What is to be done? His answer was a "return to our Islamic cultural self" which can protect our identity *vis-à-vis* the West.

Here it is important to mention Jalal Al-e Ahmad's contribution to the formation of the Islamic discourse and political culture. As a courageous and highly critical novelist he opposed Western cultural as well as politico-economic influence in Iran. His celebrated book, *Gharbzadegi* (Westoxication), was one of the most influential works of this period which opposed Western domination of Iran and the necessity of putting up resistance against it. It had a profound and far-reaching impact on the youthful intellectual generation of the 1960s and 1970s.

On the political front a number of Islamic groups emerged, after the mid 1960s, which had a radical nationalistic interpretation of Islam combined in some cases with socialistic ideas. They all opposed imperialist domination of Iran and proposed some type of Islamic government. The most notable of them included the People's Mojahedeen Organization, whose founders had split from the more liberal Freedom Movement, led by Mehdi Bazargan. They were influenced by the radical teachings of Taleqani.[21] Another, but less influential group, the Revolutionary Movement of the Muslim People (JAMA) was led by Dr Kazem Sami. An analysis of the social background of the majority of radical Islamic thinkers such as Shar'iati and Al-e Ahmad as well as most active members of the aforementioned groups reveals that most of them came from the clerical, bazaari, and traditional middle class. And finally, we should take note of the accelerated growth of various Islamic-oriented publishing houses, *Hosseiniyehs*, mosques (nearly ten thousand), study groups, and lectures during the 1970s. These provided the organizational and ideological networks of the 1978–9 revolution.

The overall picture that emerges from all this is a rejuvenated political–Islamic social movement, active for nearly two decades prior to the revolution, with its distinct political culture and ready to wage a politico-cultural challenge to the monarchy as well as other contending political groups. To secure its hegemony, the political–Islamic movement needed its leadership to coordinate various factions, energies and activities. Ayatollah Rouhollah Khomeini, who had previously challenged the Shah's authority and was thus exiled to Turkey and Iraq, provided the missing link. In a patrimonial political culture such as Iran's, charismatic patriarchal authorities are usually welcomed and emerge as lightning rods of socio-political mobilization.

Beginning with 1976, the Shah's regime came to experience an all-sided crisis which was unprecedented in scale. Not only was the regime plagued by economic recession and mounting social problems, thus antagonizing the popular strata, it was also encountering dissidence within the upper bourgeoisie, its traditional support base. The disaffected bourgeoisie in effect complained about bureaucratic intervention in business and the tight royal court's domination of society, including itself – the class that was *striving* to be the modern "ruling class" of Iran. All these domestic contradictions were exacerbated after 1976, when US President Carter's policy of "human rights" demanded of many client Third World regimes, the Shah's included, that they modify their oppressive treatment of the opposition. This further intensified the crisis and rendered the regime more vulnerable to the rising oppositional Islamic movement. It is true that by 1978 when Islamicists openly introduced the notion of an Islamic government very few had a clear idea about it. Nevertheless, what proved to be more important was not the clarity or rigor of the concept but rather the conviction among popular masses that the notion was valid and functional.

HEGEMONY OF ISLAMIC POLITICAL CULTURE

The Islamic Revolution of 1978–9 looked forward towards a fundamental reorganizing of Iranian society. The political system, social life, ideology and culture all started to change shortly after the clergy assumed political power. The Islamic Republic, assuming a hegemonic position in control of the state took cultural transformation very seriously. It sought to institutionalize an Islamic political culture. Thus, the Islamic Revolution introduced new concepts, such as *taghooti* (satanic imposters worshipping false gods), *mostaz'afeen* (the deprived masses), and *shahadat* (martyrdom); new political behaviors (demonstrations of burning the American flag, Friday prayers); new political organizations (*Komiteh*, revolutionary guards, assembly of experts); new codes of ethics, dress, entertainment, and sexuality; new political slogans and language (Death to America; War, War Till Victory; Democratic and *Melli*, Both Deception of the Masses); new national enemies, namely America and Israel; and, finally, new political values, namely independence, populism, protest against Westoxication, and the idea of the Islamic State. The Islamic Republic has effectively employed a vast range of organizations and institutions to inculcate and consolidate its political culture, particularly among the *mostaz'afeen*. A partial list includes the media, education, mosques, family, "revolutionary institutions" such as revolutionary guards, *Basij* army, *Komitehs*, charitable establishments such as the Martyrs' Foundation, Mostaz'afeen Foundation, Friday prayers, Islamic Societies in the workplace, etc.

How did this transition come about? The following chapters analyze some of the most salient aspects and most significant efforts of the transformation by the new Islamic elite. In

Chapter 2, Mehrzad Boroujerdi begins by investigating the dominant intellectual discourse of pre- and post-revolutionary Iran, *Gharbzadegi*. The genesis of this discourse is based on two interrelated issues which have confronted Iranian intellectuals since the nineteenth century: the issue of self-identity, and that of the encounter with Western civilization. The problematic of *Gharbzadegi* underlies the intellectual production not only of the concept's articulator, Jalal Al-e Ahmad, but also those of Daryush Shayegan and Reza Davari, two of the foremost intellectuals of post-World War Two Iran.

The Western social, political, economic and cultural shock to Iranian society produced searching reflections among intellectuals for change and transformation of Iran and for confronting the West. These ranged from reasserting, reforming and reviving Islam to calls for jettisoning Islam in favor of the unabashed embracing of Westernization. In all writings, the West remained as the "culture of reference" – a fact which underpins the philosophical and political critique embodied in *Gharbzadegi*. Al-e Ahmad denounced the alienation, rootlessness and inauthenticity of Westernized Iran intoxicated with the West, a fact, he believed, that was responsible for the country's inability to preserve its own historical and cultural character. Therefore, Iran's salvation, in Al-e Ahmad's opinion, was the rejection of the West and the reassertion of Islam. Similarly, Shayegan criticized occidental philosophy as devoid of the spiritual and as debased by the materialization and technicalization not only of life but also of thought. Finally, Davari rejects Western modernism and all that it is based on, the enlightenment's philosophical-political ideals and humanism. He sought to counter the West's threat through recreating *homo islamicus*, a theme wholeheartedly adopted by the Islamic Republic as we will see below in Chapter 5 by Parvin and Vaziri. Throughout the progression of the discourse against *Gharbzadegi*, the Islamic, nativistic and revivalist themes were strengthened. *Gharbzadegi* developed from a response of disenchanted intellectuals in pre-revolutionary Iran to Western encroachment to become the hegemonic discourse of the Iranian Islamic elite – a formidable intellectual base for the anti-Western populist Islamic political culture.

This metamorphosis provided the theoretical arsenal for a powerful mass movement and governmental (Islamic Republic) ideology, both of which have been much more philosophically assertive, intellectually conscious and politically confrontational than any previous revitalization movement in the history of modern Iran.

Before we get into the post-revolutionary efforts to consolidate an Islamic consensus it is useful to investigate the pre-revolutionary politicalization of Iran's religious establishment and the political emergence of Ayatollah Khomeini. Mohammad Borghei, in Chapter 3, analyzes this process and its gathering momentum since 1962, the real beginning, according to Ayatollah Khomeini himself, of the 1978-9 Islamic Revolution of Iran. Borghei argues that the events of 1961-3 within the religious establishment at the Qom seminary left permanent marks on the political culture and politics of Iran not only during the 1978-9 revolution but also in shaping the political dynamics of post-revolutionary Iran. Contrary to the clerical divisions that existed during the Constitutional movement early in the twentieth century and during the nationalist rise to power in the early 1950s, the religious establishment in the early 1960s became politicized, radicalized and relatively unified under the leadership of Ayatollah Khomeini, a sophisticated religio-political leader.

Such politicization, however, had to wait the death of the politically conservative Ayatollah Boroujerdi in Qom. Ayatollah Boroujerdi was a dominant *marja* who espoused a religious position of non-interference in politics. His death, however, coincided with socio-political turmoil in the country. It is this turmoil and the opposition to the Shah's initiative on the part of Boroujerdi's potential successors which not only politicized the religious establishment in Qom but also thrust to the fore Ayatollah Khomeini. Khomeini, one of the lesser Ayatollahs and *marjas* then in Qom, was nevertheless known for his scholarship and piety, but also especially for his advocacy of the clergy's involvement in politics. In the course of the political struggles of the period, those surrounding the Bill of Election of Municipal and Provisional Councils and the Shah's "white revolution", Khomeini emerged. The bill, which proposed elimination of the condition of being a Muslim in order to qualify for electoral candidacy, directly challenged Islam and the clergy. The clerical response to the bill, led by Khomeini, went a long way to politicize the Qom seminary and to legitimize the radical Islamic activists within it. These radicals, with Khomeini as one of their leaders, had been a minor undercurrent until that time. Khomeini's mobilization tactics, both inside the seminary and among the Iranian masses, became his trademark of political action in years to come. The oppositional political activity thrust not only Khomeini but also many of his students – for example Rafsanjani and Khamenei, the current supreme Iranian leaders – into leadership roles.

In short, Islam emerged politicized and became a base of opposition to the Shah. Islam in general, and religious events in particular, became a key impetus for mass political mobilization. All this depended on the emergence and revival of the pivotal Qom seminary as the center of religio-political authority. And that occurred largely because of the emergence of Ayatollah Khomeini himself. Ironically, although this religious movement was the cause of the Shah's political defeat in 1961–3, the Shah underestimated it, ignored it and instead actively pursued the destruction of secular opposition – a fatal and strategical political error that later came to haunt him.

During the 1960s and 1970s the Shah concentrated his regime's effort on defeating the secular, especially socialist, opposition. However, while this effort was indeed effective, there were significant other factors which helped determine the success of the Islamic political movement and the defeat of the liberal nationalists and socialists. In his chapter on the politics of nationalism and political culture (Chapter 4) Mehrdad Mashayekhi details these. The socialist movements had developed political legacies and legitimate traditions of political struggle during the 1940s in opposition to the Shah. Indeed, important segments of the population had responded to the National Front and the Tudeh Party and had built up varying political visions and political practices – distinctive political cultures. However, both these political movements lost to the Islamicists during the 1970s although they were significant members of the coalition that overwhelmed the Shah in the 1978–9 revolution. Mashayekhi focuses on the shortcomings of the socialist political culture, and by implication that of the liberal nationalist movements.

Mashayekhi's thesis is that the secular movement's radical nationalism and the discourse of dependency produced in its ideology an exaggerated emphasis on Third Worldist anti-imperialism which played into the hands of anti-Western Islamicists and underplayed other socio-political issues such as democracy and concrete everyday problems. The emergence and consolidation of Iranian nationalism has a long historical basis and was parleyed by both the secular and religious opposition to the Shah into a powerful sentiment and an all-consuming ideology. Nationalism for both the secular socialists and the religious fundamentalists set the parameters of Iranian political discourse. While this was relevant, meaningful and mobilizational for an Islamic movement concerned with socio-cultural identity, it became the theoretical failure of Iranian socialism. The overarching emphasis on nationalism for the socialists merely complemented and reinforced the political ideology of their rivals, diverted them from addressing other significant social and economic issues and emerged, in Mashayekhi's judgement, the key reason for their failure in the face of the Islamic movement.

Couched in the problematic of dependency, the Third Worldist socialist discourse of anti-imperialism and hyper-nationalism was sophisticated and seemingly unchallengeable. Yet it was flawed. A principal flaw was a blind faith in the popular will (the *khalq*) coupled with anti-intellectualism. Further, the socialist discourse was too economistic; it ignored the deeply rooted Islamic values, norms and behavior patterns even among its own ranks, and failed to articulate the democratic interests of the urban middle strata. These ideological failures, in addition to the mythification of "armed struggle", the sacredness of martyrdom and personality cultism, barely distinguished the socialists from the Islamicists. In short, the socialists' anti-imperialism may have been different in theory from the Islamicists' outright rejection of Western civilization. But in practice, this was never quite clear to the participants in the revolution.

All political tendencies expressed anti-American slogans and participated in anti-Western demonstrations in support of those who occupied the American embassy in Tehran. The intensity and drama of that political action seemed to confirm the primacy of the anti-imperialist struggle. Indeed all social, economic and political issues seemed to dissolve into the singular issue of imperialism. But anti-imperialism meant anti-Westernism; an overarching conception successfully used by the Islamic movement. Thus, in competing with political Islam for mass support the socialists were disadvantaged. Furthermore, unlike the Islamic thinkers who constantly challenged the philosophical, cultural and political foundations of the socialist movement, the socialists hardly ever engaged in a critical evaluation of Islamic thought. In short, they failed to outreach the Islamicists and thus emerged as merely secondary support for the Islamic movement and leadership of the revolution. Once the Islamicists gained power, they set out to institutionalize their political culture and eliminate all rivals – socialists and liberal-nationalists – and their ideologies. Significantly, the Islamicists proclaimed that they do not accept either the West or the East (communism).

Islamic Republican ideologues articulated their conception and desire to create anew the moral Islamic man and the just Islamic society. Parvin and Vaziri, in Chapter 5, analyze that effort. This effort was part of an overall set of goals that included also the establishment of the ideal divine rule in Iran, the restoration of Iran's independence and that of all other Islamic nations, the latter through the export of the Islamic Revolution if necessary. Each of the victorious coalition partners envisioned a different form of government. These ranged from a socialist People's Republic to a liberal Parliamentary Republic to an Islamic theocracy, *Velayat-e Faqih* of Ayatollah Khomeini, the Islamic Republic of Iran. The significance of the establishment of the *Velayat-e Faqih* ruled by theologians is the fact that Islamic justice could not be achieved and *homo islamicus* could not emerge except under its dominion.

According to Parvin and Vaziri, however, the Islamic person the Islamic Republic wishes to create is not merely one who lives by the Islamic *shar'ia* (law). It is, they contend, an Islamic person who lives by what the authors have termed "clerical culture," the internalization of the supreme value of conformity to clerical ideology. Elements of this clerical culture which the authors characterize as "Islamic Philistinism" are absolute submission to clerical authority in its unidimensional character, fractured individualism and spiritual materialism. These attributes, of course, differ in their application between Islamic men and Islamic women.

Parvin and Vaziri note that while the ruling Islamic clergy did impose this clerical culture over the population and while much of its social norms were put into daily practice, it is quite difficult to estimate the degree of its acceptance among the populace. Nonetheless, an Islamization process in accordance with the clerical Islamic culture has been instituted: the Islamic Republic's way to rehabilitate an Islamically-ill society. Such Islamism is not novel to the Iranian masses. It had been rooted, according to Parvin and Vaziri, in the folk culture and psycho-spiritual values of Iranian society. While clerical Islamism found resonance among large sectors of the population, its rejection by Islamic and secular opposition alike was severely supressed. This significantly impacted on segments of the professional, scientific and artistic strata who deserted clerical Islamic Iran. Clerical Islamic cultural hegemony is not secured in Iran, and it exhibits a multi-varied crisis; currently voluntary compliance with it differs according to social class.

With regard to Islamic economic and social justice, the Iranian masses had strong expectations from the Islamic Republic. The concept of socio-economic justice in the Islamic Republic is more problematic than that of the Islamic person. This is because Islamic law does not address this issue directly and in detail. Except for the proscription of the practice of *zakat* (almsgiving), few legal demands exist. On the contrary, according to Parvin and Vaziri, Islamic rule allows and legitimates gender and class exploitation. Not only that, they cite Iranian President Rafsanjani whose position is that wealth is created and distributed by God. Hence social class differences in society are of God's own making. While this is ultimately the case, socio-economic differentiation does derive from relations between individuals. Greedy, self-righteous and exploitative individuals become arrogant in their behavior and thus unjust, whereas humble and pious individuals are just, and thus social justice is preserved in harmony with God's will. Social justice or social conflict thus arise from individual action, not from clashes of class interests. Given this kind of conceptualization of the nature of social and economic justice, the Islamic Republic not only sanctioned (exploitative) capitalism but also failed to develop a program of economic reform and a comprehensive program of welfare. Its oil revenue had largely been used to rebuild the destroyed or damaged infrastructure as a result of the Iraq–Iran war. In short while *homo islamicus* was being created in the Islamic Republic, Islamic social justice was not.

The question of socio-economic justice may in the longer term emerge as the Achilles heel of the Islamic Republic. In the current context, the Islamic elite have concentrated on institutionalizing an Islamic political culture as a means of developing an Islamic consensus in Iranian society. The three chapters by Mohsen Milani, Rasool Nafisi and Hamid Nafici detail differing aspects of this process. Milani, in Chapter 6, analyzes the new (Islamic) constitution of the Islamic Republic of Iran. Born out of the popular revolution against the Shah, the Islamic Republic's constitution of 1979 and its revision in 1989 translated the clergy's well-articulated religious goals into constitutional principles subordinating unambiguously the state to Shi'ism (religion) and terminating the dilemma between *urfi* (secular) and *shar'i* (Islamic) laws. Milani reviews the debates and tactics of the framers of the constitution and those of their opponents – a fascinating dialogue and process which resulted in the victory of the Islamic radicals. Having established Islamic law as the foundation of the new Iranian order, the fundamentalists incorporated into the constitution the *Velayat-e Faqih* provision. This article stipulated that during the Imam's occultation "the governance and leadership of the nation devolve upon the just and pious *faqih* who is acquainted with the circumstances of his age; courageous, resourceful, and possessed of administrative ability; and recognized and accepted as leader by the majority of the people."

The constitution stipulates that real sovereignty belongs to God. God however has placed man in charge of his social destiny and has given laws that can only be interpreted by qualified *ulama* and thus the highest and legitimate authority is not the people, nor the *majles* (parliament), nor the president but the *faqih*. Thus, the people's capacity to determine their own social destiny through the institutions of the *majles* and other constitutional mechanisms are nonetheless constrained by the *faqih*, or in his absence, by the Council of Guardians (in the 1989 constitution). In short, while the constitution stipulates a "limited" notion of popular sovereignty, it elevates the *Velayat-e Faqih* to prominence and thus denies the supremacy of the will of the people. In short, the constitution, whether of 1979 or as revised in 1989, marries Shi'ism with the state and turns Iran into a theocracy legitimized both ways: by the people's will through the referendum and God's will as interpreted by the *foqaha*.

While the legitimation of Islamic government in Iran was achieved through the constitution, the revolutionary victors turned to education to inculcate, spread and consolidate mass loyalty. In Chapter 7, Rasool Nafisi compares the ideological content of education in two regimes: the Pahlavi monarchy and the Islamic Republic. For Khomeini and the rest of the ruling clergy, the modern educational system established by the former Shah was the foundation of secular Western cultural dependency which had ruined the country's Islamic tradition. It corrupted the children and drove them along a path of immorality. The educational system had therefore been a pivotal terrain of ideological conflict even before the revolution. Thus, Islamization, at least of the content of education, was of high priority for the fundamentalists. Nafisi found the elementary textbooks of the Islamic Republic deliberately doctrinaire, inculcating in children Islamic values, norms, attire and so on. Themes are more political and reflect the ideological concerns of the Islamic Revolution; for example, those of revolution against oppression, especially against the unjust and authoritarian rulers. Every aspect of nature is portrayed as a manifestation of the power and glory of God. All things are mundane but faith is sublime, and that is the *raison d'être* of the revolution.

Islamic values are not only institutionalized in the school systems; they are also encouraged through public processes. The aloof and distant state of the Shah's regime is replaced by an involving populist state of the clergy – demanding activism, ritualistic and actual sacrifice and martyrdom, themes reflected in textbooks. This combined with politics of the street and the pulpit changed the tenor, involvement and character of politics and political culture in the Islamic Republic.

Political culture in the Islamic Republic was directly and consciously constructed through the new constitution of 1979 and 1989 and directly through the changes in the content of education and the style, character and terrain of political action. Popular culture, including the culture of entertainment, on the other hand, is indirectly linked to political culture. Nevertheless, it has a profound relevance to political culture and to reproducing loyalty and legitimacy for the regime.

In Chapter 8, Hamid Naficy analyzes the process of Islamizing film culture in Iran. This is an extremely insightful chapter
which details the process not only of changing the content of
films, and therefore of censorship, but also of a conscious effort
to build institutions to produce Islamic films. Religious anti-
cinema feelings run deep in Iran. Religious leaders have long
condemned cinema as morally offensive and ethically corrupting. Ayatollah Khomeini himself had written, in two major
works prior to the revolution, of the linkage between cinema
(Western imported films) and the emergence in Iran "of corruption, licentiousness, prostitution, moral cowardice and cultural
dependance." Cinema was seen by these religious leaders as an
ideological importation by a despotic regime (the Shah's) which
in combination with other popular cultural activity – radio,
theater, popular music, dancing, mixed swimming pools and
gambling – is said to have diverted Muslims from the "straight
path." And yet such blanket denunciation, especially of cinema,
was revised to describe cinema as a tool that could be useful for
educational purposes. Thus, according to Naficy, the Islamic
Republic has encouraged, indeed developed, the "emergence of
a new, vital cinema, with its own special industrial and financial
structure and unique ideological, thematic, and production
values."

> Iranian post-revolutionary cinema is not fully-developed
> "Islamic" cinema in the sense that it is not by any means a
> monolithic, propagandistic cinema in support of a ruling
> ideology. In fact, two cinemas seem to be developing side
> by side. The "populist cinema" affirms post-revolutionary
> Islamic values more fully at the level of plot, theme,
> characterization, portrayal of women, and *mise-en-scene*.
> The "quality cinema," on the other hand, engages with
> those values and tends to critique social conditions under
> the Islamic government.

The Islamic movement and the Islamic Republic began the
process of Islamizing Iranian cinema by "cleansing" the movie
houses, controlling film imports, establishing censorship of
both imports and locally produced films, and "purifying" film
makers and entertainers (through intimidation, incarceration
and so on). Islamic Republican political consolidation between
1982 and 1989 included the direct control of or strong influence

over all the arts and broadcasting. The Ministry of Culture and Islamic Guidance developed overall control of cinematic cultural production. The Ministry created regulations governing the exhibition of movies and videos. These regulations codified Islamic values as articulated by the Islamic leaders. It also taxed ticket sales to raise funds for film making as well as for financing entertainment personnel. Thus, as important as the political control of the film and other entertainment industries is the emergence of committed Islamic film makers and entertainers.

Naficy analyzes the dominant genre and themes of indigenous Islamic feature films. These he finds are reflective of Islamic ethical values including those regarding women, and serve well the state's ideological concepts of nativism, populism, monotheism, theocracy, puritanism and independence. Thus, with the restructuring of Iranian cinema, working in films, once disdained and disparaged, has become more acceptable and respectable. An ideological repositioning of cinema occurred and "cinema, rejected in the past as part of the frivolous superstructure, has been adopted (by the Islamic Republic) as part of the necessary infrastructure of Islamic culture". Islamizing film culture is a good example, then, of the general process of Islamizing Iran, politically, socially and culturally.

In the chapters by Parvin and Vaziri, Milani, Rasool Nafisi and Hamid Nafici we noted the process of institutional and cultural restructuring, of consolidation and of Islamization by the Islamic Republic. Populism, a key political value and practice during the Islamic Revolution, continues to play an important role after the establishment of the Islamic Republic. In Chapter 9, Manochehr Dorraj analyzes this populism as it is synthesized with Islamic corporatism in post-revolutionary Iranian political culture. While populism as an ideology and practice for mobilizing the Iranian masses against an entrenched and powerful regime served the revolution well, its continued legacy and spontaneity could spell potential instability and conflict for the post-revolutionary regime. Thus, according to Dorraj, populism had to be controlled, redirected and pressed into service of the Islamic Republic. This restructuring of the ideology and practice of populism is to be achieved through Islamic corporatism.

146,567

25

Corporatism in Islamic Iran's context is a populist strategy to reconcile social class and other differences and incorporate the nation into an organic whole. Rejecting both Communism/Marxism and capitalism/liberalism, Islamic corporatism presents the Iranian masses with a "third path" of social and political development which supersedes both former visions and is in harmony with the indigenous traditions and values. The vision of Islamic corporatism is an authentic righteous Islamic *umma* on the march towards social justice on earth and toward unity with God (*kamal* or perfection). The leadership's effort towards consolidation of Islamic corporatism has been undergirded by such *real politik* practices as consensus formation, coalition building and factional compromise, Khomeini's legacy passed on to his successors. However, under the post-Khomeini leadership, an added dimension of control has now emerged: the populist elements of spontaneity, mass mobilization and street politics is gradually being replaced by increasing bureaucratization and rationalization of power. In short, the clerical revolutionaries have synthesized the populism of Shi'i folk culture with the authoritarian rule of the clergy or *foqaha*, the twin pillars of corporatism of the Islamic Republic. However, Dorraj identifies the key dilemma for this new Islamic corporatist state: much of the success or failure for the regime of the successors of Khomeini is dependent on holding the populist coalition together. Lacking Khomeini's charismatic authority, the successor leadership must provide tangible benefits to their coalition constituents.

In Chapter 10, Thomas Ricks reviews the dialectic of power politics and Iran's political culture. Ricks points out that Iran's political culture – on a popular level – focused since the 1920s on self-reliance and independence from foreign rule. The end of the Shah's regime was the product of nearly continuous resistance to European and then US intervention in Iranian economic, political, social and cultural affairs. World War Two and its aftermath brought greater US involvement in Iran, particularly with the CIA-assisted coup in 1953 which restored the Shah to power. In his chapter Ricks argues that US policy towards Iran remained remarkably consistent in supporting the monarchy from 1909 to 1979. This took place when the Iranian people over the same period of time changed their views regarding the monarchy, the role of foreign powers and themselves.

Indeed, it was the emergence of an authentic Iranian political culture first in the 1910s and 1920s, and then in the 1950s through to the 1970s that "demonized" and cursed the United States long before the terms of "Great Satan" or "Death to America" made US evening news headlines.

Iranians, according to Ricks, were anti-US in the sense of opposing the widespread and aggressive Americanization of Iran. In short, the steady and precipitous erosion of the image of the US as a supporter of the Iranian people's aspiration for self-determination, coupled with increasing support for the despotic monarchs, is crucial to the emergence of anti-Americanism among the Iranian revolutionary activists: liberal nationalists, socialists and Islamicists. While Iranian political culture included a strong anti-foreign, anti-European, component before World War Two, it turned anti-American after that.

America's fall from grace – from the beatification of the US in 1907–9 to its demonization since 1978–9 – is persuasively traced by Ricks. He shows the role of the US in the power politics of oil, anti-communism and the monarchy in Iran leading it to the support of a despotic regime in opposition to the popular will. Hence the Iranian popular struggle against despotism and the monarchy became essentially a struggle against the United States.

In conclusion, Iranian popular political culture in opposition to the Shah, and later as a pillar of the new Islamic Republican regime, became the basis for an overarching political consensus which has been in large part responsible for the regime's popularity, stability and legitimacy. Until such a consensus cracks or disintegrates under the successors of the Ayatollah Khomeini, the Islamic Republic is here to stay for some time to come.

NOTES

1 L. Pye and S. Verba (eds), *Political Culture and Political Development* (Princeton University Press, Princeton, 1965), p. 513.
2 H. Katouzian, *The Political Economy of Modern Iran* (New York

University Press, New York, 1981); H. Bashiriyeh, *The State and Revolution in Iran* (Croom Helm, London, 1984); see also an earlier work, F. Halliday, *Iran: Dictatorship and Development* (Penguin Books, New York, 1979).

3 E. Abrahamian, *Iran Between Two Revolutions* (Princeton University Press, Princeton, 1982); N. Keddie, *Roots of Revolution* (Yale University Press, New Haven, CT, 1981).

4 M. Fischer, *Iran: From Religious Dispute to Revolution* (Harvard University Press, Cambridge, MA, 1980).

5 R. Looney, *Economic Origins of Iranian Revolution* (Pergamon Press, New York, 1982); F. Kazemi, *Poverty and Revolution in Iran* (New York University Press, New York, 1980).

6 S. Zabih, *Iran Since the Revolution* (Johns Hopkins University Press, Baltimore, 1982); G. Afkhami, *The Iranian Revolution: Thanatos on a National Scale* (Middle East Institute, Washington, DC, 1985).

7 The best is S. Bakhash, *The Reign of the Ayatollahs* (Basic Books, New York, 1984).

8 C. Benard and Z. Khalilzad, *The Government of God* (Columbia University Press, New York, 1984).

9 Among the issue-oriented books see E. Hoogland, *Land and Revolution in Iran* (University of Texas Press, Austin, 1982); A. Bayat, *Workers and Revolution in Iran* (Zed Press, London, 1987). See also A. Tabari and N. Yeganeh (eds), *In the Shadow of Islam* (Zed Press, London, 1982).

10 M. Parsa, *Social Origins of the Iranian Revolution* (Rutgers University Press, New Brunswick, NJ, 1989); E. Abrahamian, *Radical Islam: The Iranian Mojahedeen* (I. B. Taurus, London, 1989).

11 R. Mottahedeh, *The Mantle of the Prophet* (Pantheon Books, New York, 1985); S. A. Arjomand, *The Turban For The Crown* (Oxford University Press, Oxford, 1988); M. Fischer and M. Abedi, *Debating Muslims* (University of Wisconsin Press, Madison, 1990).

12 M. Dorraj, *From Zarathustra to Khomeini: Populism and Dissent in Iran* (Lynne Rienner, Boulder, CO, 1990); M. R. Behnam, *Cultural Foundation of Iranian Politics* (University of Utah Press, Salt Lake City, 1986); S. A. Arjomand, *Authority and Political Culture in Shi'ism* (State University of New York Press, Albany, 1988).

13 M. Lowy, *The Politics of Combined and Uneven Development* (Verso Books, London, 1981); A. G. Frank, *Crisis in the Third World* (Heinemann, London, 1981); J. Taylor, *From Modernization to Modes of Production* (Humanities Press, Atlantic Heights, NJ, 1979).

14 J. Taylor, *ibid*, pp. 101–4.

15 A. Soroush, "Seh Farhang," in *Ayneh-e Andisheh*, February–March, nos 3 and 4, 1991.

16 J. Gibbens (ed.), *Contemporary Political Culture* (Sage Publications, London, 1989), p. 5.

17 L. Binder, "Iran," in *The Political Economy of The Middle East: 1973–1978* (US Congress, Washington, DC, 1980), p. 163.

18 M. Fischer, *op. cit.*, p. 185.

19 F. Halliday, "The Iranian Revolution: Uneven Development and

Religious Populism," in F. Halliday and H. Alavi (eds), *State and Ideology In The Middle East and Pakistan* (Monthly Review Press, New York, 1988), p. 46.
20 S. Akhavi, *Religion and Politics in Contemporary Iran* (State University of New York Press, Albany, 1980), ch. 5.
21 E. Abrahamian, *op. cit*, 1989, ch. 3.

2

GHARBZADEGI

The Dominant Intellectual Discourse of Pre- and Post-Revolutionary Iran

Mehrzad Boroujerdi

INTRODUCTION

Michel Foucault, the late French philosopher, in a series of works exploring the history of madness, illness, crime, and sexuality, attempted to excavate the genealogy of various modern scientific disciplines. Through a critical analysis of their assumptions, discourses, and actions, Foucault brought a historical indictment against such disciplines as medicine, pedagogy, criminology, psychiatry, and demography. He showed that the prevalent Western definitions of rationality, perversion, appropriate codes of sexual behavior, and delinquency were all formulated through the subjugation of an "other": i.e. the "madman," the "deviant," the "born criminal," the "delinquent" or the "hermaphrodite."[1] This "other" is "always pushed aside, marginalized, forcibly homogenized and devalued as that cognitive machinery does its work."[2]

Formatively influenced by the works of Foucault on the "Constitution of Otherness", Edward Said, a Palestinian scholar, attempted to apply the same methodology to a different subject-matter. In his widely-acclaimed book *Orientalism*,[3] Said set out to deconstruct Western representations of the Orient and Orientals. He launched his attack with a devastating critique of the basic ontological premises of Orientalism, which he defined as a "an enormously systematic discipline by which European culture was able to manage – and even produce – the Orient politically, sociologically, militarily, ideologically, scientifically and imaginatively during the post-Enlightenment period."[4] Said first called into question the dualistic *Weltanschauung* of Orientalism which suggests there exists a radical, ontological difference between the nature, cultures, and peoples of the Orient and the Occident. He showed how this epistemology of differentiation prevalent in all Orientalist writings is in reality the artifact of an "imaginative geography" stretching back several centuries. For Said, the essentialist categories of "Orient" and "Occident" which constitute the very basic foundations of Orientalism's schematization are humanly-mediated, discursive productions conceived in the process of cultural encounter.[5] This arbitrary division of humanity into Oriental and Occidental beings at best represents a credulous acclimation, and at worst pure racism and naked discrimination. Following Foucault, Said argues that "otherness" requires (as well as reinforces) particularity and difference since the "self" is usually constituted in negative identity to the "other". Hence, the "constitution of otherness" is an attempt to (re-)determine the "self."[6]

While Said looked at the process of formation of the "Oriental other" for Westerners, I shall examine the formation of the "Occidental other" within the social imagery of the Iranian intellectuals.[7] Hence, this chapter will provide a critical analysis of contemporary Iranian political and intellectual thought. The study will focus on the emergence of an intellectual discourse known as *gharbzadegi* which came to dominate the intellectual panorama of pre- and post-revolutionary Iranian society.[8] The genesis of this new mode of thought will be traced back to two dominant, interrelated issues that have been confronting modern Iranian intellectuals since the last century: (1) the issue of self-identity; and (2) that of encounter with Western civilization.

The ontological, epistemological and political underpinnings of *gharbzadegi* will be addressed through a critical rendition of the works of three Iranian intellectuals: Jalal Al-e Ahmad, Daryush Shayegan and Reza Davari-Ardakani. The selection of these intellectuals was not based on their popularity, but rather by the following criteria: (1) they articulated some of the most philosophically-consequential ideas on the discourse of *gharbzadegi*; (2) they represent different views and political affiliations; and (3) they exemplify the predominate response of Iranian intellectuals during the 1960s, 1970s and 1980s to the problem of encounter with the West.[9] Jalal Al-e Ahmad was Iran's most prominent social critic of the 1950s and 1960s. Daryush Shayegan, a former university professor as well as

Director of the Iranian Center for the Study of Civilizations, presented one of the more philosophically-refined expositions of the Orient/Occident problematic. Reza Davari-Ardakani (hereafter Davari), a professor of philosophy at Tehran University has emerged as one of the two leading, non-clerical ideologues of the Islamic Republic of Iran.[10]

IN SEARCH OF AN "ORIENTAL IDENTITY"

As a social category, intellectuals almost constantly struggle with external or self-imposed tensions. These tensions emanate in part from the universal role of intellectuals as promoters and narrators of culture, and in part from the particular economic, social and political conditions of their respective societies. The Iranian intellectuals of this century are a case in point. The economic and cultural decadence of Iranian society in the nineteenth century along with the simultaneous advent of the Western powers paved the way for the introduction of European thought into Iran. Almost immediately a debate originated as to whether and how to limit or imitate its intellectual onslaught. A prognosis of the theoretical ventures of Iranian intellectuals at the end of the nineteenth and the beginning of the twentieth century would substantiate the essential thrust of such an assertion.[11] Some intellectuals became overwhelmingly convinced that the only way to redemption was through a three-phase process: (1) a break with the past; (2) total emulation of the West; and (3) the avoidance of any indigenous innovations in this process of acculturation.

Their ambition was to remake Iran in the image of the West. Hence, one early Iranian traveler to Great Britain gave the following advice to his countrymen:

> This writer believes if Iranian citizens were to have peace of mind and were to adapt the deeds of the British all of their daily matters would be done in the right way.[12]

The Iranian modernist Mirza Malkum Khan (1833–1908) spoke of the need for adoption of European civilization without Iranian adaptation.[13] The renowned Iranian writer and statesman, Sayyid Hasan Taqizadeh (1878–1970), exemplified this infatuation with the West when he laid out his blueprint for building a new Iran with the following pronouncement:

> we need to recognize that we have fallen behind the Western civilization both spiritually and physically by some hundred thousand *farsangs* [each *farsang* is equivalent to 6.24 kilometers] in knowledge, technology, music, poetry, manners, life, spirit, politics, and industry. We should therefore only strive to retain our *milliyat* (nationality), that is, our racial identity, language and history, and beyond that seek to pursue the European advancements and civilization without the slightest doubt or hesitation. We must surrender to the Western civilization totally and unconditionally.[14]

As a group, these thinkers were representing the views of newly-emerging élites in Iran and in the Arab world.[15] Their liberal ideas on free enterprise, education, rationalism and parliamentary government soon found staunch supporters among the intelligentsia, professionals, aristocrats and even circles among the ruling classes in Iran, Turkey, and Egypt.[16] In Iran, these developments laid the foundations for sweeping socio-economic and cultural changes which were introduced first by the constitutional movement of 1905–11 and later by Reza Shah.

Meanwhile, a more eclectic venture was molded which attempted to articulate oriental mysticism with Enlightenment's humanism and socialism. Among its leading proponents one can find such respectable intellectual figures as Mirza Fath Ali Akhundzadeh (1812–78), Mirza Aqa Khan Kermani (1853–96), and Ahmad Kasravi (1890–1946). Faced with Europe's scientific ascendancy and temporal power, they searched for a middle ground between the spiritual East and the materialistic West. While sharing the first group's belief in the necessity of imitating the universalist West, they nevertheless maintained their critical outlook. Kasravi, a prolific writer and social thinker, articulated the second group's manifesto at the time with the following words:

> Another problem is this issue of the East and the West. Since Easterners have not kept pace with Westerners in their acquiring of science and knowledge and are still

struggling in the midst of aberration and darkness of the past centuries, the latter are looking down at them, always wishing to dominate them. As an Easterner I confess that we are very backward. I confess that we are swimming in [a sea of] ignorance. But you [Westerners] should also confess that in the past two centuries, since Europeans have found their way here, instead of trying to awaken and emancipate Easterners from their aberration and darkness, they have insisted that the Easterners remain in that entanglement. They have realized that it is in their interest to keep Easterners ignorant, and have used all means toward that end.[17]

Their predicament arose from the fact that they were suspended between two civilizations, attempting to reconcile modern rationalism with antiquated traditions. Yet they did not fully belong to either one of these schools of thought. They manifested their eclecticism through their: (1) advocation of pre-Islamic Persian glory; a strong sense of Persian chauvinism; hatred of Arabs; and (2) borrowing of Enlightenment's language of secularism, nationalism, democracy, socialism and scientism. They were living in a "Levantine sub-culture," sharply criticizing their decadent society for its despotic political machinery, rigid socioeconomic structures, archaic ideologies and foreign-infected (as well as unscientific) language, and poetry.[18] Inspired by the ideals of the French Revolution, they advocated peasants' interests and social justice, and envisioned a revolutionary solution to Iran's miseries.

A third intellectual campaign was also formed which has come to be known as "Islamicism" or "Islamic Modernism." While the second group spoke the language of nationalism, deism, secularism, and at times socialism, this third group was positively Islamic in its outlook and political agenda. Among its leading proponents were such acclaimed figures as Sayyid Jamal ad-Din al-Afghani (Assad-Abadi) in Iran, Muhammad Abduh and Rashid Rida in Egypt, and Muhammad Iqbal in Pakistan. Faced with the imminent threat of the Western powers and the eradication of the traditional insularity of their societies, along with the aloofness of a good number of the ulama, these thinkers attempted to awaken their countrymen from their hypnotic trance and historical nightmare. While influenced by European doctrines, they nevertheless remained opposed to the inclusive appropriation of the East by the West. Viewing cultural abstinence as no longer a practical alternative, they advocated selective adoption of those Western scientific and cultural traits which were compatible with the Shari'ah. Al-Afghani (1839–97) engaged the famous French Orientalist, Ernest Renan, in a brilliant polemic in which al-Afghani attacked the Western perception of its own "civilizing" mission, its claim to a universalist philosophy, and its historicist outlook.[19] For him and his disciples, Islam constituted a mobilizing ideology capable of standing up to the West. They believed the avant-garde intellectuals of the first two groups had lost touch with the majority of the Iranian masses who were still firm believers in Islam, traditional normative values and habits. It was to this perceived need that they addressed themselves. Following the widespread tendency of intellectuals to speak for the "others" and to have a sense of political mission, they advocated pan-Islamism as their revolutionary "utopia."

While promoting modernization through selective adoption from the West in economic and technological fields, the Islamicists remained steadfast in their opposition to modernity and modernism. They were not willing to acknowledge that "modernity" as a culture and "modernism" as a consciousness were only the by-products of "modernization" as an economic process.[20] Unable to comprehend the interrelatedness of cultural properties, they subscribed to the maxim of Thomas Hobbes "out of the past we make a future" and attempted to pursue a visionary future through a mystical past.

What brings these three intellectual undertakings together, despite their different political beliefs, is the way they denote the West as the "other." For those who viewed it as a perfect model to be wholeheartedly embraced, those who advocated cautious acculturation, and those who attempted to dismantle and transcend it as the "antagonistic other," the West constantly returned as the "culture of reference," positing itself as universally valid. It seemed then, as now, that no way existed to circumvent the West, and its perpetual Eurocentric discourse(s). The West had become a source of inspiration as well as a vantage point from which non-Western societies could examine themselves in order to diagnose their cultural-historical "illness."

A trajectory of the discursive terrains of modern Iranian intellectual thought from the late nineteenth century to the present would demonstrate its epistemological and political continuities as well as its ruptures and transformations. Despite the current flourishing of a genre of revisionist historical studies which have tried to deny or downplay the role of liberal and eclectic modernists of modern Iran, the fact remains that these intellectuals have left their mark upon Iranian political culture in no uncertain way. Their impact on the language, values, rituals, terminology, practices and imagery of modern Iranian political culture is irrefutable. The ascendancy of Islamicism to power in 1979 did not take place in an intellectual-theoretical vacuum. The earlier reactions and oppositional cries of al-Afghani and his disciples about the West were gradually transformed into a more articulate, antimodernist, political and philosophical paradigm which laid the intellectual groundwork for the 1979 Revolution. It is to an examination of this paradigm and its intellectual precursors that we now turn.

Al-e Ahmad: an iconoclast *homme de lettres*

In the fall of 1962, amid a social transformation which was rapidly altering the configuration of Iranian society, a monograph entitled *Gharbzadegi* was published by Jalal Al-e Ahmad.[21] The book proved to be an intellectual bombshell immediately upon its release because it called into question the basic foundations of Iranian social and intellectual history. This quality made *Gharbzadegi* the intellectual bible of several generations of Iranian intellectuals.

Gharbzadegi performed a variety of functions. First, it depicted the dilemma of a changing society by providing a critical chronicle of a century of Iranian enlightenment. Second, by putting the question of national and ethnic identity once again on the agenda, *Gharbzadegi* enunciated a nativistic alternative to the universalism of the Iranian left so popular in the previous decade. Third, by providing a passionate eulogy for a passing era and its customs, *Gharbzadegi* articulated an anti-modernist, populist discourse very much sceptical of all that the West had to offer. Finally, it exhorted many Iranian intellectuals to reassess their passive and unreflective embrace of Western ideas and culture, and called for an awakening and resistance to the hegemony of an alien culture which increasingly dominated the intellectual, social, political and economic life of the Iranian society.

Al-e Ahmad begins his defiant monograph with a definition of *gharbzadegi* as "the aggregate of events in the life, culture, civilization, and mode of thought of a people having no supporting tradition, no historical continuity, no gradient of transformation. . . ."[22] His clear intention was to sensitize the Iranian public to the problem of growing rootlessness in their country, which he perceived as a "disease."

> I speak of "gharbzadegi" as of tuberculosis. . . . I am speaking of a disease: an accident from without, spreading in an environment rendered susceptible to it. Let us seek a diagnosis for this complaint and its cause – and, if possible, its cure.[23]

Influenced by Heidegger, Al-e Ahmad viewed technology and machinism as the two essences of Western civilization. For him, the West was not just an imperialist entity, but also the heart of technological development. Al-e Ahmad maintained that technology did not allow for an equal exchange among nations, since some were exporters of it while others were its importers. Similarly, machines were not just mere instruments, but rather the embodiment of a mode of thought. Viewing machinery and technology as a talisman to the Westoxicated, he formulated his basic concern in the following terms:

> We have been unable to preserve our own historico-cultural character in the face of the machine and its fateful onslaught. Rather, we have been routed. We have been unable to take a considered stand in the face of this contemporary monster. So long as we do not comprehend the real essence, basis, and philosophy of Western civiliza-tion, only aping the West outwardly and formally (by consuming its machines), we shall be like the ass going about in a lion's skin.[24]

Al-e Ahmad believed that this disease could result in the eradication of Iran's cultural authenticity, political sovereignty, and economic well-being. His usage of a medical analogy to symbolize a cultural, political, and an economic ailment deliberately emphasized intellectual vigilance. Grounding his discussion in the familiar dichotomy of "us" versus "them" or "East" versus "West," Al-e Ahmad depicts himself as "an Easterner with his feet planted firmly in tradition, eager to make a two- or three-hundred year leap and obliged to make up for so much anxiety and straggling." Later, continuing his comparative reasoning, Al-e Ahmad writes: "As the West stood, we sat down. As the West awoke in an industrial resurrection, we passed into the slumber of the Seven Sleepers."[25]

In criticizing the "we," however, Al-e Ahmad first and foremost incriminated those Iranian intellectuals who were looking to the West as an alternative. He viewed these intellectuals as the agents most responsible for creating an environment susceptible to Western ingress and domination. Based on such a conviction, Al-e Ahmad denounces all notable thinkers of the constitutional era as being "Westoxicated." Broadening the perimeter of his criticism from intellectuals to the common people, he wrote:

1 A Westoxicated person stands on thin air.
2 A Westoxicated person is devious.
3 A Westoxicated person seeks ease.
4 A Westoxicated person normally has no specialty.
5 A Westoxicated person has no character.
6 A Westoxicated person is effete.
7 A Westoxicated person is a man totally without belief or conviction.
8 A Westoxicated person hangs on the words and handouts of the West.[26]

Al-e Ahmad viewed intellectuals as the promoters of *gharbzadegi*; yet he was not willing to accept that, as a social group, they were only a reflection of the internal contradictions and incoherence of their own society. He criticized intellectuals while ignoring the fact that in a society such as Iran, which was rapidly becoming urbanized, industrialized, and incorporated into the world capitalist system, new social classes were emerging which demanded a new definition of self. Inappropriately, Al-e Ahmad held Iranian intellectuals solely accountable for all the anguish and misery of their society. It is as if there were no relationship between these intellectuals and their place of upbringing – as if they were weeds that grew at will. Al-e Ahmad's chiding critique puts the intellectuals, rather than social relations, on trial. Perhaps it was in an imaginary debate with Al-e Ahmad that Jean-Paul Sartre declared:

> Produit de sociétés dechirées, l'intellectuel temoigne d'elles parce qu'il a intériorise leur déchirure. C'est donc un produit historique. En ce sens aucune société ne peut se plaindre de ses intellectuels sans s'accuser elle-même car elle n'a que ceux qu'elle fait.[27]

As the first eloquent critic of machinism in Iran, Al-e Ahmad lamented the crumbling of his traditional society at the hands of machines:

> as the machine entrenches itself in the towns and villages, be it in the form of a mechanized mill or a textile plant, it puts the worker in local craft industries out of work. It closes the village mill. It renders the spinning wheel useless. Production of pile carpets, flat carpets, felt carpets is at an end.[28]

Al-e Ahmad, however, was willingly oblivious to the reality that these "alien" machines also curtailed workers' hardships by reducing their work hours and increasing their productivity. He wanted to put the machine, a monstrous giant, back in the genie bottle, and turn it into an obedient servant ready to obey its master at any time. However, Al-e Ahmad did not discuss how this could be accomplished. In the entire *Gharbzadegi* essay, no mention is made of the positive results of machinery. Al-e Ahmad perceived the machine in a similar vein as the Orientalist viewed Easterners: as tools or people which, out of necessity, one was forced to employ in order to accomplish one's needs or goals.

His preoccupation with the role of machines prevented Al-e Ahmad from appreciating the complexity of advanced capitalism. Although he did not make any comments on such 1960s debates as the dependency theory, the North–South debate, or the New International Economic Order, Al-e Ahmad was clearly influenced by the amalgamation of these debates.

His theory of *gharbzadegi* could be viewed as a less systematic version of dependency theory, which was captivating many other Iranian intellectuals besides Al-e Ahmad at that time. Furthermore, from the perspective of political psychology, this resistance to machinism can be perceived as a byproduct of the mentality of many Third World intellectuals of that era. One Iranian thinker explained this dilemma regarding machinism in the following way:

> In its encounter with the West, the Westoxicated world sees its problem as one of confrontation with the former's power. They [the people] either become captivated or intimidated by it, or become fascinated and ready to sacrifice everything they have for the sake of obtaining this power. This power can best be witnessed in the technology and sophisticated machinery of the West. It is thus that, in the eyes of the Westoxicated world, the totality of the West is equated with machinism, technology and capitalism.[29]

His encounter with Western thought and the modernization process compelled Al-e Ahmad to turn toward nativism. Judging from the progression of his ideas one realizes that Al-e Ahmad came more and more to believe that the preservation of indigenous customs would be possible only through a turn toward Shi'ism. Maintaining an instrumentalist view of religion, Al-e Ahmad prescribed the revival of Shi'i Islam as Iran's most effective "vaccine" against the epidemic of *gharbzadegi*. Logically, he considered the clergy, as the meticulous guardians of faith, to be the most qualified as "doctors" who could distribute this identity-saving vaccine. His high esteem for the clergy stemmed from his regard for the ulama as the only group in Iran that did not succumb to Western domination. With a sense of deep regret over the hanging of the conservative Sheikh Fazlollah Nuri at the hands of progressive minded Constitutionalists, Al-e Ahmad declared: "I look on that great man's body on the gallows as a flag raised over our nation proclaiming the triumph of *gharbzadegi* after two hundred years of struggle."[30]

As Iran's leading intellectual of the 1960s, Al-e Ahmad epitomized the puzzling state of mind which besieged Iranian intellectuals in the post-World War II era. This was a generation tormented by the Cold War, the prospect of nuclear annihilation, de-Stalinization, neo-colonialism, Western self-doubt, endemic dictatorships, economic dependency, and nationalist uprisings. Al-e Ahmad belonged to a generation that was at once inspired by the West yet politically opposed to it; a generation xenophobic toward the West, yet drawing inspirations from the thoughts of its leading thinkers; a generation dodging religion and traditionalism, yet pulled toward them; a generation aspiring for such modernist goals as democracy, freedom, and social justice, yet skeptical of their historical precedents and contemporary problems; and finally a generation in need and search of a definition of "self" and "other." Al-e Ahmad's *Gharbzadegi* underscored the dilemma of Iran's divided intellectual polity by delimiting the choice to two alternative models: the model of the contemporary Western societies, or that of the supposed "perfect utopia" of early Islam.

Shayegan: an Oriental critic of Occidental philosophy

As one of the few Iranian intellectuals who balanced his interest in Western philosophy with an equal attention to Asian philosophy, Daryush Shayegan remains an intellectual exception worthy of in-depth consideration.[31] From 1976 to 1978 he served as the director of the Iranian Center for the Study of Civilizations, a small institute aimed at familiarizing Iranians with the civilizations of Eastern and Asian countries such as China, Japan, India and Egypt. One of the first books published by the Center was a collection of essays by Shayegan himself on the socio-cultural mutations of the traditional societies of Asia.[32]

In this book, Shayegan turned Al-e Ahmad's political critique of the West into a more elaborate philosophical critique. He warned Iranian (and Asian) intellectuals about the "double illusion" of trying to acquire Western technology while maintaining their own cultural identity. Shayegan contended that the traditional societies of Asia have fallen behind Western history and that this has become their predicament ever since. He writes:

My years-long research on the nature of Western

thought, which from the point of view of its variety, richness, searching and mesmerizing power is a unique and exceptional phenomenon in our earthly world, made me conscious of the fact that the process of Western thought has been moving in the direction of gradual negation of all articles of faith which make up the spiritual heritage of Asian civilizations.[33]

Shayegan maintained that the elements of Western thought which were gradually negating all Oriental articles of faith were to be found in "technical thinking." Following Heidegger, he called this mode of thinking the "inevitable end of Western thought." Disagreeing with the early twentieth century Iranian intellectuals who argued that one can borrow such elements as technology from the West as long as they are compatible with one's indigenous cultural heritage, he rebutted: "One cannot say that we borrow technology but would abstain from its annihilating consequences, since technology is a product of a transformation of thinking and the outcome of a process lasting a millennium."[34]

Reminiscent of French sociologist Jacques Ellul's character-ization of a "technological society" based on automatism, self-augmentation, universalism, autonomy and monism, Shayegan put forward a philosophical critique of "technical thinking."[35] He viewed technical thought as a by-product of the amalgama-tion of four descending trends in the evolution of Western thought:

1 *Technicalization of Thought*: The process of descendance from intuitive insight to technical thought, and of reducing nature into material objects.

2 *Materialization of the World*: The process of descendance from substantial forms into mathematical-mechanical concepts, which causes the negation of all mystical and magical qualities of nature.

3 *Naturalization of Man*: The process of descendance from spir-itual drives to instinctive drives, which negates all the divine qualities of celestial man.

4 *De-Mythologization*: The process of descendance from resurrec-tion and concern with future life (based on cyclical time) to historicism and a conception of time which is empty of any otherworldly meaning (based on linear time.)

Shayegan's philosophical reading of history was based on a dualistic ontology which candidly accepted the West as its culture of reference. For him, Oriental identity could only be constructed and upheld through differentiation from the West. He maintained:

> In the Orient, science never developed in the same way it evolved in the West because the Orient never became mundane, and nature never got separated from the spirit governing it, and the manifestations of divine blessing never left the realm of our universe. The Orient never produced a philosophy of history, since existence was never reduced to a mere subjectivity or a process such as in the philosophy of Hegel.[37]

In other words, "we" (Orientals) have avoided the destructive repercussions of the four descending trends of Western thought, and so much better for "us." According to Shayegan, the essence of science and philosophy in Asian civilizations was altogether different from that of the rest of the world. On the status of science he wrote:

> In the great Asian civilizations of Islam, Hinduism and Buddhism, science has always been subordinate to religion and philosophy. Science never obtained the independence and possession which it gained in Western culture, and subsequently led to its mutiny against religion and philosophy, making humans into the sole owners and possessors of the universe.[38]

Turning to philosophy, Shayegan maintained that in Asian civilizations, philosophy has an entirely different telos: "Asian thought is essentially gnostic and its goal is salvation."[39] "If Occidental philosophy is a question of existence and being, and if philosophy answers 'why' questions, in Islamic mysticism the questioner is God, and humankind only answers."[40] In other words, according to Shayegan, Occidental philosophy is based on rationalist thinking while Oriental philosophy is grounded in revelation and faith.[41] The first began with relativity and secularized all knowledge, while the latter began with prophecy and divine revelation and viewed all knowledge as sacred. In the Islamic theosophical tradition which is based upon belief in a set of esoteric truths supported by such axiomatic principles as prophecy, holiness and celestial revelation, there cannot be any "unknowns," since the answers were supposedly provided long before the questions were formulated.

Shayegan asserted that since the sixteenth century, when the West replaced religious order with civil society, it has been losing its spiritual trustworthiness. The outcome, according to him, is the present crisis of the West which has manifested itself in four forms: cultural degeneration, the twilight of gods, the demise of myths, and the collapse of spirituality.[42] Viewing the Orient as the only remaining depository of humanity, authenticity and spirituality, he warned Asian intellectuals to safeguard their cultural identity, ethnic memories and heritage in the face of the intellectual assault of Western thought. Shayegan's basic premise was that the survivors of the great Asian civilizations are living in a no-man's land, between the agony of God(s) and its (their) imminent death. For him, *gharbzadegi* was the commanding spirit of this transitional phase. Speaking of *gharbzadegi*, he wrote: "it is another side of unawareness about the historical destiny of the West . . . *gharbzadegi* equals ignorance about the West, not knowing the dominant elements of a way of thought which is the most dominant and aggressive world view on Earth."[43]

Hence Shayegan appears to be more anti-technological than Al-e Ahmad ever was. While the latter wanted only to make an obedient servant out of Western technology, Shayegan contended that Western technology and science constitute an inseparable whole. To reject one is to reject the other. The solution, according to Shayegan, was to return to cultural spirituality, which represented the only effective weapon possessed by the Orient against the intrusive West. He maintained that ethnic memories would expedite the flourishing of Asia's ancient, glorious heritage. In the case of Iran, Shayegan viewed Islam, and in particular Shi'ism, to be the constitutive source of Iranians' collective ethnic memory. For Shayegan, just like Al-e Ahmad, Islamic Iran and Iranian Islam have been so mixed with one another (for over fourteen centuries) that it is no longer possible to distinguish between the two. In a Hegelian fashion he describes the relationship between Shi'ism and Iran:

Contact with this atmosphere means contact with the

spirit of Iran which, whether we like it or not, blossomed
in the context of Islamic thought and is still influential
since Iran is in reality the trustee of the Muhammadian
truth, and the light of mysticism in Islam. It is for this
reason that Iran gives priority to the descendants of
Muhammad and its last heavenly appearance (i.e. the
Twelfth Imam).[44]

Similarly, Shayegan's upholding of religion as the Iranians'
source of identity led him to the same position previously
undertaken by Al-e Ahmad. If Shi'ism was Iran's sole spiritual
asset, then the ulama by necessity would be its most con-
scientious custodians. Shayegan wrote: "Today the class that is
more or less the protector of the ancient trust and, despite its
weak health, keeps alive the treasure of traditional thought is
to be found in the Islamic theological centers of Qom and
Mashhad."[45] He concludes his critique with a piece of philosophical-political advice: "Against a [Western] culture which is
threatening our existence in the most aggressive way, we have
no right to remain silent."[46]

Shayegan's philosophical expositions lead him to construct
the "West" as an "ontological other" (see Table 2.1). This
othering' of the West and his subsequent castigation of the
influences wrought by it compelled Shayegan to: (1) con-
gratulate Islamic and Oriental cultures (for avoiding the four
descending trends of Western thought); (2) promote an
oppositional counterdiscourse; and (3) call for an alliance with
the clergy, whom he views as the rightful custodians of the
treasure-house of traditional thought.

Shayegan's construction of the West is reminiscent of Georg
Lukacs's "reification." Inspired by Marx's theory of "fetishism
of commodities," Lukacs coined this term to describe the idea
that humans come to perceive the products and realities "made"
by themselves to have a separate existence from them. As the
new objects, humans are then alienated from, controlled by,
and live at the mercy of their own former products.[47] It seems
that Shayegan's grandiose postulation about the nature of
things Occidental has led to a reification of the "West." The
"West" is not considered as an assorted amalgamation of
disparate entities and qualities but rather as an essence, or a
Hegelian *Geist*.

Table 2.1 A taxonomy of Shayegan's philosophy[a]

	Occident	Orient
Ontological and epistemological bases of philosophy	Subjectivity, historicism, materialism	Intuition, revelation, resurrection, prophecy
Goal of philosophy	Acquisition of greater dominance through knowledge	Acquisition of truth and salvation
Nature of questioner	Mankind as questioner seeking answer to "Why" questions (Being, Existence)	Questioner is God, mankind only answers
Nature of knowledge	Profane and mundane	Sacred and gnostic
Position of science	Independent of and privileged over religion and philosophy	Dependent and subordinate to religion and philosophy
Descending trends	Technicalization of thought, secularization of the world, naturalization of man, de-mythologizing	Questioning and abandonment of cultural spirituality
Causes of present crisis	Cultural degeneration, twilight of gods, demise of myths, rise of self-centered humanity, collapse of spirituality	Infiltration by Western philosophical doctrines

[a] This table represents my reconstruction of Shayegan's positions based on his following books: *Asiya dar Barabar-e Gharb*; and *Botha-ye Zehni va Khatirah-e Azali*.

Only in the aftermath of the 1979 Revolution, when his theoretical exhortations were turned into a political reality, did Shayegan realize the shortcomings of his earlier reifications. Incriminating himself as well as his fellow travelers, he wrote:

The deep shocks that the Iranian Revolution caused in regard to our thinking, and values, as well as everyday practices, should lead us to rethink the state of relationships among civilizations. This means that we should not view these civilizations as two distinct geographical

46

worlds or opposing cultural poles. Instead, we should view them as two constellations whose stars constantly enter each other's universe and create eclectic and unclear concepts which to a sharp observer represent the non-cohesiveness of ideas present within the foundation of each civilization.[48]

Davari: an ideologue in pursuit of *homo islamicus*

If Al-e Ahmad endeavored to awaken Iranian intellectuals from their historical coma by vehemently attacking *gharbzadegi*, and Shayegan attempted to delineate an ontological difference between Orient and Occident, Reza Davari has set himself a more ambitious goal.[49] His objective is to transcend both Al-e Ahmad's politicized critique and Shayegan's ontological counterclaims through a more immanent philosophical critique aimed at, what he perceives to be, the pivotal truths of Western thought, i.e. humanism and modernity. For Davari humanism is the "blueprint for another man, a man to whom all the philosophies, theories, logic and new sciences are subordinated. Humanism is present in all philosophies and theories. . . . Even religion is interpreted based on humanism. Humanism is Westoxication. . ."[50]

After viewing humanism as tantamount to *gharbzadegi*, Davari moves on to an indictment of modernity. He writes:

> Modernity is a tree which was planted in the West and has spread everywhere. For many years we have been living under one of the dying and faded branches of this tree, and its dried shadow which is still hanging over our heads. While we have taken refuge in Islam, the shadow of this branch has still not yet totally disappeared from over our heads. In fact, neither we nor it have left each other alone. What can be done with this dried branch?[51]

The answer is obvious: not only the branch, but also the tree of modernity itself should be eradicated. How may this be done? Through the formation of a distinctive intellect, one that is distinguishable and superior to the "Western intellect." An intellect which instead of believing in humanism and the separation of politics and religion is grounded in the axioms of guardianship and prophecy.[52] As an anti-modernist philosopher aspiring toward the absolute edification of the minds of the Iranian intellectuals, Davari contends that a renaissance in Islamic philosophy can only occur through repudiating humanism, modernity and the totality of the Enlightenment accomplishments (i.e. rationalism, secularism, and individualism).

In a way, Davari is conversing with the ghost of Al-e Ahmad. He begins with rectifying the latter's definition of the West.

> The West is a way of thinking and a historical practice which started in Europe more than four-hundred years ago, and has since expanded more or less universally. Its accomplishment is to possess everything included in the celestial cosmos. Even if it were to prove the existence of God, it will be done not with the intention of obedience and submission, but in order to prove itself.[53]

According to Davari's Hegelian view of history, the West is not a partial or a political entity but rather a "totality." Davari thus goes way beyond Al-e Ahmad and Shayegan in appropriating and domesticating the West as an oppositional "other." He blames the West not only for its imperialistic ambitions *vis-à-vis* the Third World, but also for its anthromorphization of god.

Having laid down these epistemological groundwork, Davari proceeds to reprimand Al-e Ahmad's theory of *gharbzadegi* through the following statement: "'Contrary to what Al-e Ahmad thought, *gharbzadegi* is not a sickness and does not have any particular remedy;[54] and "it is not enough to limit ourselves to a purely political struggle against it. *Gharbzadegi* is not a personal physical complication, and it is not limited to certain groups".[55] Making his criticism even more pointed, Davari writes: "Not everyone who is against *gharbzadegi* or proclaims himself to be is by necessity outside its domain. Anyone who is guided by the 'Western intellect' and is conquered by Western materialism and consciously or unconsciously evaluates everyday events based on the evolution of Western history is Westoxicated."[56]

After challenging the totality of Al-e Ahmad's theory of *gharbzadegi* and politely taunting him as being "Westoxicated," Davari implicates Al-e Ahmad's historical evaluation of the Iranian intellectual movement. He claims that, for Al-e Ahmad, politics is the guarantor of fulfillment of all decency and truth, as well as wickedness.[57] Davari considers intellectuals as offspring of modern Western history who did not live before it. He designates an intellectual as one who begins with the principle of separation of politics and religion (with the help of an intellect that has taken the place of revelation). Davari credits Al-e Ahmad with having presented a brilliant description of Iranian intellectuals but maintains that the latter has failed to understand the essence of intellectualism, which Davari contends has now reached a dead end.[58]

Davari argues instead of blaming or counseling intellectuals, like Al-e Ahmad did, one has to move toward altercating with intellectualism altogether. He maintains that in the aftermath of the 1979 Revolution it is no longer sufficient just to complain about *gharbzadegi*. Instead one should indulge in a process of critical reflection on the very essence and reality of Western history. According to Davari a serious critique of *gharbzadegi* can only be effective when it is undertaken in the name of a return to the essence of Islam. He writes: "If we were not to enjoy the guidance of religion, we would unwillingly remain within the trap of the West".[59] For him, Islamic identity can only be constructed and protected through first perceiving (constituting) and then nullifying the Western "other."

Davari's philosophical account is full of sweeping generalizations. He writes: "There is not even one just [system of] government and politics in the political East or West;"[60] "no revolution can occur in the world unless the foundation of the West is transformed".[61] Davari speaks of the "spirit of the West," "Western Philosophy", "Western civilization," "destiny of the West" and the "essence of the West" as if it were a homogenous totality with well-defined cultural and intellectual boundaries. Having assumed that the "West" is a unified whole, Davari comes to the conclusion that non-Western societies should reject the West in its totality.

> What in non-Western countries are generally regarded as "modernity", "progress", "revolutionary ideology", "liberalism" and "democracy" are in reality the dispersed, superficial, and defective forms of *gharbzadegi* which can be called defective or passive *gharbzadegi*.[62]

However, Davari does not illustrate (1) why the West should be viewed as a unified whole; (2) why is it that its history has or should come to an end. His Hegelian/Heideggerian construction of a unified and totalizing "West" leaves us with no chance but either to fully accept or fully reject the "West."

Davari's philosophical axioms do not lend themselves to any type of analytical criticism. As soon as one tries to scrutinize Davari's grandiose postulates through any social science methodology, he rebuts with yet another barrage of sweeping propositions which do not enhance the terms or the topics of discourse in any reasonable fashion. Such propositions as "the scientific method of inquiry is itself a product of the West and a manifestation of its spiritual decline and technological domination" are all too frequent and fallacious to warrant a response. Furthermore, Davari's philosophical propositions has grave political ramifications for a democratic system of government. His anti-modernist stand does not and can not acknowledge any space for doubt, dissent, irreverence, or pluralism; since these are the very same achievements of the Enlightenment era he is so dauntlessly trying to disavow.

CONCLUSION

This tripartite typology attempted to trace the trajectory of the metadiscourse of *gharbzadegi* which dominated the Iranian intellectual panorama from the early 1960s onward. It was argued that *gharbzadegi* was far from being monolithic. Quite the contrary, it was a paradigm full of internal contradictions and currents that was refined at each turn by its advocates. *Gharbzadegi* metamorphosed from Al-e Ahmad's chilling political critique into Shayegan's philosophical formulations, and came to rest temporarily with Davari's ontological denunciation of the West. The first blamed the West, the second mourned its self-inflicted death, and the third called for its abandonment.

Under the aegis of depicting an Oriental identity, all three thinkers discussed here have come to depict the West as a radical other. The internal/external figurative speech of *gharbzadegi* has forged a discursive space in which a radical mental boundary separates "we" and "they." The result has been the gradual essentialization and purification of the categorical dualism of *gharbzadegi*. This dualistic perception has been both indispensable and detrimental to the endeavor of Iranian intellectuals to construct a collective identity of their own. It has been indispensable since their alibi involved devaluation of the "other" from the very beginning, and detrimental since they have been consumed with this imaginary "other."

On the face of such theoretical lacuna and intellectual stagnation, it should not come as a surprise that the majority of both religious and secular Iranian intellectuals have turned toward nativism, traditionalism and Islamicism. As a result of this dynamic transformation, the status of the discourse of *gharbzadegi* is no longer the same in post-revolutionary Iran as it was in the pre-revolutionary era. It grew from being an acculturated response of disenchanted intellectuals to becoming the hegemonic discourse of a revolutionary élite. The former uneasy squabbles of a number of critical intellectuals were now transformed to the theoretical stockpile of a revolutionary movement.

It is inconceivable to begin to comprehend the true causes of the unmistakable phobias, distrust, enmity, sensibilities, and defiant behavior of post-revolutionary Iranian leaders toward the West without first scrutinizing the discourse of *gharbzadegi*. Such slogans as "Death to the Great Satan" and "Neither East nor West," which captivated the minds of so many people, were not merely an Iranian replica of Third World nationalistic sentiments. They were also enriched with a strong dosage of the ontological principles of *gharbzadegi*. Khomeini's articulation of Iran's Islamic and national identities with one another and his suspicion of the outside world and commitment to the notion of a besieged nation engaged in an unequal combat helped to inculcate a garrison state mentality among many Iranians already accustomed to a universally dichotomizing mind-set.

Despite its triumphant political status, *gharbzadegi* remains intellectually tormented. It is based on too many untenable, questionable ontological and epistemological premises to sustain itself for long. Its nostalgia for the past, attachment to things native, idealization of identity, and ethical rejection of modernity are all problematical. Having grown jaded by the fiery rhetoric of *gharbzadegi*, an increasing number of Iranian citizens, intellectuals and politicians have come to abandon this discourse altogether. They view its dichotomizing mind-set, redolent romanticism and unabashed anti-modernism, as short-sighted, unpopular and irrelevant. The end may be at hand for a discourse too ill-suited for the needs of a rapidly transforming polity.

NOTES

1 See the following works by Michel Foucault: *Discipline & Punish: The Birth of the Prison* (Vintage Books, New York, 1979); *The History of Sexuality*, vol. 1 (Vintage Books, New York, 1980); *Madness and Civilization: A History of Insanity in the Age of Reason* (Pantheon, New York, 1965); and *The Birth of the Clinic: An Archaeology of Medical Perception* (Vintage Books, New York, 1975).

2 Stephen K. White, 'Poststructuralism and Political Reflection'. *Political Theory*, vol. 16, no. 2 (1988), pp. 190.

3 Edward Said, *Orientalism* (Vintage Books, New York, 1979).

4 Ibid, p. 3.

5 Throughout this chapter the two dichotomies of Orient/Occident and East/West will be used interchangeably in order to remain loyal to the literal translations and the tone of the works cited. The 'East' or the 'Orient' encompasses all of the Middle and Near East, Asia, Far East, and North Africa, while the 'West' or the 'Occident' refers mainly to Western Europe and North America. As we shall see later, however, the term 'West' is also (mis)used very ambiguously by a number of Iranian intellectuals. While it represents a geographical entity for some, others take a more symbolic or mystical view of it, and regard it as a way of life or a set of ontological doctrines.

6 For two thought-provoking works on the 'constitution of otherness' see Tzvetan Todorov, *The Conquest of America: The Question of the Other* (Harper & Row, New York, 1984) and Michael J. Shapiro, *The Politics of Representation: Writing Practices in Biography, Photography, and Policy Analysis* (University of Wisconsin Press, Madison, 1988).

7 Throughout this chapter I have used the term 'intellectual' as the English equivalent of the Persian term *'rowshanfekr'* which has a more generic connotation than its English counterpart. The category of *'rowshanfekran'* encompasses both the intelligentsia and the intellectuals. Hence, such groups as writers, poets, literary critics, artists, teachers, professors, researchers, translators, and journalists have been categorized as intellectuals.

8 The progenitor of the term *gharbzadegi* is a contemporary Iranian philosopher named Ahmad Fardid (b. 1912). However, it was popularized by Jalal Al-e Ahmad in a book by the same title published in 1962. *Gharbzadegi* has been rendered into various English translations such as: 'Weststruckness,' in *Gharbzadegi [Weststruckness]*, trans. by J. Green and A. Alizadeh (Mazda Publishers, Lexington, 1982); 'Occidentosis,' in *Occidentosis: A Plague From the West*, trans. by R. Campbell (Mizan Press, Berkeley, 1984); 'Plagued by the West,' in *Plagued By the West*, trans. by Paul Sprachman (Caravan Books, Delmar, 1982); 'Westernmania', in James Bill,

The Eagle and the Lion: The Tragedy of American-Iranian Relations (Yale University Press, New Haven, 1988); 'Euromania,' in Roy Mottahedeh, *The Mantle of the Prophet* (Pantheon Books, New York, 1985); 'Xenomenia,' in *Islam and Revolution: Writings and Declarations of Imam Khomeini*, trans. by Hamid Algar (Mizan Press, Berkeley, 1981); 'Westitis' in Edward Mortimer, *Faith & Power* (Vintage Books, New York, 1982); and 'Westoxication,' in Nikki Keddie, *Roots of Revolution* (Yale University Press, New Haven, 1981). In all instances the term *gharbzadegi* was generally meant to convey Iranian society's and its intellectuals' indiscriminate borrowing from the West. I prefer 'Westoxication' since it most closely resembles Al-e Ahmad's usage of *gharbzadegi* as a medical metaphor denoting a social illness. However, throughout this chapter I will continue to use the original Persian term *gharbzadegi* since its use somewhat differs from one author to another.

9 One notable exclusion in this regard is Dr Ali Shariati whose work came to exert a lot of influence upon Iranian intellectuals during the 1970s.

10 The other being Dr Abd al-Karim Surush, a British educated philosopher and historian of science. I have dealt with the ideas of Surush and Shariati, among others, in my forthcoming book *Iranian Intellectuals and the West: A Study in Orientalism in Reverse* (State University of New York Press, Albany, 1992).

11 For a systematic treatment of the life and ideas of some of the more influential Iranian intellectuals of this era see the following works of Fereydoun Adamiyat: *Andishahha-ye Mirza Aqa Khan Kermani* [The Thought of Mirza Aqa Khan Kermani], (Zar, Tehran, 1978), *Andishahha-ye Talebuf-e Tabrizi* [The Thought of Talebuf-e Tabrizi], (Damavand, Tehran, 1984), *Fekr-e Demukrasi-e Ejtema'i dar Nahzat-e Mashrutiyyat-e Iran* [The Idea of Social Democracy in the Iranian Constitutional Movement], (Payam, Tehran, 1984), and *Andishah-ye Taraqqi va Hokumat-e Qanun* [The Idea of Progress and the Rule of Law], (Khvarazmi, Tehran, 1977).

12 Abo'l-Hasan Khan Ilchi, *Heyrat'nameh: Safarnameh-ye Abo'l-Hasan Khan Ilchi beh Landan* [The Book of Perplexities: Travel Memoirs of Abo'l-Hasan Khan Ilchei To London], edited by Hasan Mursalvand (Mu'assasah-ye Khadamat-e Farhangi-e Rasa, Tehran, 1985), p. 221.

13 See Hamid Algar, *Mirza Malkum Khan: A Study in the History of Iranian Modernism* (University of California Press, Berkeley, 1973).

14 Cited in Gholamreza Vatandoust, 'Sayyid Hasan Taqizadah and *KAVEH*: Modernism in Post-Constitutional Iran (1916–1921),' unpublished Ph.D dissertation, University of Washington, 1977, p. 47.

15 In the Arab world, Rifa'ah Rafi' al-Tahtawi, Taha Hussein and Ahmad Lutfi al-Said suggested a similar undertaking in taking a short cut to civil society. See Ibrahim Abu-Lughod, *Arab Rediscovery of Europe: A Study in Cultural Encounters* (Princeton University Press, Princeton, 1963).

16 The simultaneous rise of Muhammad Ali's movement in Egypt, and the Young Ottomans, the Young Turks and Ataturk in Turkey led to enormous cultural transformations in these two respective societies. For an exposition of the ideas of Arab and Turkish intellectuals during this era see: Albert Hourani, *Arab Thought in the Liberal Age 1798-1939* (Cambridge University Press, Cambridge, 1984); and Serif Mardin, *The Genesis of Young Ottoman Thought: A Study in the Modernization of Turkish Political Ideas* (Princeton University Press, Princeton, 1962).

17 Ahmad Kasravi, *Payam be Daneshmandan-e Urupa va Amrika* [A Message To European and American Scientists], (n.a., Tehran, 1958), p.35.

18 See H. Algar, 'Malkum Khan, Akhundzadeh and the Proposed Reform of the Arabic Alphabet,' *Middle Eastern Studies*, vol. 5, no. 5 (1969), pp. 116-130; and M. A. Jazayery, 'Ahmad Kasravi and the Controversy Over Persian Poetry', *International Journal of Middle East Studies*, vol. 4, no. 4 (1973), pp. 190-203.

19 See H. Pakdaman Natiq, *Jamal ed-Din Assad Abadi dit Afghani* (Maisonneuve et Lgrose, Paris, 1969); and N. Keddie, *An Islamic Response to Imperialism: Political and Religious Writings of Sayyid Jamal ad-Din al-Afghani* (University of California Press, Berkeley, 1983).

20 For a philosophical discussion of 'modernism,' 'modernization,' and 'modernity' see Marshall Berman, *All That is Solid Melts into Air: The Experience of Modernity* (Simon and Schuster, New York, 1982).

21 Jalal Al-e Ahmad (1923-69) was born into a religious family from northern Iran. Upon graduating from high school he broke with religion and joined the ranks of the Marxist Tudeh Party, where he soon rose to a high position within the party's publicity department. In 1947, however, he left the party and retired from the political arena only to return a few years later during the oil nationalization campaign led by Dr Muhammad Mossadeq. His reorientation toward Islam gradually took place after the 1953 coup and reached its focal point with the publication of *Gharbzadegi*. By this time, as a teacher, belletrist, translator and ethnographer he had earned a reputation for being the unofficial, leading spokesman of anti-establishment Iranian intellectuals, and served as a mentor to a great many of them.

22 Jalal Al-I Ahmad, *Occidentosis: A Plague From the West*, p. 34.

23 Ibid, p. 27.

24 Ibid, p. 31.

25 Ibid, p. 55.

26 Ibid, pp. 92-7.

27 Jean-Paul Sartre, *Plaidoyer pour les intellectuels* (Gallimard, Paris, 1972), p. 41.

28 Al-I Ahmad, *Occidentosis*, p. 68.

29 Daryush Ashuri, 'Dar Amadi be Ma'na-ye Jahan-e Sevvom', [A Preface to the Meaning of the 'Third World,'] *Kitab-e Agah* (Agah, Tehran, 1983), p. 206.

30 Al-I Ahmad, *Occidentosis*, p. 57.

31 Born in 1935 in Tehran, Shayegan was educated in Iran, England, Switzerland and France, respectively. In 1968, he received his doctorate in Hindu and Sufi philosophy from the Sorbonne under the supervision of Professors Corbin and Lacombe. Upon his return to Iran he became a professor of mythology, Indology and comparative philosophy at Tehran University. After the revolution he served as the Director of the Institute of Ismaili Studies in Paris, and is presently the editor of *Iran Nameh*, a Persian journal of Iranian Studies published by the Foundation for Iranian Studies in Maryland, USA.

32 Daryush Shayegan, *Asiya dar Barabar-e Gharb* [Asia Facing the West], (Amir Kabir, Tehran, 1977).

33 Ibid, p. 3.

34 Ibid, p. 46.

35 See Jacques Ellul, *The Technological Society* (Knopf, New York, 1964).

36 Shayegan, *Asiya dar Barabar-e Gharb*, pp. 47–8.

37 Daryush Shayegan, 'Din va Falsafeh va Elm dar Sharq va Gharb' [Religion, Philosophy and Science in East and West], *Alefba*, vol. 1, no. 6 (1977), p. 108.

38 Ibid, p. 102.

39 Shayegan, *Asiya dar Barabar-e Gharb*, p. 233.

40 Shayegan, *Din va Falsafeh va Elm dar Sharq va Gharb*, p. 109.

41 See Daryush Shayegan, *Botha-ye Zehni va Khatirah-'e Azali* [Idols of Mind and Perennial Memory] (Tehran: Amir Kabir, 1976).

42 Shayegan, *Asiya dar Barabar-e Gharb*, p. 168.

43 Ibid, p. 51.

44 Ibid, p. 190.

45 Ibid, p. 296.

46 Ibid, p. 51.

47 See Georg Lukacs, *History and Class Consciousness* (MIT Press, Cambridge, 1968), pp. 83–110.

48 Daryush Shayegan, 'Ideolozhik Shodan-e Sonnat' [The Ideologization of Tradition], *Zaman-E Now*, no. 12 (1986), p. 45. For a more comprehensive treatment of this topic see his *Qu'est-ce qu'une revolution religieuse?*, (Les Presses d'aujourd'hui, Paris, 1982).

49 Born in Ardakan (near Isfahan) in 1933, Davari finished his primary and secondary education in his place of birth. His dissertation, completed in 1967, dealt with the influence of Greek philosophy on the political philosophy of such early Islamic thinkers as Farabi. Since his graduation, Davari has been a professor of philosophy at his alma mater, Tehran University, where he mainly teaches courses on the history of modern philosophy. After the revolution, while maintaining his academic post, Davari served in such capacities as a researcher in the Iranian Academy of Philosophy; member of the newly-found Iranian Academy of Sciences; as well as a member of a number of scientific and academic delegations representing Iran in international conventions.

50 Reza Davari, *Enqelab-e Islami va Vaz'-e Konuni-e Alam* [Islamic Revolu-

tion and the Present Status of the World], (Entesharat-e Markaz-e Farhang-ye Allamah Tabataba'i, Tehran, 1982), p. 59.

51 Ibid, p. 83.

52 Ibid, p. 85.

53 Reza Davari, 'Lavazem va Natayej-e Enkar-e Gharb' [The Necessities and Consequences of Refuting the West], *Kayhan-e Farhangi*, vol. 1, no. 3 (1984), p. 18.

54 Davari, *Enqelab-e Islami va Vaz'-e Konuni-e Alam*, p.56.

55 Ibid, p. 83.

56 Ibid, p. 80.

57 Ibid, p. 48.

58 Reza Davari, *Shammah-ey az Tarikh-e Gharbzadegi-e Ma (Vaz'-e Konuni-e Tafakkor dar Iran)* [A Short Account of Our Westoxicated History (The Present Status of Thought in Iran)], (Surush, Tehran, 1984), p. 8.

59 For more on Davari's views see the following two articles of his: 'Eshterak-e Mabade-ye Gharb va Sharq-e Siyasi' [The Common Origin of Political West and East], *Kayhan-e Havai*, 6 Aug. 1986; and 'Ilteqat: Tajavoz-e az Had' [Eclecticism: Exceeding the Limits], *Kayhan-e Havai* 23 Sept. 1986.

60 Davari, *Shammah-ey az Tarikh-e Gharbzadegi-e Ma*, p. 22.

61 Ibid, p. 15.

62 Davari, *Enqelab-e Islami va Vaz'-e Konuni-e Alam*, p. 113.

3

IRAN'S RELIGIOUS ESTABLISHMENT
The Dialectics of Politicization
Mohammad Borghei

INTRODUCTION

Ayatollah Khomeini and his associates invariably state that the Iranian Revolution began in 1962.[1] Also, specific reference is made to that effect in the preamble of the Constitution of the Islamic Republic of Iran. But the literature concerning the Islamic Revolution is generally silent about that year and the preceding years. The literature, at the most, dates to the events of June 5, 1963. In effect, those events were the culmination of a movement that began earlier in 1961, found its direction in practice in 1962 and engulfed a wide spectrum of the religious establishment. The main question is how did the Qom Seminary and the religious establishment, that had remained politically aloof until 1961, appear on the political scene within a period of one year, and how was it able to start a movement which was unprecedented on such a scale since the Mossadeq era in the early 1950s? This chapter deals with the developments within the religious community, and in particular within the Qom Seminary after the death of Ayatollah Boroujerdi in 1961, in the process of the rise of political Islam.

We will examine the religious atmosphere of Iran and, in particular, of the Qom Seminary, during the leadership of Ayatollah Boroujerdi. It will also be demonstrated how an alert leader such as Ayatollah Khomeini, by taking advantage of the favorable conditions within the Seminary as well as the political situation of the country, was able to transform the Seminary from a politically aloof institution into an active and interventionist one.

This results from the fact that the emergence of a *Marja* (religious leader of reference) is more a function of his understanding of the socio-political situation of the Seminary and the country in general and his skillful handling of the situation rather than the mere depth of his religious knowledge. Although the time-frame of this paper is basically the 1961–3 period, nevertheless the events and developments that took place in the religious establishment in Iran left their permanent marks on the politics and political culture of Iran during the 1978–9 Revolution and its aftermath, and in a sense shaped the dynamics of post-revolutionary Iran.

Two points concerning the research methodology are also in order:

1 Since our primary objective is the examination of the politicization of the Seminary and the religious establishment, the events have been viewed from that standpoint and outside developments have been treated only in terms of their impact and effects on the Seminary.
2 Sources concerning the developments within the Seminary during this period are very limited. On the one hand, the Shah's government, the media, writers and essayists in general belonged to the modern sector of the society and were unfamiliar with the Seminary and religious community. Therefore, little was written by them on the subject either then or subsequently. On the other hand, the Seminary and the religious community with their traditionalist approach treated the events orally in face-to-face, intragroup discussions and did not care to record them.

Consequently, the information supplied in this chapter is based largely on personal observations and participation in those gatherings. Wherever possible, available resources and the works of other authors have been utilized in the preparation of this paper.

PROFILE OF THE OLD ORDER

In order to understand the course of the subsequent developments in the Qom Seminary as well as in the religious establishment of the country as a whole and the way that each of the newly emerging leaders attained power and influence, it is necessary to examine the situation in Qom and in the religious establishments of the country at the time of Ayatollah Boroujerdi's death in March 1961.

Ayatollah Boroujerdi was considered the most influential and powerful *Marja* since the Constitutional Revolution. His domain was not limited to Iran but encompassed Iraq, Pakistan Lebanon and, perhaps, other parts of the world; wherever Shi'ite Muslims lived. He was known as *Al-Mojadded* (the innovator), for his concentrated efforts in the reconstruction and expansion of the theological center. Although Boroujerdi spearheaded the expansion of the Qom Seminary and was the mainstay of its power and strength, nevertheless the religious establishment of the country inherited a number of basic problems. In general, following the policies of great *Marjas* of the post-Constitutional era, he alienated the religious establishment from society and turned that body into a stagnant institution. This was particularly true *vis-à-vis* the realm of politics and the modernization movement.

Non-interference in politics

Ayatollah Boroujerdi refrained from involvement either in politics or in the affairs of government. In the exceptional cases when a law or a bill appeared to be in direct variance with religious rules, he expressed his views and did so within the traditionally recognized limits of the clergy. He, along with the majority of the *ulama* (religious authorities) of the post-Constitutional era, believed in non-interference in politics.[2] This approach was in line with the recommendations the great Shi'ite theologian Ayatollah Seyyed Kazem Yazdi (d. 1919) made to the *ulama* in the post-constitutional era and with that of Ayatollah Haeri (d. 1945), the great religious authority of the period.[3]

Even after the abdication of Reza Shah in 1941, when various social and political forces became highly active, and involvement in political affairs became a hot issue among religious groups, Ayatollah Boroujerdi opened a conference in February 1949 to consider the issue. After lengthy discussions, the participants, all prominent clergymen, voted in favor of non-interference in politics.[4] Ayatollah Boroujerdi's track record and his strong belief in non-interference in politics made it impossible for political forces to organize and take root in the theological center. Those clergymen or groups that took an active interest and role in politics were banished from the center. The following constitute clear examples.

Ayatollah Kashani, a highly respected religious authority and politician, received written praise from several religious authorities from Najaf when he returned to Iran in 1919.[5] But the Qom Center remained indifferent towards him. Even when Ayatollah Kashani was at the peak of his political power and was elected as the speaker of the *Majles*, Ayatollah Boroujerdi kept his distance.

Ayatollah Seyyed Ali-Akbar Borghei, a well-known and respected lecturer at the Seminary and the author of several important books, was ostracized after his involvement in politics in 1953. Theological students attacked his home as well as the bookstore owned by his son in the Qom bazaar, and the Ayatollah had no recourse but to flee Qom. During the years when he was active in politics, Borghei was abandoned by the clergymen from the Qom Center.[6]

The *Fedaiyan-e Eslam* Group (the Devotees of Islam) was founded by two or three young clergymen in 1945. Since these men did not command any prestige in the Qom Center, they failed to establish any power base there. Moreover, none of the prestigious clergymen joined their ranks. It was rumored that when Vahedi, a Fedaiyan leader, tried to disrupt the procession arranged at the time of bringing the remains of Reza Shah to Qom, the Lorestani theological students, under order from Ayatollah Boroujerdi, drove Vahedi out of the city.[7]

In 1947, Ayatollah Boroujerdi rejected the idea of politicizing the Palestine issue. It was precisely for this reason that he left the gathering in which Ayatollah Eshraqi was delivering a sermon.[8] Well-known religious authorities, such as Ayatollah Zanjani who supported the National Front, irrespective of their reputation for scholarship, did not have intimate connections with the Seminary. The idea of keeping politics out of the Seminary resulted in alienating politically-motivated religious forces.

Lagging behind the time

Historically speaking, opposition of the clergy to modernism had it roots in the Constitutional Revolution. As a result of the removal of the clergy from the political scene following the Constitutional Revolution and the severe suppression of the clergy by Reza Shah, the clergy was characterized as having rejected modernization to the extent that they banned radio programs, considered modern education as a corrupt institution and regarded civil service work as a vulgar activity.

Even clerics such as Ayatollahs Sanglaji, Qomshe'i, and a few other prominent ones who were in favor of the modern educational system, the introduction of reform into the Seminary, and modification of religious orthodoxy among the people, were totally ostracized and were branded as nonconformists by the majority of the clergy. The following examples simply illustrate the continuation of the aforementioned trend at the time of Ayatollah Boroujerdi's leadership.

In 1955, among 32 students in a class in an Islamic school in Tehran, the families of some 12 students prevented their children from pursuing their education in modern institutions.[9]

When Ayatollah Borhan opened a school for girls on Lorzadeh Street in Tehran in the early 1950s, he was vehemently opposed by the Seminary and many devout Muslims.

By 1961, a large number of pious Muslims were on the government's payroll. Each month they would take their entire salaries to reliable clergymen for "purification."

In 1959, a tailor in Qom, who was listening to the radio in his shop was attacked and beaten up by a clergyman.

During those years, Haj Ansari, the greatest orator among those who met with approval of the Seminary, kept tongue-lashing the inhabitants of Qom who secretly owned television sets. He called modern schools "centers of infidelity and faithlessness". He assailed the prevalence of moral turpitude in girls' schools.

Nevertheless, modernism as a requirement of the time and assisted by the government was making headway. This could be observed in the fact that prominent religious authorities such as Ayatollahs Najafi and Khomeini were sending their youngest children to high school, and the sons of Ayatollah Shariatmadari and Haeri were enrolled in local and foreign universities.

Undoubtedly, the Seminary and the main body of the clerical establishment were neither in touch with the young generation that had been educated in the modern educational system nor did they understand that generation's needs. Therefore, the religious youth turned to the translation of works from Arabic. Works of Jurjc Zaydan and other Egyptian authors about the biographies of prominent figures in Islam were in great demand.

While during the 1940s and 1950s large quantities of voluminous books were being published on subjects like *On the Manners of Toilet,*[10] the magazine *Maktab-e Eslam* (*The Islamic School*) was the only publication in the Seminary that was able to establish a link with the new generation. Under these conditions, religious forces outside the Seminary that tried to fill the gap and meet the demands of the young generation not only were abandoned but also were driven out of the main body of the religious establishment. The Association for Islamic Education (*Jame-e-ye Ta'limat-e Eslami*) which operated some 170 primary and secondary schools[11] was founded by Haj Sheikh Abbas-Ali Eslami, a relatively unknown clergyman. The main body of the clergy rarely participated in the activities and expansion of the association. In the interest of reaching out and establishing contact with the new generation, Hedayat Mosque was constructed in an area where many movie theaters were located and was thought to be the center of modern Tehran. But fundraising for the completion of the mosque proved to be extremely difficult in 1961; religiously-inclined, educated individuals were complaining that the amount of money collected in a matter of few days for financing the repair work in Seyyed Aziz-Allah Mosque in the bazaar of Tehran far exceeded the amount that had been collected for the construction of Hedayat Mosque over a period of several years.

Thus, it became increasingly obvious that the changes and developments that took place in society over the previous decades necessitated the introduction of reform measures into the Seminary in political, social, and educational areas.

The monthly lectures (*Goftar-e Mah*) that began in 1960 in Tehran and attracted enlightened religious reformist figures such as Mahmoud Taleqani, Mehdi Bazargan, and Morteza Motahhari proved to be extremely popular. When the first volume of the collected lectures was published, it became a bestseller. These lectures covered such issues as reforming the Seminary, establishing a council to perform the functions of the *Marja*, and concern about public issues.[12] However, with the presence of a man of Ayatollah Boroujerdi's stature, it was impossible to take any action. It was only after his departure that the main obstacle was removed and all reformists were set free.

THE POLITICIZATION OF THE RELIGIOUS ESTABLISHMENT

The internal transformations of the religious establishment came at a time when society as a whole was in political turmoil. In the early 1960s, the regime was facing severe economic and social problems. It had no choice but to initiate wide-ranging reforms. The Shah, who was aware that his "White Revolution" reform programs were going to face resistance from the clergy, found it to his advantage to have the most eminent *Marja-e Taqlid* (source of imitation) reside in the far-away town of Najaf in Iraq rather than in Qom, which is located within spitting distance of Tehran. So, he chose Ayatollah Hakim, the then prominent *Marja-e Taqlid* in the Shi'ite world and a resident of Najaf, to send his condolences on the death of Ayatollah Boroujerdi.[13] The timing coincided with the extreme unpopularity of the Shah, following his dissolution of the Majiles in May 1961, and directly involving himself in political issues. Therefore, his telegram of condolences to Ayatollah Hakim and the response of the Ayatollah was interpreted as the Ayatollah being supportive of the Shah. This impression ruined Ayatollah Hakim's chances for leadership.

In order to understand the mechanisms and criteria governing the election of a *Marja*, it is imperative to consider the contenders for leadership in the context of both internal clerical network as well as external societal links and involvements.

A number of clergymen attain a degree of distinction among their colleagues by a combination of factors, including scholarship and piety in the Seminary. Such distinction entitles them to the title of the grand Ayatollah. The ordinary Shi'ite Muslim is required to choose a *Marja-e Taqlid*. This task is accomplished through a chain of enquiry, i.e the seeker would ask his local *mollah* for guidance in his search. The local *mollah*, in turn, seeks the opinion of a trusted higher ranking *mollah*. The latter would recommend one of the distinguished Ayatollahs. When the

Marja is chosen in this manner, the followers begin sending their religious dues to the chosen *Marja* through the same network of the clergy. The proper handling of a social or political issue by a prominent clergyman can improve his popularity and prestige. Or, as the case of Ayatollah Hakim indicated, a poorly handled issue may destroy his standing in the eyes of the public.

Marjas and their handling of current issues

With Ayatollah Hakim's exit from the race, the field was left open to the *Marjas* in Qom to step into the shoes of the late Ayatollah Boroujerdi. Ayatollahs Shariatmadari, Golpaygani, and Najafi were eminent among the theologians and far ahead of other contenders in the race.

One of these men, namely Ayatollah Najafi, was a good-natured individual with the qualities of a sage who did not nurture any desire for leadership and had not even tried to organize a power base. Ayatollah Golpaygani on the other hand was interested in holding the position of leadership. He was utterly conservative and therefore his followers came from like-minded conservative groups. When the race for leadership was in progress, Ayatollah Golpaygani issued a *Fatva* (religious ruling or opinion) which was strongly opposed by the youth and the enlightened believers. In his *Fatva*, Ayatollah Golpaygani ruled that since paper money can neither be weighed nor measured, it is not subject to the law of usury. This meant that a man could not be held in violation of religious laws concerning usury if he loaned 1,000 rials to another man and later claimed and received 1,200 rials in exchange.

The Ayatollah, despite the complete prohibition of usury in Islam, was condoning it as an official and legal practice. The entire episode demonstrated vividly that Ayatollah Golpaygani was out of touch with modern times and with the pace of development in society and that he did not understand the people, even the very religious ones. Consequently, several public statements were made against this ruling by individuals and groups.[14]

While Ayatollah Golpaygani's blunder eliminated his chances of succession, it helped Ayatollah Shariatmadari, known for his shrewdness and eminence in the Seminary. His administrative skills and, most importantly, his immense following among the Azarbaijanis, which was ethnically motivated, propelled him far ahead of the remaining contenders. But a number of religious, political, and educated groups who for reasons mentioned earlier were dissatisfied with the Seminary and were not happy with Ayatollah Shariatmadari's victory. They believed that Ayatollah Shariatmadari was advocating very nearly the policies of the late Ayatollah Boroujerdi.

However, there were other men, such as Ayatollah Khomeini, who were very little known outside the scholastic centers of the clergy. Even in Qom, Ayatollah Khomeini was only addressed as Haj Aqa Ruhollah with no titles attached to his name. Despite his unassuming circumstances he was moving forward slowly but steadily. He did not receive any *Sahm-e imam* (religious dues) and therefore did not pay any allowances to theological students. He had not yet established any close link with either the public or the main body of the clerical network.

Nonetheless, he was well-known among the notables for his scholarship and piety as well as for his advocacy of the clergy's involvement in politics and revision of certain religious rules to meet the requirements of modern times. Although Ayatollah Khomeini held his lectures in the isolated Khanum Mosque, they were the most heavily attended lectures in Qom. He was interested in the issues in which the young and educated generation were concerned. To strike up a conversation with members of the younger generation he would, when the need arose, even listen to the news about soccer matches.[15] The religious people who were dismayed with the backwardness and the reactionary stand of the clergy gradually became aware of Khomeini's views and gathered around him. In the meantime, some laymen also joined the ranks of his followers simply because Khomeini in his ecclesiastic treatise had discarded some of the well-grounded religious traditions concerning such issues as the inedibility of raisins when they are swollen as a result of cooking and the untouchability of the sweat of a man produced by the exertion in an unlawful intercourse. At the same time, certain political events led to two movements among religious groups. The first movement which lasted fifty-four days was against the Bill of the Election of the Municipal and Provisional Council. The second move-

ment was against the Shah's "White Revolution". These movements resulted in the politicization of religion and caused an
otherwise unknown *Marja* to suddenly become a prominent
political and religious leader.

First movement: a two-month clergy movement

In October 1962, the Council of Ministers adopted a bill
concerning the elections of the municipal and provincial
councils. Religious groups under the leadership of the clergy
rallied against the bill, opposing it on three grounds:

1 In the bill, the words "heavenly scripture" had been substituted for the word "Koran."
2 Women had been enfranchised.
3 The condition of being a Muslim in order to be qualified for
  candidacy and election had been eliminated.

Each political group interpreted the bill differently. The Shah,
who was planning to introduce his "Shah–People Revolution"
within the next few months, was using the bill to test the social
and political climate and gauge the strength of the opposition.
The clergy and religious groups believed that the bill not only
negated the fundamental tenets of their faith but also was an
intentional attempt to weaken Islam and impose limitations on
the application of Islamic laws. Secular political forces such as
the second National Front and the Toilers' Party, which at the
time were very active and believed to be very strong, were
facing a dilemma. True, they strongly opposed the regime of
the Shah, but had no grounds to object to a progressive law. In
fact item two had been on their own agenda even before the bill
was drafted. It was obvious that they had serious disagreement
with clergy on that issue. Consequently, even though they
were aware of the fact that the Shah was using the bill as a
means for political maneuvering and by its implementation the
Shah would score a victory, they were not only unable to form
an alliance with the clergy against the government but were
also in accord with the government view on the issue and
wholeheartedly opposed that of the clergy. Before examining
the method of operation of *Marjas* and the clergy in opposing

the above-mentioned bill, a brief accounting of the course of events related to the movement against it is in order.

On October 8, 1962, the draft of the bill was made public by the government. It immediately encountered severe objection by the clergy. The *Marjas* and other clergymen began addressing the Shah and the Prime Minister Alam. Alam left their telegrams unanswered but started an extensive media campaign against the superficiality of the hardcore believers and their opposition to women's rights.[16] As a countermeasure the clergy began to mobilize the believers and to use the pulpits and mosques as their bases for attacking the government. The bazaars were closed in the cities of Tehran, Qom, and Tabriz in support of the clergy. The clergy with their second round of telegrams to the Shah and the Prime Minister increased their pressure on the government. In the end, the government retreated by announcing that it was left to the *Majles* to adopt and/or reject the draft bill. But the *Majles* had been dissolved in May 1961, and no date had been set for election of a new *Majles*. Alam in his answer to the *Marjas'* telegrams alleged that the participation of women in elections had been approved before in connection with the municipal elections by the mere fact that at the time no objection was raised against it by Ayatollah Boroujerdi. The Shah also responded to the telegrams of the clergy and called the attention of the *ulama* to the changed circumstances of women and also implicitly accused the *ulama* of backwardness and obscurantism. The clergy, however, did not yield and reacted by shutting down classes at the Seminary, refusing to hold public prayers, increasing pressure on the government through their speeches in the pulpits, organizing rallies and demonstrations, and closing the bazaars. On November 26, the Prime Minister announced the cancellation of the draft bill. The clergy did not accept the mere announcement of cancellation as a sufficient measure. Finally on December 1, the Council of Ministers adopted a bill which formally declared the draft bill as null and void.

It appears that Khomeini was perhaps the only leader who played his hands in this political game admirably. In view of the differences between Ayatollah Khomeini's style of leadership and that of the other *"Marja-e Taqlids"* that continued all through the subsequent years, it is enlightening to discuss his methods more fully.

The political emergence of Khomeini

Ayatollah Khomeini was well aware of the fact that the institution of religion, with its vast network which reached the far corners of the country, had tremendous influence at all levels of society. If those influences were to be exploited politically, it would unleash the widest, strongest and the most fundamental movements. On the other hand, as was mentioned earlier, in the past several decades, the institution of religion had been totally uninterested in wielding power and had mainly confined its efforts to religion and personal affairs. If this rusted old sword were sharpened, it could be turned into an awesome weapon. Also because of the necessity of imitation and the need for *Marja-e Taqlid* in Shi'ism, the clergy remained the central decision-making body with the Seminary as its bastion. Therefore without control over the decision-making body, any movement would only touch the periphery and would thus be ineffective.

Thus Ayatollah Khomeini, prior to becoming actively involved in politics, first, was elevated to the highest rank in the membership of the religious organization, i.e., he established himself as the *Marja-e Taqlid*. But as long as Ayatollah Boroujerdi, the undisputed leader, was alive Khomeini restrained himself and did not engage in any political activities. Later, when the first opportunity for involvement in politics appeared, he took the fullest advantage of the situation but avoided extremism and individualism. Thus, to change the seminary and make it politically active, Khomeini adopted tactics similar to those of knowledgeable party activists. To affect this, first he needed to establish channels of communication with people, and then use their force to unseat his prominent competitors. Further, he needed the concurrence of his colleagues. He could earn it either by convincing them or by enticing the people to apply pressure on them, which would bring about the gradual elimination of his opponents. In his fight to change the religious establishment, Khomeini deemed it necessary to not only keep the totality of the institution intact, but also to strengthen its organizational structure and demand more obedience and docility from its members.

Therefore, in his initial attack against the bill concerning the elections for the provincial and municipal councils, Khomeini immediately met with Ayatollah Shari'atmadari and other *Marjas* and joined them in the issuance of a common declaration and followed their lead. Ayatollah Khomeini in all of his statements repeatedly mentioned that: "The Islamic *ulama* will not remain silent," or "The Iranian clergy and those of the holy shrines will show the government its proper place." In early 1963, whispers of opposition to his unorthodox and totally political behavior were growing louder among certain *Marjas* at the Seminary and among religious groups in Tehran. In particular, Ayatollah Seyyed Ahmad Khonsari openly criticized Ayatollah Khomeini's methods. In response, politically active believers in the bazaars of Qom and Tehran attacked those leaders. But Ayatollah Khomeini made no attempt to support these forces. It was only after seizing absolute power following the revolution of February 1979, that he complained about the "heart bleed" that he had suffered at the hands of those *ulama* and by their opposition.[17] On all occasions, Ayatollah Khomeini credited the clergy and the Seminary for any political progress made by the movement. By doing so he supported the leadership that initiated the movement and, at the same time, attempted to take the leadership of the organization into his own hands and politicize it even further. By offering a taste of power to the body of the organization, Ayatollah recruited its young and active constituencies and, by manipulating them, compelled the competing *Marjas* to cooperate or otherwise face isolation and expulsion.

A reading of Ayatollah Khomeini's statements during the critical 1962–3 events reveals that in all movements he observed certain rules and made his moves accordingly. His primary goal was to attract those religious forces that were at odds with the Seminary. He also tried to gain the indirect support of mainly secular parties and political forces with the expectation that with the help of such forces he would be able to mend and grease the broken and corroded wheels of the religious establishment.[18] He was confident that when the engine started he would have no further use for such forces. He also attracted reform-minded religious groups and progressive religious individuals who had links with the young generation inside and outside the country. In the meantime, Ayatollah Khomeini was mindful of maintaining his ties with the most conservative forces within the seminary as well as the rest of the religious establishment.

An examination of the statements issued during the nine months preceding the June 5 incident reveals the calculated and careful nature of Ayatollah Khomeini's moves. They show that he always moved one step and only one step ahead of the accepted limit of the political demands of the clergy. During the movement against the bill concerning the elections for the provincial and municipal councils, when the statements were generally related to the anti-religious contents of the bill, Ayatollah Khomeini raised the issue in more general terms by emphasizing the disastrous economic conditions of the country and lack of freedom, and on such premises he attacked the government's actions in their entirety. During the next movement against the "Shah–People Revolution" and the storming of Faizieh School by paratroopers, however, Ayatollah Khomeini directed his attacks against Israel and the person of the Shah while other clergymen in their statements mainly complained about the dictatorship of the government and violation of the law.

Achievements of the clergy

The achievements of the religious establishment during the 54-day long movement may be summarized as follows:

1 The clergy and the religious establishment throughout the country as well as in Najaf joined the movement, but the movement did not have grassroots involvement and most of the clergy at the local mosque levels did not join the movement. Yet the movement achieved an important political victory for the clergy and revived a feeling of strength in them. Ayatollah Shari'atmadari in his December 2 speech said: "We made progress which has been unprecedented during the fifty years since the establishment of the Constitution."[19]

2 Although the basic tenet of the movement was the defense of Islamic laws, in the statements of Ayatollahs Shariatmadari, and Khomeini, and radical clergymen in cities such as Tabriz, Shiraz, and Terhran in contrast to the tradition of the Seminary in the previous two decades, political issues such as

suppression of the press and the despotic rule of the government were raised, and Ayatollah Khomeini was the only *Marja* who also referred to Palestine, Zionism, and the chaotic economic conditions in the country.

3 Ayatollah Shari'atmadari moved far ahead of the other competing *Marja* such as Ayatollahs Najafi and Golpaygani. Ayatollah Khomeini, who was one of the last men in line, pushed ahead and occupied the second position.

4 Religious forces and individuals who were in favor of reform and political involvement and who had abandoned the Seminary in the previous two decades returned to the sanctuary. The Freedom Movement group, in its November statement, defended the clergy[20] and, in its second statement the same month, congratulated the clergy for their intervention in the political scene.[21] The speakers of the *Goftar-e Mah* lecture series expressed their optimism for the implementation of their programs regarding the introduction of reform measures into the Seminary and the position of the *Marja-e Taqlid*.[22]

5 Ayatollah Khomeini succeeded in establishing direct contacts with the masses and adopted a method of campaigning which became his trademark for political struggle in the years to come.

The second movement of the clergy and the "Shah–People Revolution"

In order to adhere to President Kennedy's policy, which had made the advancing of a $35 million loan contingent upon the introduction of politico-economic reform[23] to attract masses of workers and peasants and to bring a semblance of order to the chaotic situation of the country, the "Revolution of the Shah and People" was declared on January 9, 1963. It was announced that a referendum would be held on January 26. However, the Shah knew that any opposition to the stated principles by either political or religious forces would undermine their political positions. Therefore, while he was persistently trying to extract a *Fatva* from the *ulama* against his land reform program, he was also encouraging publication of newspaper articles denouncing the reactionary supporters of the landlords. But the clergy were consciously avoiding the entrapment, except

Ayatollah Ahmad Khonsari who simple-mindedly fell into the trap.

Marja-e Taqlids together with political forces carefully avoided attacking the declared "principles"; rather, they challenged the illegal method by which they were adopted. They noted that the referendum was unconstitutional, the *Majles* was in a state of interregnum, that the Shah was not legally accountable for the actions of the government, and finally that the Shah was becoming increasingly despotic.

The clergy had already experienced the glory of a political victory during their previous fifty-four-days movement. The ice had been broken and the clergy were no longer apolitical and had proved their ability in the mobilization of the masses. Therefore, they actively took up the challenge. All *Marjas* sent telegrams to the Shah and declared their opposition to the illegal referendum and the Shah's dictatorship. Even Ayatollah Khoie issued a strongly worded statement from Najaf and condemned the referendum.[24] Finally, the clergy from the provinces issued a joint statement in opposition to the referendum. The waves of opposition rose throughout the country. On January 21, 1963, the bazaar of Tehran closed for three days as a show of solidarity with the opposition. On January 23, the bazaar of Qom joined the strike. In Qom a large number of inhabitants demonstrated against the referendum. The demonstrators were crying: "We are followers of the Quran, and we do not want a referendum." A clash occurred between the police and the demonstrators. Tehran University was embroiled and, on January 24, the police attacked the university. Tanks and armored cars were positioned on the streets of Tehran. Political parties such as the National Front and the Toilers' Party, however, lacked the ability to assume the leadership of the movement. Both parties nurtured conservative views and therefore were unable to satisfy the demands of the youth that constituted the main social group in the political struggle.

The clergy, on the other hand, were becoming increasingly organized. The *Marjas* and prominent clergymen in the provinces were holding weekly meetings in order to coordinate their activities. For the first time, nine *Marjas* and prominent clergymen of Qom issued a joint declaration against the "Shah–People Revolution."[25] The statement made it clear that clergymen such as Ayatollahs Lankarani and Zanjani, who had been active in the National Front and had been involved in politics independent of the Seminary, had rejoined the Seminary and together with conservative and apolitical clergymen, such as Ayatollahs Damad, Haeri, and Allameh-Tabatabai signed the joint declaration.

The Shah angrily arrived in Qom on January 24 and in a speech called religious groups "black reactionaries" who were more dangerous than the "red reactionaries", i.e., the communists. He said that the followers of the clergy were just "a bunch of stupid bearded bazaaris," who were anti-Iranian and political pawns in the hands of foreigners. He accused them of collaboration with the Russians in the Azerbaijan incident and added that their ideal leader was Jamal Abdel-Nasser of Egypt.[26]

The referendum was held on January 26, despite the fact that it had been boycotted by all political and religious forces. Shortly after, political unrest spread throughout the country. Even Ayatollah Mohsen Hakim, the greatest *Marja* in the Najaf Seminary and indeed in the entire Shi'ite world sent a telegram to Ayatollah Shari'atmadari in Qom denouncing the Shah's referendum.[27] Ayatollahs Shari'atmadari and Khomeini issued statements against the illegal action of the government and declared that they would not celebrate the New Year festivities that year and that they would be in mourning.[28] However, despite the presence of the Seminary on the country's political stage, the main body of the clergy was not comfortable with radicalism and, in particular, with Ayatollah Khomeini's tactics. Consequently, a plan for the issuance of a joint statement by the *Marjas* and leading clergymen failed. Prominent individuals at the Seminary, conservative lecturers and essayists such as Nasser Makarem-Shirazi, Hadi Khosrowshahi, and Ali Davani gathered around Ayatollah Shari'atmadari. Shari'atmadari, despite his strongly worded statements, was moving more conservatively and closer to the tradition of the Seminary in the areas of religion and politics. At the same time, Ayatollah Khomeini was surrounded by radical clerics, politically active religious groups, and young theology students such as Rabbani-Shirazi, Mohammadi-Gilani, Rouhani, Khalkhali, Rafsanjani, Khamenei, and Morvarid. But what had changed drastically in connection with the activities of these forces within the Seminary and throughout the religious establishment and what disturbed the traditional relationships and methods of the Seminary was the fact that these young theological students and radical clergy were able to develop into a strong cohesive force and engage in political activities. In the past, these elements, who were scholastically unimportant and financially weak, were not able to apply pressure to the *Marjas* and prominent *ulama*. But now, by attaching themselves to and standing behind a *Marja*, they succeeded in legitimizing their political presence and actions. Although the pressure group was at the early stages of its formation, its influence was already strongly felt. *Marjas* were under pressure, orators were forced to talk about politics on the pulpits, and anti-government pamphlets were distributed in mosques despite the unwillingness of conservative prayer leaders.

Meantime, Ayatollah Khomeini, who demanded maximum political advantage from the situation in order to strike a blow at the government, issued a statement titled: "The Clergy Will Not Celebrate New Year's Festivities." In that statement he raised an issue that he knew full well would excite the public and direct their anger against the government. He said: "The government wants to draft 18-year-old girls into the army and place them in the barracks."[29] This means that the government is forcing virtuous Muslim girls into prostitution at bayonet point. Given the public understanding of army barracks and their fanatical concern about girls, the statement proved to be so damaging that, two days later, the Shah in a speech in the city of Mashhad called the allegations a big lie and added: "These absurd rumors and incredible lies are evidence of the weakness of those who spread these fabrications."[30]

In the evening of the second day of the New Year, paratroopers and security forces stormed a mourning gathering at Faizieh School and brutally beat the clergy. Soon many telegrams in denunciation of the incident began to pour into Qom from within the country and abroad. Ayatollah Hakim in a telegram invited the clergy to leave Qom and collectively settle in the city of Najaf. But the invitation was declined by the *Marjas*. Ayatollah Khomeini, in response to the above telegram, declared: "We shall resist till death."[31] Public prayers were suspended for a week. At this stage, Ayatollahs Khoie and Shahroudi from Najaf as well as clergymen from the provinces of Fars and Kermanshahan sent messages of support to *Marjas*, singling out the Ayatollah Khomeini by name.[32]

In commemoration of the fortieth day of the Faizieh School incident, Ayatollah Khomeini issued a statement and for the first time pointed his finger at the Shah as the man responsible and added that if the Shah was not guilty, he had to publicly deny his involvement in the incident.[33] Two months after the storming of Faizieh School when the month of Moharram began, the government announced its intention of banning the formation of mourning sessions and assemblies.

The month of Moharram (when the largest religous demonstrations are organized throughout the country) was an excellent occasion to be exploited politically by the clergy. Ayatollahs Shari'atmadari and Khomeini issued statements in which they encouraged people to defy the government and participate in mourning sessions. A confrontation of this nature transformed mourning sessions into political and anti-government gatherings. The recitations of the leaders of the breast-beating procession took a completely political tone. They cried: "Hossein the master of free men sacrificed the lives of his children, his brother, and his own for the cause of freedom." The maxim "life is nothing but belief and struggle" was substituted for traditional recitations about Hussein's martyrdom while his lips were parched with extreme thirst.[34]

The same afternoon, security forces were stationed all over the city of Qom and armed soldiers were brought to the city from the Manzarieh garrison located 30 kilometers from Qom to reinforce the existing security forces. In order to prevent Ayatollah Khomeini from going to Faizieh School, where he had planned to deliver a speech, soldiers were stationed at all intersections throughout the city. The fear of a widespread bloodbath hung over the city. At this juncture, Ayatollah Khomeini by announcing that: "Even if blood becomes knee-deep in the city, it will not stop me from going to Faizieh School," broke the state of indecision and fear. Following the announcement, shouts of "God is great!" were heard from the residence of the Ayatollah. Some two hundred volunteers signed their last will and testament and surrounded the Ayatollah's house. Under the protection of these volunteers, the Ayatollah was taken to Eram Street where he was put in a convertible car and the procession headed in the direction of the Shrine of Massoumeh. As the crowd approached the shrine, the armed soldiers suddenly retreated and left the city altogether.[35]

Ayatollah Khomeini entered Faizieh School and, for the first time at a huge public gathering, addressed the Shah directly: "I advise you wretched, miserable 45-year old man to stop and ponder a little. These people prefer to brand you as a jew, in which case I am required to declare you as an infidel. Then you will be kicked out of the country and will suffer its consequences."[36] Although the speech generally avoided any direct attack on the monarchy, took a tone of advice, and demanded a declaration from the Shah for his non-involvement in the incident, it employed bold and harsh language in which not only radical religious groups but also secular politicians saw the signs of political leadership in Ayatollah Khomeini. The sharp edge of the speech was directed against Israel and Zionism – a subject close to the hearts of all political forces.

Two days later, Ayatollah Khomeini was arrested and taken to Tehran. In the wake of his arrest, the June 5 unrest occurred. The unrest spread over different parts of the country, and a large number of people were killed, injured, and arrested. All Shi'ite clergymen both in Iran and Iraq condemned the killings. Even Sheikh Mahmoud Shaltut the rector of the Al-azhar University in Cairo in a telegram he sent to the *ulama* in Qom condemned the Shah's action.[37] The bazaars in many large cities were closed in protest against the government. Ayatollah Khomeini's leadership was recognized not only within the Seminary but all political forces accepted him as a major political figure. The Toilers' Party declared Ayatollah Khomeini the "Absolute *Marja-e Taqlid*." The National Front which refused to back the clergy during the period of unrest and ignored the clergy-inspired movement, in a statement declared that the United States was responsible for the June 5 tragedy.[38]

CONCLUSION

In the light of the aforementioned movements and developments, the religious establishment went through fundamental changes whose effects were echoed in the 1978–9 revolution and its aftermath. The most important conclusions may be summarized as follows.

The emergence of political Islam

The non-political attitude of the Seminary since the Constitutional Revolution, which defined its distinguishing characteristic under the leadership of Ayatollah Boroujerdi, was discarded. Since the political movements had been initiated by the top echelon of the religious pyramid, i.e, by the *Marja-e Taqlid*, and in view of the hierarchical structure of Shi'ite Islam, the movement gained popular legitimacy down to the lowest layers of the religious structure. Political protests by means of recitations of breast-beating groups and words of the orators in the pulpits engulfed the far reaches of the country and even the most ardent conservative was politicized. The demeanor of the movement was such that in religious organizations, the power of politically active religous circles was increasingly on the rise while conservative groups were losing their power steadily. Thus, following the example of Qom, the *ulama* from large provincial cities held monthly, and at the height of the unrest, weekly meetings to coordinate their activities. As a result, numerous political mistakes by various groups and individuals were avoided.

Furthermore, the coordination meetings were the best forums for politically active, experienced and courageous religious individuals to take political power into their own hands. Outside these meetings, the general trend of the movement in the country and in the Seminary became more radicalized under the helmsmanship of Ayatollahs Shari'atmadari and particularly Khomeini. Conservative religious groups became increasingly weaker and finally lost their grip on the political lever. Ayatollah Behbahani, a close friend of the court, and Ayatollah Khonsari, a conservative clergyman with a total lack of political sophistication, lost their power in Tehran as did Ayatollahs Najafi and Golpaygani in Qom. On the other hand, Ayatollahs Milani and Qomi in Mashhad, Ayatollah Sadouq in Yazd, and Ayatollahs Rabbani and Madani in Shiraz, due to their political courage, became more widely known.

All in all, the politicization trend continued until the 1979 uprising, when, due to general crisis in the society and the absence of alternative political parties, the radical clergy assumed leadership.

The revival of the Seminary as the center of political authority

As a result of gradual and calculated moves to politicize the Seminary, the unity and plurality of the clergy was maintained. It was spared from division and disunity which plagued the clergy during the Constitutional Revolution and during the 1951 movement for nationalization of the oil industry. Moreover, preservation of the unity caused the Seminary to become the center for the political movement and to gain confidence in leading the 1978–9 revolution.

Religion as an impetus to the mass movement

The June 5 incident demonstrated how the clergy with its vast religious organizations and networks was able to engineer a widespread and popular movement and draw the members of the lower strata of society into action. For example, for the first time, even women from the poorest and the most deprived sections of the city of Qom took part in the demonstrations against the government and in the clashes with the security forces. Even the well-known mobsters Tayyeb and Haj Esmail, who drew their strength from their influence among the urban poor, and were generally either apolitical or pro-government, were drawn into action on the basis of their religious beliefs. Later these groups also played an important role during the revolution and supplied the active members for the first combative forces of revolutionary committees and guards.

Organizing traditional forces

Finally, the movement further strengthened the old division between the modernist and traditionalist forces in society. It proved the ability and skill of the latter force to mobilize the masses by using religion. It further showed the failure of government officials as well as modern secular intellectuals who belonged to the first category to appreciate that ability. The movement with all its immensity and influence showed that its roots were grounded in the traditional segment of society and had very few followers among the modernist strata. In Tehran, for example, all activities of the movement were concentrated in the old part of the city, i.e, the downtown and bazaar areas and the nearby villages. The northern part of the city, where most of the modernist strata lived, remained unaffected even at the height of the movement. Despite the gathering strength of the movement, the political literature of the 1960s and 1970s, with scant exception, remained silent about it. This was mainly due to the fact that most writers and intellectuals belonged to the modernist strata of society,[39] and had no interest in a clergy-led movement. Jalal Al-e Ahmad, with his deep traditional roots, and Bijan Jazani, with his considerable knowledge of society among the leftist groups, were among the few exceptions. Whereas, a smaller guerrilla movement by leftists started in 1972, namely the *Fedaiyan-e Khalq* movement, which was close to the hearts of the modernist writers, was generously treated in the political literature of the country. Consequently, modernist politicians never fully understood the depth of the movement that in the eyes of many religous groups constituted the backbone of the February 1979 revolution. Likewise, the Shah's government ignored the growing power of the religious groups and concentrated its energies on neutralizing the political activities of the radical and secular forces which, in fact, did not have deep roots in society.

NOTES

1 Many political groups, including religious ones such as *Nehzat-e Azadi*, do not share this view.

2 Ali Davani, *Nehzat-e Rouhaniun-e Iran*, (10 vols, Bonyad-e Farhangi-e Imam Reza, Tehran, 1981/1360), vol. 2, p. 338.

3 Said Amir-Arjomand, "Traditionalism in Twentieth-Century Iran," in Amir Arjomand (ed.) *From Nationalism to Revolutionary Islam* (State University of New York Press, Albany, 1984), p. 203.

4 Shahrough Akhavi, *Religion and Politics in Contemporary Iran: Clergy-State Relation in the Pahlavi Period*, (State University of New York Press, Albany 1980), p. 63.

5 *Ibid*, p. 68.

6 *Ibid*, pp. 65–6.

7 Interview with Dr Sadr (Minister of Commerce in the Bazargan Cabinet and a member of the Central Committee of *Nehzat-e Azadi*), Feb. 1989.

8 *Ibid*.

9 Author's own observation.

10 *Adab-e Bayt-ol Khala*. (Matbuati-e Hekmat, Qom, 1955).

11 Michael M. J. Fischer, *Iran: From Religious Dispute to Revolution* (Harvard University Press, Cambridge, MA 1980), p. 121.

12 Mahmoud Taleqani, "Tamarkoz va Adam-e Tamarkoz-e Marjaiyat Va Fatva" in *Bahsi Darbareh-e Marjaiyat Va Rouhaniyat*, (Tehran, 1962), pp. 131–5.

13 Hamid Algar, "The Opposition Role of the *Ulama* in the Twentieth Century," in *Scholars, Saints and Sufis*, Nikki Keddie (ed.), (University of California Press, Berkley, 1971), p. 252.

14 *Sarcheshmeh*, Oct. 15, 1962.

15 Eyewitness account.

16 Khomeini, in his public statements, made no reference to the issue of granting voting rights to women. But after the Bill was withdrawn, in an introductory statement on December 1, 1962, prior to the resumption of his lectures, he told his students that: "Wherever women have been employed in government offices, work has been disrupted . . . when women work in an office they become a source of disturbance. Do you want to secure your independence with the help of women?" (A Davani, *Nehzat-e Rouhanion Iran*, vol. 3, p. 40). When he was making such statements orally he was well aware of the fact that those statements were intended for private consumption in the Seminary and were not supposed to leak out and become available to the public.

17 *Kayhan Havaie*, March 1 and Jan. 25, 1989.

18 Ayatollah Khomeini emphasized such issues as observing the Constitution, the Palestine issue, Zionism, and suppression of the Press. His first political move showed that he was basically different from the majority of the clergy and religious leaders. It also demonstrated that he was not only interested in reform measures as related to anti-religious matters but he had political ambitions and was seeking power. When lectures were resumed in the Seminary after a long break, Khomeini devoted his lecture to political issues and raised the question of the power of the clergy and the fact that the government must submit to their demands. He said: "The *ulama* have always been the guarantors of the nation's independence. The people have always supported the *ulama* and have trusted them ten times more than they have trusted the government. The people volunteered to wrap themselves in shrouds and fight if the *ulama* so permitted. But we [the *ulama*] did not allow it." He then added: "We have the nation's sympathetic ear. We received a letter from Rey which indicated that some 5,000 men wrapped in shrouds were ready to march. The people of Japelagh wrote that we are 100,000 strong and awaiting your order to march. A letter from Loreston indicated that the Lor tribe was wrapped in shrouds and was ready to march [against the government]" (S. H. Rouhani, *Nehzat-e Imam Khomeini*, pp. 157–8).

19 Davani, *Nehzat-e Rouhanion-e Iran*, vol. 3, p. 166.

20 S. H. Rouhani, *Nehzat-e Imam Khomeini*, p. 166.

21 *Ibid.*, p. 185.

22 It should be noted that these forces and individuals were neither in

a position to mobilize all the religious forces nor did they hold a position of prestige among the mainly secular political and social forces. For example, Bazargan, one of the leaders of the Freedom Movement group, in spite of his distinguished record in the political struggles of the National Front, his position as a university professor, and the authorship of numerous works, was at the bottom of the list of those elected to the Congress of the Second National Front. The leaders of the National Front such Dr Azar, interviewed by the author on February 1989, referred to Mr Bazargan as reactionary and narrow minded. Bazargan and his associates objected to the presence of women in the Congress, left the session, and finally forced the Congress to make separate seating arrangements for each sex.

23 Fred Halliday, *Iran: Dictatorship and Development* (Penguin, New York, 1979).
24 Davani, *Nezhat-e Rhouhanioun-e Iran*, vol. 3, p. 206.
25 Rouhani, *Nehzat-e Imam Khomeini*, pp. 294–302. This statement was signed by Ayatollahs Morteza Husseini Langroodi, Ahmad Hosseini Zanjani, Mohammad Hossein Tabatabaie, Mohammad ousavi Yazdi (also known as "Damad," Son-in-Law of Ayatollah Hairi), Mohammad Reza Mousavi Golpaygani, Seyyed Kazem Shari'atmadari, Hashem Amoli, Morteza Haeri, and Rouhollah Mousavi Khomeini. On Ayatollah Khomeini's suggestion, the statement was signed in accordance with the seating arrangement, rather than the traditional method which is based on the religous rank.
26 *Kayhan*, Jan. 24, 1963.
27 Davani, *Nehzat-e Rouhanioun-e Iran*, vol. 3, p. 215.
28 *Ibid*, pp. 245-6.
29 Rohani, *Nehzat-e Imam Khomeini*, p. 317.
30 *Kayhan*, April 12, 1963.
31 Davani, *Nehzat-e Rouhanioun-e Iran*, vol. 3, pp. 315–21.
32 *Ibid*, pp. 284–90.
33 Maraz-e-Madarek-e Farhang-e-Enqelab-e-Eslami, *Sahif-e-nur*, (Vezarat-e-Ershad-e-Eslami, Tehran, 1982/1361), vol. 1, pp. 46–7.
34 From the author's collection of recitations.
35 Eyewitness account.
36 Rohani, *Nehzat-e Imam Khomeini*, pp. 456–60.
37 *Ibid.*, pp. 533–6.
38 Bulletin of the National Front, Dec. 7, 1963.
39 Interview with Dr Mohammad Baheri. Washington, DC December 1988.

4

THE POLITICS OF
NATIONALISM AND
POLITICAL CULTURE

Mehrdad Mashayekhi

> The political culture of modern Iran, one in which myths
> about the power and motives of foreign states have vivid
> life, is in part a product of . . . earlier, and by no means
> imagined, external interventions. This supposedly para-
> noid streak in Iranian nationalism has its historical ratio-
> nal roots, just as the anxiety and illusions of individuals
> can have roots in their own earlier traumatic experiences.
>
> (Fred Halliday)

INTRODUCTION

The Iranian Revolution of 1978–9 was a massive revolutionary
upheaval which put an end to 2,500 years of monarchy. Under
the banner of "Independence, Freedom, Islamic Republic" it
mobilized various classes, strata, ethnic and religious minorities, and people of all ages with heterogeneous idealogies,
politics and interests. Despite the lack of a cohesive political
party, or a clear political platform, the clerical leadership
succeeded in maintaining the necessary political unity among
the diverse ranks of participants. Instrumental in preserving
the unity, and ultimately the actualization of the "populistic
pact" among major contenders for power, was the articulation
of an anti-imperialist and anti-dictatorial discourse cloaked in
Islamic terms, images and symbols. This radical Islamic discourse united various forces, rendered a populist bloc possible,
and facilitated the transition to a new theocratic society, ruled
by the Shi'ite clergy, and characterized by a dominant Islamic
political culture.

The populistic character of the Iranian Revolution has been

discussed in a number of works.[1] For our purpose, we define a populist movement as a multi-class movement, led by a charismatic figure, in which participants are viewed in a homogeneous fashion as "masses" or "common people." Populist movements in the Third World often mobilize "a united 'people' in which class tensions are overcome in the euphoria of heightened nationalism where hostility is directed against the imperialist outside and their lackeys within."[2]

The *de facto* alliance that took place in late fall of 1979 in Iran was a clear manifestation of a populist movement. The alliance was formed primarily among various clerical factions, the liberal Islamic Freedom Movement and JAMA (Revolutionary Movement of the Muslim People), and the secular liberal National Front and independent individuals. Lay Islamic radicals such as the Mojahedeen-e Khalq organization and socialists supported the clerical hegemony and the charismatic role of Ayatollah Khomeini. There were two central unifying principles in this alliance: opposition to the Pahlavi Court, in particular to the Shah; and a strong anti-imperialist and nationalistic sentiment, directed against the United States. Given the tactical nature of this political alliance, the demise of the populist bloc was expected. The revolution's victory was soon followed by power struggles and the gradual disintegration of the populist alliance into its constituent elements. This was anticipated, since these various political forces represented different interests, ideologies, social bases and political traditions.

The dominant approaches among observers of the Iranian Revolution have traditionally focused either on various socioeconomic and political (domestic and international) contradictions responsible for the downfall of the Shah's regime (structural approach), or the active mobilizationary role of the Islamic forces during the 1960s and 1970s (social movement approach).[3] One dimension of the revolution that is often ignored is placing the movement Islamicist in the post-1953 historical dynamics of rivalry among major political movements vying for power, namely, the liberal–nationalist and socialist movements. Why did the Islamicists emerge victorious? The answer necessitates a close examination of the rivals' shortcomings and/or their differential treatment by the state. Obviously, all sources of internal weakness among the above

movements had indirectly contributed to the relative invigo-
ration of the Islamicists (before and during the revolution) and
to their consolidation of power in the post-revolutionary era.
Fischer best captures this multi-movement approach: "[W]hat
produced the Islamic form of the revolution was not Islamic
revivalism so much as repression of other modes of political
discourse."[4]

This chapter deals with one of the major political movements
in the post-1953 period in Iran, the socialist movement. Our
focus will be on the nature of its political (sub-)culture,
especially on the role of its radical nationalistic frame of
thought and its affinities with the emerging Islamic political
culture of the revolution. Further, we will demonstrate that the
socialist movement's underlying political (sub-)culture, i.e. the
politically relevant "system of empirical beliefs, expressive
symbols, and values which define the situation in which political action takes place,"[5] had a strong impact on the socialists'
political behavior. This practice included their *de facto* alliance
with the clergy-led coalition during the revolutionary process
of 1978–9 as well as their post-revolutionary performance
which resulted in their early departure from the political scene.
In the examination of socialist sub-culture, we identify two
major points: an *exaggerated* emphasis on a radical Third Worldist
anti-imperialist view, which resulted in the overlooking of
other social and political issues, particularly democracy; and, a
similarity between some aspects of the socialist and Islamic
political sub-cultures. These internal shortcomings alienated
the socialist movement's supporters and facilitated the clergy's
hegemony in the revolutionary process.

Since radical Third Worldist nationalism constituted the
socialist sub-culture's most salient element, it is to this version
of nationalism that we turn to next.

EMERGENCE OF NATIONALISM

Throughout its history, Iran has witnessed waves of invasions
from the outside. Thanks to their rich cultural heritage, however, Iranians have survived such devastating experiences and
each time have adapted themselves to the new conditions,
meanwhile preserving some aspects of their ancient civilization, most notably the Persian language.

Nevertheless, major invasions by Greeks (334–330 BC), Arabs (seventh century), Turks (eleventh century), and Mongols (thirteenth century) contributed to the formation of a foreign-suspicious collective memory; a mass psychological defense mechanism that helped Iranians adjust themselves to the alien forces undermining their collective identity.

The transition from the formation of the historical memory based on a negative and exaggerated fear of foreigners, and modern *nationalism*, a positively conscious discourse for creating a truly sovereign nation-state independent of foreign domination, and in control of its resources, polity and culture was facilitated by two major episodes. The first was the sixteenth-century reunification of the Iranian territory under the Safavid dynasty which was accompanied by the elevation of Twelver Shi'ism to the official state religion. The second, beginning in the last half of the nineteenth century, was the acceleration by Iranian society of an all-sided contact with the European colonial powers. The latter's role in the emergence of nationalistic sentiments and values is twofold. First, the incorporation of Iranian economy into the international capitalist markets threatened the economic interests of urban middle-class propertied and commercial strata – a pivotal social grouping which became very active in resisting Western intervention. Second, in a positive manner, through the spread of modern values and ideologies (such as liberalism, socialism and nationalism) by the intelligentsia. "[T]hey not only introduced into the vocabulary of contemporary Iran numerous Western words . . . but also injected modern meanings into many old words. For example, *istibdad* changed in meaning from "monarchy" to "despotic monarchy"; *mellat* from "religious community" to "secular nationality"; and *mardom* from the "people" without any political connotations to "the People" with its democratic and patriotic connotations."[6] In fact, the experience of decolonization of the Third World indicates that most often intellectuals emerge as the leaders of anti-imperialist nationalist movements.

Since nationalism is not a total ideology, it can surface in a variety of ideological systems. We can verify this point by demonstrating nationalism's presence among diverse ideological groupings active in the twentieth century Iran. At least four major nationalistic trends can be identified:

85

1 Liberal–nationalism, which originated in the works of thinkers and politicians such as Mirza Malkom Khan and Hassan Taqizadeh. Of the thirty newspapers published in Tehran in 1907, twenty-seven were liberal – nationalist. Some of them include: *Fatherland, Civilization, Language of the Nation*.[7] Liberal–nationalism was best manifested in the oil-nationalization movement led by the National Front and Dr Mohammad Mossadeq (1951–3).[8]

2 Persian–nationalism of thinkers such as Aqa Khan Kermani, Fath-Ali, Akundzadeh, and Zain al-Abedin-e Maraghehi, identified Iran with its pre-Islamic past and blamed all the social ills of Iran on Islam and the Arab invasion.

   After the Constitutional Movement, the Chauvinistic Persian–nationalistic tendency was articulated with diverse ideologies, politics and personalities. It was integrated into Pahlavi state ideology, the political platform of a number of small right-wing parties active in the 1940s, such as the Arya Party, the Sumka Party, and the Pan-Iranist Party.[9] Also, some notable writers and intellectuals including Sadeq Hedayat and Ahmad Kasravi expanded its anti-Shi'i and anti-Arab elements.

3 Islamic (and Pan-Islamic) nationalism of Sayyed Hassan Modarres and Jamal al-Din Assad-Abadi believed that Islam could be the only basis for uniting Asian peoples against the inroads of the West.[10]

   Islamic–nationalism was later echoed among diverse religious parties, movements and figures. Most notable are Ayatollah Kashani's Society of Muslim Warriors, a member of the National Front; People's Mojahedeen Organization, a radical socialistic-oriented Islamic group, active since the early 1970s; and finally, the nationalistic themes in various writings of the leaders of the 1978–9 revolution, such as Ayatollah Khomeini, Hashemi-Rafsanjani, Motahhari, Taleqani, etc.

4 Socialist–nationalism originated in the works of writers and activists such as Talebov, Haydar Amu-Oghli and Ali-Akbar Dehkhoda. It reproduced itself most strongly in the writings of Khalil Maleki, a socialist intellectual and activist, especially during the 1940s and 1950s, and finally in the Third Worldist discourse of the Fedaiyan guerrilla movement of the 1970s.[11]

It is to this movement and its associated political sub-culture that we turn to in this chapter.

Third Worldist discourse in Iran

Following World War Two, there was a resurgence of national liberation movements in the colonies, which along with political efforts by nationalist forces and/or governments in nominally independent states, attempted to extend their control over their own society, politics, culture and natural resources, and/or to re-negotiate the terms of trade with the advanced capitalist countries. Dr Mossadeq's nationalization of Iranian oil (1951) and Nasser's nationalization of the Egyptian Suez Canal (1956) are clear examples. One can also include the 1955 Bandung Conference of African and Asian countries, which acted as the collective politico-economic alliance of the recently decolonized states.

What all these various Third World movements shared was the final goal of "national independence." Supposedly this goal was to be achieved through a policy of non-alignment, via a "third way," distinct from both Western capitalism and Eastern socialism. This loosely defined discourse has been termed "Third Worldism."[12] One political variant within this general discursive order was Third Worldist Marxism, adopted by those liberation movements in the periphery, which were characterized by revolutionary socialist leadership (China, Vietnam, Cuba). Thus, the distinctive feature of this tendency can be identified as a radical project for achieving *national independence*: politically, economically and culturally, usually through violent means and using a Marxist discourse. The utopia of a sovereign nation-state, fully controlling its resources and competing on a global scale with the advanced countries, constantly inspired these nationalistic movements. Adoption of radical developmentalist ideologies, including Soviet communism, therefore, was a post-World War Two attempt by Third World intellectuals to respond to the enigma of "how to compress historical time."[13]

The first political group influenced by Third Worldist discourse in Iran was a splinter group from the pro-Soviet Tudeh Party, led by Khalil Maleki, a European-educated intellectual, who initially formed the *Hezb-e Zahmatkeshan-e Mellat-e* Iran

(Party of the Toiling Masses of Iran). Inspired to some extent by the anti-colonialist movements in the periphery, as well as by the Yugoslav rebellion against Stalinist authoritarianism, this party represented the first organized socialist and nationalist intellectual force to side specifically with the peoples of Asia, Africa and Latin America against both "Western imperialism" and "Eastern socialism." Eventually, in 1960, these intellectuals formed the Society of Iranian Socialists. A number of radical nationalist intellectuals, most with social democratic and some with Islamic tendencies (e.g. Hussein Malek, Asghar Haj-Seyyed-Javadi, Amir Pishdad, and Jalal Al-e Ahmad, the author of the famous *Gharbzadegi*, worked closely with the Society.

Third Worldism, however, was most systematically developed in the guerrilla movement of the 1970s in general, and among the socialist Fedaiyan-e Khalq organization in particular.

THE FORMATION OF THE THIRD WORLDIST-SOCIALIST GROUPINGS

The infamous coup d'etat of August 1953 put an abrupt end to the popular oil-nationalization movement led by Dr Mossadeq and the National Front, and brought the Shah back to power. The coup's success further reinforced the element of mistrust toward foreign powers that was already present in the popular political culture.

The Shah, anxious to overcome his crisis of legitimacy, insured the state's stability through a combination of ruthless repression and expanded economic projects. All evidence indicates that repression most affected the socialist movement and, to a lesser extent, the liberal National Front. Given the fact that prior to the coup, opposition to the court primarily came from these groups, their post-coup severe suppression was no surprise. By the mid 1950s all opposition parties and clubs, unions and syndicates, newspapers and magazines were banned. The state-sponsored terror resulted in the profound organizational and discursive decline of both the socialist and liberal-nationalist movements. Whereas, the Islamic movement, more or less, remained immune to state repression, due to a large extent to the 1953–8 clergy's withdrawal from direct political activity to the mosques and religious schools. At the same time, a number of the clerics and lay-Islamic thinkers instituted Islamic centers and think tanks, many of them anti-socialist in politics and ideology.[14]

However, in the late 1950s, new socialist and revolutionary circles and groupings, predominantly of an intellectual–student constituency, resumed their activities. Reactivation of the left coincided with the acceleration of armed struggle in Algeria, Cuba and Vietnam, where movements for national liberation were in process. Meanwhile, the Shah's regime, facing economic difficulties and American pressure to liberalize the political system, legalized political activity (excluding socialist groupings) in 1960 (basically to please Washington). This provided the (Second) National Front an opportunity to resume its activities, this time without Dr Mossadeq and also without any clear political platform. In these years, the new generation of socialist activists participated in the political struggles somewhat in affiliation with and around the Front. Following the formation of the Student Organization of the National Front (*Sazman-e Daneshjooyan-e Jebhey-e Melli*) in 1961, many radical, nationalist, and socialist activists from the ranks of the intelligentsia became actively involved. In the words of Bizhan Jazani, an active member himself, the Student Organization constituted "the supporting force of the Front's left wing."[15] This organization regularly published a political journal called *Payam-e Daneshjoo (Students' Message)* and concentrated its activities in the universities and high schools. But why such an interest in students?

The opposition politics of the post-coup era in general, and that of the socialist left in particular, were characterized by an inflation in the activities of students. This stands in contrast to the pre-coup period (1941–53) when the nationalist opposition movement primarily incorporated the *bazaar* and the new middle-class intelligentsia. In the post-coup period, the students became the new agents of radical–nationalistic politics. Their nationalism, expressed in anti-imperialist and populistic slogans, was much more abstract than the oil nationalization movement, led by the National Front. In the early 1970s, James Bill referred to students as the most alienated and explosive section of the new middle-class in Iran.[16] An early manifestation of student radical nationalism was the Tehran

University's student demonstration in December 1953, against the arrival of Richard Nixon, which resulted in the death of three students.

The students' superactivism in the post-coup era stems from two factors: their numerical growth and the ideological shift of the intelligentsia. The first factor was largely due to the quantitative expansion of the educational system that was undertaken by the regime. Several factors are responsible for such rapid expansion of the educational system and the increasing number of students. One was the high rate of population growth combined with improved health conditions which changed the composition of the population in favor of the youth. Between 1956 and 1975 the average rate of annual population growth in Iran was approximately 3 per cent. In the same period, the 15–24 age group's proportion increased from 15.4 per cent of the population to 18.9 per cent.[17]

Iran's expanding economy, along with the aforementioned change of the population's composition, necessitated an expansion of the educational system. Consequently, the state's new economic and social projects, especially during the 1960s, radically increased the number of institutions training students and the jobs which employed intellectuals. Nowhere can we detect this dramatic increase better than in the institutions of higher education. Between the years 1953-4 and 1978-9, the number of students in institutions of higher education increased from 9,996 to 175,000, which were receiving education in 236 colleges and universities.[18] The number of students studying abroad also showed a dramatic increase, from 2,818 in 1956 to over 80,000 in 1978. Further, students at the junior high and high school levels grew from 369,000 in 1963-4 to 831,000 in 1978-9.[19] This expansion, however, contributed to the concentration of students in big cities. During the 1970s, two-thirds of all college students and one-third of all high school students studied in Tehran. The rest were mostly concentrated in other major urban centers such as Isfahan, Tabriz, Shiraz and Ahvaz.

The increased youth in the population, combined with a rise in the number of high school and college students, and their concentration in big cities, all provided the necessary conditions which only required political and organizational mobilization to result in a socio-political explosion. In fact, the political alienation that prevailed among the youth in general and students in particular made them very susceptible to political mobilization. During the 1970s, various socialist and Islamic groups and circles responded to this need by actively organizing the alienated students.

The second factor responsible for the students' superactivism was the political and theoretical shift of the new generation of socialist intelligentsia. Strongly influenced by a populistic-nationalistic perspective rooted in the Third Worldist ideology of the 1960s, the young radical Iranian intellectuals increasingly identified themselves with an "anti-imperialist" project, defining the central political question as liberation of the nation (from imperialist domination) by the *khalq* (people). They called their utopia *Khalq's Republic*, which was based on the Soviet model of post-revolutionary society, adjusted to the underdeveloped economic conditions of Iran. The associated subculture also included beliefs and values supportive of: violence (as a means of resolving society's fundamental political contradictions); martyrdom; anti-intellectualism (manifested as admiration for direct *action*); and economistic emphasis on development.

Once the newly emerging socialist groups defined their political project as an "anti-imperialist revolution," students and intellectuals were logically elevated to the vanguard role of the opposition to the regime. This shift obviously required a theoretical rejection of the workers' role in social change. Frantz Fanon's notion regarding "embourgeoisement of workers in the colonized countries,"[20] to Regis Debray's thesis about the negative impact of the city on politics and morals of the "proletarians"[21] all contributed to the new perspective. Likewise, Amir-Pariz Pouyan, a socialist intellectual and activist, argued that Iranian workers, by accepting the dominant culture of the society, have "mostly acquired lumpen characteristics."[22] Thus, during the 1960s and 1970s, the socialist intellectuals substituted the *students* for other revolutionary agents, particularly the workers.

The brief "breathing period" of 1960-3 did not last long; neither was it intended to. The Shah's regime, facing new waves of opposition by the clergy, commercial bourgeoisie, students, and intellectuals, relied on its bureaucratic–repressive apparatuses as well as American support to maintain social order. The bloody suppression of the clergy-led June 1963 uprising against the Shah's reforms marked the official end of this interval. The new socialist circles and organizations found themselves in a highly repressive environment. The regime's recourse to repression in a way also conditioned the mode of struggle by the radical opposition. The idea of armed struggle found its way into the minds of the radical intelligentsia.

Among socialist circles and groups formed in these years the most notable were SAKA (the Organization for the Liberation of the Iranian People), *Goruh-e Arman-e Khalq* (Group of the People's Ideal), the Palestine Group, and most important of all, the Organization of the Iranian People's Fedaii Guerrillas (OIPFG), generally known as the *Fedaiyan* (self-sacrificers).

The *Fedaiyan* were considered the major socialist grouping of the 1970s, and were highly active among university students. The OIPFG was formed out of the merger of two circles in April, 1971: the Jazani–Zarifi (J–Z) circle and Ahmadzadeh–Pouyan (A–P) circle. While the former was characterized by pro-Soviet tendencies and some of its members had a history of affiliation with the Tudeh Party Youth Organization, the latter had Maoist inclinations and its members were previously active with the (second) National Front, with pro-Mossadeq tendencies.

Interestingly, the *Fedaiyan* kept publishing *Payam-e Danshjoo* (originally published by the Student Organization). They were of the opinion that "the role of revolutionary students and intellectuals . . . is decisive in spreading the struggle among the masses; and any procrastination in this regard is a major betrayal of national interests and the interests of Iranian proletariat."[23] Further, they argued that "to mobilize the masses for struggle we have a long way to go and *the vanguard forces in this process should predominantly come from among the vast masses of students*"[24] (emphasis ours). Thus, it would be no exaggeration to call the *Fedaiyan's* discourse "*student politics.*"

Abrahamian has gathered valuable information on the class origin of the dead guerrillas during the Shah's rule. Out of 306 dead guerrillas about whom there is sufficient information, 280 (81 per cent) belonged to the ranks of the intelligentsia. Over 48 per cent of them were college and high school students. For the Fedaii Organization, out of 160 dead guerrillas, 148 (92 per cent) came from the intelligentsia. More than 46 per cent of them were either college or high school students.[25]

The ten pioneer members of the Fedaiyan who were killed by the regime had the following employment and educational backgrounds: Bizhan Jazani, philosophy graduate; Hassan Zarifi, lawyer; Sa'id Kalantary, radio and television technician; Abbas Sourki, political science student and employee of the Central Bank; Mohammad Chupanzadeh and Aziz Sarmadi, workers; Ahmad Jalil-Afshar, high school student; Ali Akbar Safaii, engineering student; Mohammad Ashtiyani, law student; and Hamid Ashraf, engineering student.[26]

The politics of most socialist (as well as radical Islamic) groups were centered on a radical Third Worldist nationalism which viewed imperialism, led by the United States, as the "main enemy." Domestically, the Shah's regime was nothing but the "executive committee" of foreign interest and/or the "dependent bourgeoisie." All in all, dependency was considered to be the key to most problems and misfortunes of the society. Indeed, it is our contention that the *problematic of dependency*, as the political–theoretical discourse of Third Worldist nationalism, constituted the banner around which radicalized intellectuals of the 1960s and 1970s in general, and the socialist intellectuals and students in particular, were mobilized. It is to this exposition of radical nationalistic frame of thought, the most salient feature of the socialist political sub-culture, that we turn to next.

THE PROBLEMATIC OF DEPENDENCY

The concept of "problematic" has been defined as a "particular way of looking at the world defined by the fundamental question asked, and which includes concepts, methods and theories."[27] It is our contention that in the early 1960s, when Al-e Ahmad's "Westoxication" notion became popular among critical intellectuals, the dependency problematic was in the formative stage. By the early 1970s when concepts of "dependent capitalism" and "dependent state" were promoted by socialist theoreticians, in particular by Bizhan Jazani, the dependency perspective was at the very height of its popularity. In fact, the dissident political culture, comprised of socialist, Islamic, and liberal sub-cultures, was marked by the idea of *national independence* that is an end to national dependence; this theme clearly dominated the issues and subjects debated by politicized urban strata, particularly the intellectuals and students. Writing in 1971, Zonis remarked: "Perhaps the single most salient political issue in contemporary Iran is the evaluation of . . . instances of foreign encroachment on Iranian sovereignty and their relevance for domestic politics."[28]

This preoccupation with the loss of socio-cultural identity and political sovereignty was rooted in the rapid and fundamental transformations taking place in Iran, mostly under the influence of the state. The Pahlavi state's developmentalist strategy could not succeed without concurrent political and socio-cultural "modernization". While the Shah was not convinced to change the rigid political structures, he was quite willing to embark upon a cultural transformation of the society, based on a shallow interpretation of "Westernization." By the early 1970s, this commercialization of the culture was well under way. This was most evident in the educational system, entertainment, art, film, consumption habits, relations with the opposite sex, and even everyday conversation. Daryush Homayoun, the Shah's last Minister of Information, in his critique of such policies has stated:

> In this modernization effort, radio's musical programs, television shows, film festivals, consumer goods, and expensive projects (only to import a corner of America or Europe), and obviously Western-modeled organizations have all absorbed more time, energy, and money than transforming people's minds and helping them to think in more National terms and in acting in more scientific ways.[29]

This cultural "modernist" project needed the consent of the urban strata regarding this metamorphosis. Various social institutions were at work to this end. For example, the state-controlled mass media's underlying objective was to impose a "collective consciousness" among the urban Iranians regarding the desirability of the state's policies and its version of "Westernization." The qualitative growth of the mass media in the post-1963 period should be viewed in the light of this policy. During the 1960s, the number of radios grew from two million to four million, and televisions from 120,000 to

94

1,700,000. According to a study by Assef Bayat, among Tehrani factory workers, 80 per cent owned a television set in their homes.[30] Cinema was used as a strong instrument for political socialization. According to Hamid Nafici, themes such as traditional versus modern living, cabarets and nightclubs, Western influence, and Iran's progressive image were among the most popular ones.[31] According to one survey about popular programs on the National Iranian Television conducted in the early 1970s, eight programs out of fifteen were US-made serials. The rapid disintegration of the traditional indigenous culture and the introduction of superficial and selective aspects of Western culture gave rise to alienation and anomie, which in turn led to frustration, anger and rebellion, particularly among the urban strata. Such conditions could not but ignite a politico-cultural reaction among traditional sectors of the population, as well as the intelligentsia. Reaction to cultural alienation during the 1960s and 1970s was so widespread that even weekly popular magazines printed satirical stories ridiculing *Massachustti*, a typical American-educated technocrat who was out of touch with even very basic social and cultural values of Iran.[32]

Al-e Ahmad, of course, tried to characterize the "Westoxicated man" with every possible negative feature. Who is a "Westoxicated" individual? He is "confused," "sneaky," "submissive," "religiously indifferent," "mixed up," "a jack-of-all-trades," "prissy," and finally "always looks as if he just came out of the box, or out of some European fashion house."[33] Ali Shariati, an Islamicist sociologist, referred to the typical "Westoxicated" youth as an "assimilated, foreign, second-hand type, dubbed into Farsi. This type, trapped in the consumerist culture, exactly resembles a model; a plastered mannequin on whom they put on any dress and make-up they wish."[34] Thus, the dependency problematic proposed answers for the ills afflicting state, society, economy, culture and individual character.

Interestingly, this project shared a fundamental element with that of the Constitutional Movement era: its reference point was the West, only with the opposite political conclusion. Hence, the West - in its totality - was blamed for "contaminating" the otherwise pure indigenous Iranian culture, society, and character. At that time Malkom Khan, a French-educated reformer, advocated "the adoption of Western Civilization and industry without Iranian alteration",[35] but less than a century later, Massoud Ahmadzadeh, a Fedaii theoretician, condemned Western influence for having "disrupted the natural development of the Eastern societies" and also for having created an artificial growth."[36] Apparently, Ahmadzadeh and many other critical intellectuals of this period were convinced that had imperialism not penetrated Iran, there would be a "natural" path of development, resulting in progress, prosperity, and a flourishing culture. This nostalgic sign for the past is best echoed in Safaii-Farahani's characterization of the old society in which: "the deprived and the well-to-do know common manners, customs, and values. Zeal (*ghairat*), chastity (*namoos*), and purity (*effat*) were common concepts for all society . . . Both classes enjoyed common tales, songs, and music."[37]

Reza Baraheni, a leading socialist novelist, critic, and avant-garde intellectual, in his *Masculine History* (*Tarikh-e Mozakkar*), falls in a traditionalist trap of criticizing the West in its totality and praising the East – Third World – on the basis of its indigenous values. Baraheni confesses to the profound influence of Al-e Ahmad's ideas regarding "Westoxication" on his work which is subtitled a "Treatise Regarding Cultural Distortion in Iran."[38] Similarly, Samad Behrangi, an Azerbaijani school teacher and intellectual, strongly criticizes the educational system and questions the state's educational policy: "Is it wise to translate textbooks written by American educators for Iranian schools, teachers, and educators, and even including them in the curriculum of Teachers' Training College?"[39] Mostafa Rahimi, another socialist writer, confronts Western domination: "The specter dominating the twentieth century's second half, is the specter of [Eastern] nations' liberation; liberation from any form of [Western] domination."[40] Most Iranian poets, including Ahmad Shamlu, Said Soltanpour, M. Azarm, Khosrow Golesorkhi, and M. Omid, strongly criticized and condemned Western cultural and political influences in Iran. In his periodization of modern Iranian literature, Sepanloo, a leading Iranian writer, believes that what distinguishes the 1960s from other periods is the decade's "alertness regarding Westoxication and transcending of inferiority complex toward the West's intellectual exports and gaining of an Eastern, Asian, Islamic, Iranian identity."[41]

Dependent capitalism

While practically all radical intellectuals, religious and secular, were concerned with Iranian dependence on the West, they were not all in accord on the exact *mechanisms* and *relations* through which dependency was reproduced. Islamic thinkers relied on cultural–ideological explanations. Socialist intelligentsia, on the other hand, considered dependency as a predominantly politico-economic phenomenon. The goal of an independent Iranian nation-state controlling its market, resources, and political destiny dominated the young socialists' thought structure. Ali-Akbar Safaii-Farahani, an active Fedaii member, raised the question that most clearly expressed this concern: "Can the present Iranian bourgeoisie attain the classic growth of the Western bourgeoisie?"[42] He responded negatively.

Bizhan Jazani, the architect of the "dependent capitalism" thesis in Iran, characterizes dependent capitalism as "a semiformation or . . . an unstable and transitory one" which can emerge in the periphery in the period between feudalism and socialism.[43] The following features characterize "dependent capitalism": first, the rise and consequent rule of a new ruling class, i.e., "comprador bourgeoisie"; second, the establishment of capitalist relations in the agricultural sector and the subsequent fragmentation of peasantry; third, the expansion of foreign investment and an increase in "foreign exploitation"; fourth, the formation of a "minority consumer" class which functions as a base for neo-colonialist culture; and finally, political dictatorship as the most pronounced feature of the state.[44]

Apparently, the advocates of the "dependent capitalism" thesis were convinced that there were two types of capitalism: "classical capitalism" (advanced capitalist societies) and "dependent capitalism" (located in the Third World). This thesis is not only limited to a description of the economic system but, in fact, becomes the very theoretical foundation for a specific political strategy: the anti-imperialist revolution. While most observers of Iranian society during the 1960s and 1970s correctly recognized the growing dependence of Iran on the West, nevertheless the *strategic priority* placed on the issue of dependence was questionable. Only the arrival of the revolution revealed the shortcomings of this perspective.

Revolution and dependency

While the participating masses in the revolution of 1978–9 did not have a clearly-formed view of the future society, their opposition to the status quo was based on rather firm ground. Their slogans reflected their vehement anti-dictatorial and anti-imperialist sentiments. American support for the dictator, along with exploitative and alienating features of Western presence in Iran, could not but fix the demand for independence in the political consciousness of participants in the revolution. This only reinforced the deeply held nationalistic values in the popular political culture. The clergy, closely in touch with the masses, did not hesitate to include this demand in the main tripartite slogan of the mass movement. Thus "Independence, Freedom, Islamic Republic" became the rallying cry which temporarily united classes and groups. Also, the strategic slogan "Neither Eastern, Nor Western" tried to convince the participants that the post-revolutionary society would cherish indigenous values. According to a study on the slogans of the revolution, 400 slogans out of a total of 800 (50 per cent) were anti-dictatorial; whereas only 92 slogans (11.5 per cent) had an anti-imperialistic content.[45] The socialist movement's reading of the mass movement, however, was different. By over-emphasizing the pro-independence and nationalistic tendencies, the left underestimated the anti-dictatorial and democratic nature of the movement. Logically, they gave uncritical support to the clergy's *anti-foreign* strategy. The *Fedaiyan's* "minimum program," in the morrow of the uprising, echoes this preoccupation with foreign domination.[46] In the first two items we read:

1 The fundamental goal of the revolution is the annihilation of the dependent capitalist system via the elimination of the rule of imperialism and its lackeys, and the total establishment of *khalq's* rule.

2 In this glorious revolution of our *khalq*, we support the just struggle and measures taken by Ayatollah Khomeini in the overthrowing of the monarchial system and in the struggle against imperialism and its internal lackeys, and we support his just measures with all our might.

In the aftermath of the revolution, the ranks of the organized revolutionaries multiplied rapidly. Within weeks, dozens of socialist parties, groups, and circles with diverse perspectives presented themselves to the politically anxious youth. Other than the *Fedaiyan* and the Tudeh Party, which enjoyed a tradition of active presence in Iran, others were either new groups or European-based circles which were least familiar with the social, cultural and political milieu in Iran. Some of the major post-revolutionary socialist organizations included the *Paykar* Organization, the Organization of Communist Unity, *Ranjbaran* Party *Rah-e Kargar* Organization, and the Kurdestan-based *Koomeleh* (later affiliated with the Communist Party of Iran). Less than a year after the February uprising, the left could count on considerable numbers of activists and sympath-izers, especially among the students, intellectuals, new middle class, professionals, industrial workers, and some national minorities such as Kurds, Turkomans and Baluchis who believed the left could respond to their demands. Among the various political organizations, the *Fedaiyan*, thanks to their heroic struggles of the 1970s, were the dominant force to be reckoned with.

In fact, the socialist movement, after four decades of repres-sion and sporadic underground activity, found a favorable situation to institutionalize itself, develop a mass base, and influence the politics of society. This could only materialize if (1) the Islamic state would tolerate the opposition, and (2) the left would act in a realistic, non-romantic and mature way. This required the left to develop a minimum level of unity among its ranks; define the nature, goals, potentials, contradictions, and the actual direction of the revolution; identify its allies and foes; and develop a critical assessment of its strengths and vulner-abilities. A critical re-examination of the pre-revolutionary socialist sub-culture also needed to be on the agenda of the post-revolutionary socialist movement. Based on the existing documents, this hardly ever materialized. Partly as a result of the early arrival of repression, and partly due to simple ignoring of the issues, in essence, the traditional pre-revolu-tionary political strategy and culture reproduced itself in the hearts and minds of the left. Thus, it remained trapped in an ineffective frame of discourse and practice and gradually alie-nated a considerable segment of its supporters. In the remainder of this chapter we will examine the post-revolutionary socialist political culture and politics.

SOCIALIST POLITICAL SUB-CULTURE

Socialist politics and political culture in Iran owe their real origins to the practices of the Tudeh Party beginning in 1941, when under the favorable political atmosphere created by the Soviet presence in Iran, the party institutionalized itself and spread its ideas particularly among workers, new middle strata and the intelligentsia. Despite the fact that the Iranian socialist movement has a longer history, those earlier groups and activists (such as the Communist Party of Iran in the 1930s) operated at a much smaller scale and were less influential. Thus the Tudeh Party introduced the Stalinist version of Marxism into Iran.

As was discussed before, in the late 1950s the Third Worldist ideology and its socialist variant appeared in Iran, basically through the impact of the Chinese, Cuban and Vietnamese revolutions. However, in this period, the movement was not a cohesive, firmly rooted, and well-defined socialist movement and/or political culture, either in comparison with the Islamic movement or with the more developed socialist movement of the 1940s.

Intensified political repression by the state, along with an underground guerrilla mode of struggle, deprived the left of the ability to develop a mass base or to value cultural and ideological issues. This happened exactly when the Islamicists were actively redefining their political culture partly by borrowing ideas from Third Worldism. It is therefore of no surprise to find out that in the interaction between the two movements, both during and after the revolution, it was the Islamic political culture that influenced, and to some extent "Islamized," the socialist sub-culture. According to a recent critique: "The youth interested in political and intellectual issues were indeed attracted to the Stalinist version of Marxism without a radical breaking with this [Islamic–Iranian] native culture."[47] Thus the young socialist activist unconsciously borrowed ideas, values, and morals from the deep-rooted Islamic cultural reservoir. In the post-revolutionary period, one could identify a range of politico-cultural elements in the socialist sub-culture that were indeed similar or somewhat similar to those of the Islamic political culture:

Anti-dependency perspective

Preoccupation with the "anti-imperialist" struggle (particularly the Tudeh's anti-Americanism which at times bordered on the clergy's "anti-foreign" sentiments) constituted the central concern of the socialist movement during the 1970s. According to a self-critique: "Foreign enemies have always been an indispensable element of our existence. Even when such enemies have not had a practical existence, we have somehow contributed to their formation; as if our identity assumes its meaning only in opposition to the 'other'."[48] This had much in common with Ayatollah Khomeini's oft-quoted statement: "All of our troubles today are caused by America."

A populistic definition of revolution and justice

Although the concept of class was formally invoked, in the deeper layers of the socialist sub-culture and its collective consciousness justice would only be served by a populistic redistribution of wealth, power and prestige among the *khalq*. Maurice Meisner thus explains the conditions of emergence and motivation of populists in the Third World, which in fact fit Iran:

> a traditional peasant-based society disintegrating under the forces of modern capitalism introduced from without and generally perceived as alien; . . . the emergence of an intelligentsia alienated from traditional values and existing society; and the desire of members of that intelligentsia to bridge the gulf that separates them from society.[49]

The socialist concept *khalq* (the deprived and oppressed masses) was very much in line with the Islamic term *mostazafeen* (the disinherited and oppressed section of the Islamic community). The criterion employed was first and foremost in terms of poverty and oppression (rich versus poor). Manochehr Dorraj thus compares the two versions of populism in Iran:

Whereas the religious sector of the intelligentsia held that the only way to serve God is to serve his creatures, the secular populace extolled the *khalq* as the force of historical transformation. While the secular populists saw the rule of the oppressed as a matter of historical necessity, the Muslim populists perceived of it as a matter of Islamic duty and moral obligation.[50]

During the 1960s and 1970s, many socialist-oriented students spent some time in the lower-class *qahveh-khaneh* (tea houses) in search of the *khalq*. In fact, only a small percentage of industrial workers spent their time in tea houses.[51] By spending their time with rural migrants, radical students tried to bridge the gap between themselves and the *khalq*.

Anti-intellectualism

This refers to a "resentment and suspicion of the life of the mind and those who are considered to represent it."[52] Paradoxically, anti-intellectualism can be found within the socialist movement, a movement which is predominantly of an intellectual nature. However, closer scrutiny allows one to understand the contradictory nature of anti-intellectualism and the fact that most often anti-intellectualism does not present itself in a pure form. Anti-intellectual tendencies in the Iranian socialist political culture derive from a number of sources. First, its populist character convinces the socialist of the authenticity of the masses. They were looked upon as the *real* teachers of politics and culture. In Iran, Maoism further strengthened this existing tendency.[53] Second, the dogmatic nature of Stalinism regarding the role of the vanguard party, and the "proletarian ideology," with its monopoly over "correct politics", strongly prevented socialist activists and intellectuals from coming to terms with theoretical and ideological debates and challenges. Third, the historical continuity of political and cultural repression in Iran, in the form of state censorship, thwarted the institutionalization of pluralism and by implication intellectual diversity, tolerance and criticism. Religion also prevented the spread of ideas that were secular and/or Western in origin. The pre-revolutionary Iranian Constitution testifies to this point.[54] According to article 20:

All publications, except heretical books and matters hurtful to the perspicacious religion of Islam are free, and are exempt from censorship.

In article 21 we read:

Societies and associations which are not productive of mischief to Religion or the State and are not injurious to good order are free throughout the whole country.

However, whether Islam is inherently anti-intellectual is debatable. A number of secular thinkers, in recent years, have argued that "our culture begins with religious outlook and is diminished as a result of this outlook." Such a society is supposedly the "cemetery of unborn thoughts and never could have produced thinkers."[55] Accordingly, the impact of a "religious culture" on various social institutions, especially the educational system, further retards analytical thinking and the emergence of thinkers.

On the other hand, students of Shi'ism reject the above abstract reasoning and its narrow definition of "thinking" and "thinker." In contrast, they argue that:

The victory of the Usuli movement over the rival Akhbari school in the late seventeenth and early eighteenth centuries [confirmed] . . . that Shi'ism is more responsive to social reality, more flexible, more "creative," as it were, than Sunnism. The Usuli school, affirming the need for *mujtahids* to exercise independent judgement on matters of the law, advanced *aql* (reason) as a source for the development of Islamic jurisprudence.[56]

All in all, anti-intellectualism was so deep-rooted in the socialist sub-culture that the concept of intellectual (*rowshanfekr*) was generally used in a pejorative way. The *Paykar* Organization, not an exception in any way, characterized intellectuals with "anti-disciplinary self-centeredness, lack of persistence, paranoia, anarchism, etc."[57] Ahmadzadeh's statement best captures this viewpoint:

Doesn't this imply that from a pure theoretical point of view, the international Communist movement . . . neither has the opportunity nor the need [for theory]? Doesn't this mean that today, more than any other time, we need the practitioner more than the theoretician?[58]

Violence as the means of resolving conflicts

Violence has been defined as "any behavior, physical or non-physical, direct or indirect, collective or individual designed to injure, damage, or destroy persons or property."[59] Violence becomes political when it aims at political power. Violence has historically constituted an element in the Iranian culture in general, and in the political culture in particular. The youth are socialized within institutions such as the family and school, which resort to physical punishment as a method of discipline. Later, religious ceremonies and teachings glorify and justify the use of violence against the opponents of religion. Islamic concepts such as *Jehad* (holy war on behalf of the Islamic community), *qessass* (a tit-for-tat type of retaliation), *shahadat* (martyrdom) and stoning (as a method of punishment) provide some examples. Further, during this political socialization, the young Iranian learns that law is not respected by the citizens because it does not represent them. In fact, he sees an arbitrary interpretation of law by the governments in power. Further, criticism of and opposition to the government is usually met with various violent and repressive measures. There is no surprise, then, that the typical Iranian socialist adopted those interpretations of Third Worldist thought most harmonious with his past social and cultural experiences. Fanon's words, to the effect that for the people of the Third World violence "invests their characters with positive and creative qualities,"[60] were invoked; and further, the guerrilla movement echoed Mao, Debray, Stalin, Che, Lenin, and others regarding the indispensability of violence to the question of power. Other than the guerrilla movement of the 1970s which popularized terms such as armed struggle, armed propaganda, class violence, armed resistance, etc, there were many other concepts and slogans which implied violence that were frequently used by both the socialist left and Islamicists in the post-revolutionary period. Slogans that began with "Down with . . ." or "Death to . . .", were typical examples. Moreover, socialists' frowning upon the ideas of *negotiation* with one's opponent, compromise, or the idea of non-violent transition to the future society all imply a strong and deeply rooted conviction regarding the desirability of violence in the process of social change.

Martyrdom (*shahadat*)

Ayatollah Motahhari, a leading theoretician of the Islamic movement, thus defines the philosophy of martyrdom:

> There is a concept in Islam enjoying a special sacredness. If someone is familiar with Islamic concepts . . . he can sense that a halo of light has engulfed this word, and that of "*shahid*" [martyr] . . . From Islam's point of view, whoever achieves the status of "*shahadat*" . . . achieves one of the highest statuses and ranks that a human might reach in his ascending trajectory.[61]

The Islamic culture promotes an ascetic philosophy of life centered on the high worth of sacrifices and suffering; stoicism, fasting, self-flagellation, and the cult of martyrdom are manifestations of this viewpoint that has penetrated many aspects of everyday life as well as the secular dissident political culture.

In comparing the literature and discourse of Islamic and socialist groups in Iran one is struck by the similar emphasis placed on martyrdom. Since there is very little in the Russian or Third Worldist revolutionary literature on martyrdom, its prevalence in the dissident political culture could only derive from Shi'i Islamic culture. Martyrdom for socialists became an integral political value. Even more, it was a psychological mechanism which helped prepare them for the arduous course of struggle and legitimized their efforts. In 1971, Roqieh Daneshgary, a Fedaii member, wrote the following poem on torture:

> Pain is a transitory phenomenon,
> But disgrace is a scar which remains.
> The pain of torture is a tolerable pain
> About which if you don't think, you won't even feel it.[62]

The concept of *fedaii*, used by the guerrilla group, itself has heavy religious connotations. It refers to a selfless devotee, a volunteer for self-sacrificing. Mehdi Rezall, a member of the Mojahedeen Organization, echoed this theme in his defense:

"Let them torture me, let them sacrifice my flesh and blood for the masses."[63]

Other commonalities

We can also identify other important values, attitudes and ideas among socialists that had affinities and similarities with those of the Islamic political culture. Among them we can refer to *sectarianism*, prevalence of the *cult of personality, rejection of liberal– democratic values, romantic utopianism*, a *dogmatic* approach to ideological texts, and placing priority on *collectivity* and society rather than the individual.

One mechanism by which Islamic ideas, attitudes, and moralities have penetrated the socialist sub-culture has been the social and familial backgrounds of those who joined the left. This was particularly true about the (A–P) Circle, whose leadership, at least up to two years before the formation of the circle in 1967, was of an Islamic orientation. Another example is provided by the 1975 "change of ideology," in the Mojahedeen Organization. As a result, a segment of the Islamic Mojahedeen adopted a socialist viewpoint and took over the whole organization, and reverted to physical elimination of their "ex-members." The end result in the post-revolutionary years was the Paykar Organization, one of the most dogmatic and traditionalist groupings of the socialist movement.

The socialist practice

In this study we treated political culture as a system of ideas, attitudes and values which *conditions* political behavior. To what extent, then, has socialist political sub-culture shaped socialist practices in the post-revolutionary years?

Following the February 1979 Revolution, the majority of socialist parties embraced a supportive and non-critical attitude *vis-à-vis* the clerical faction in the new regime. The Tudeh Party, which enjoyed a *de facto* theoretical domination over the majority of the Iranian left, argued that "the dominant aspect of the national and democratic revolution in Iran is its independence-seeking and anti-imperialist aspect."[64]

Consequently, the clergy in power were called "revolutionary democrats" who were expected to take a "non-capitalist path" to development. The *Fedaiyan*, likewise, by emphasizing the anti-imperialist nature of the revolution found *khalqi* roots in the new regime. They propagated the view that "After the Shah it is America's turn!" The left, not in touch with the concrete demands and interests of the new middle class and the working class, still pursued abstract policies that were akin to its old *student politics* perspective. The existence in 1979 of approximately 19 per cent of the population in the 15–24 age group (half of them urban residents, and over a million of them high-school and college students) with radical and abstract values, was a factor that further reinforced this political tendency among the left. As a result, many concrete democratic demands of potential supporters were either ignored or relegated to an unknown future. In the first year of the revolution, examples of support for secular independent women's movement, for progressive newspapers and magazines and the lack of the left's the left–liberal National Democratic Front testified to the left's confusion about its priorities. Such a failure reflected the left's dominant critical perspective about the democratic rights, as justified by the dependency perspective. According to this view, democratization of civil society was impossible as long as the dependent economic relations and institutions were in place.

The above political views were also common among the smaller parties with apparently different political "lines," including groups supportive of China, Albania, Cuba, or Trotskyism. The pro-China, Revolutionary Organization (later called *Ranjbaran*), defined its strategic slogan as "Not America, not Russia; an independent and self-reliant Iran". Speaking about the new post-revolutionary culture, it proposed:

> Our independent culture should be satiated from the clear limpid spring of scientificity, national–popular traits in order to maintain its parity and be generative and dynamic and keep away from unoriginality. Our independent culture, inspired by our national, popular, and historical originalities . . . should expand in order to perform its outstanding role in constructing an independent, free . . . Iran.[65]

Later, an Iranian historian, sympathetic to the above perspective, devoted an entire book to demonstrating that Iranian history was characterized by a fundamental conflict between two opposing political forces: pro-independence and pro-dependence. "In the final analysis, the future of the Iranian Revolution and reconstruction, to a large extent [depends] on the struggle between these two political lines."[66]

In November 1979, Islamic students, "followers of the Imam's line", occupied the American embassy in Tehran. Once again the vast majority of the left supported the action, vowing only to "deepen" it. The *Fedaiyan* declared: "All weapons and pens should aim at US imperialism and its domestic allies."[67] By the latter they meant the owners of the already-nationalized large factories. Other major socialist parties took similar positions. Nevertheless, this "second revolution" benefitted the clergy in various ways: it led to the departure of Islamic liberals from the government; it diverted the people's attention from their economic grievances to a new issue; and it disarmed the left and isolated it among its potential supporters. This episode also intensified political conflicts within the highly divided left and contributed to an existing division among the *Fedaiyan* ranks.

In the summer of 1980, a major split divided the *Fedaiyan* into the pro-government Majority faction and a more militant Minority faction. Subsequent developments, however, proved that the differences were only at the political tactics level and did not affect the deeper layers of the theoretical (dependency) perspective. The minority faction soon declared that it "considers imperialist domination and dependent capitalism to be the primary obstacles on the road of society's development"[68] and by doing so reaffirmed that no major theoretical break with the past had occurred.

The brief period of political coexistence sharply came to an end when, beginning in June 1981, the Islamic regime embarked on a systematic series of attacks against the opposition, including the left. A number of smaller groupings soon departed the political scene, some permanently. Others, suffering heavy casualties, went underground. The Tudeh Party and Fedaii (Majority) were the only parties that temporarily remained immune, thanks to their supportive attitude for the state. But this also came to an end when, in 1983, many of the top cadres of these parties were arrested and later executed. By then the socialist movement and the dependency problematic were in total disarray. This signified not only a political defeat, but also a cultural–ideological one.

These developments affected the socialist movement in an uneven fashion: on the one hand, they gave rise to self-critical intellectual and political responses, mostly in the form of new theoretical journals or small factions challenging the left's dominant politics and political values; on the other hand, for the majority of the traditional leaderships even the enormous shock of these events could not modify their analytical categories and thought structure. They basically maintained the old discourse and emphasized a return to the "fundamentals." This polarization further strengthened the sectarian tendency and at times even led to armed conflicts.[69] After 1985, with Gorbachev's assumption of power in the Soviet Union and the introduction of *glasnost*, the left's process of atomization and self-critique was further accelerated. Shortly thereafter, new notions of "democracy," "pluralism," "tolerance," and "deideologization" found their way into the left's discourse and gradually were used as a new point of reference. This marked the final demise of the dependency perspective.

Meanwhile, the deeper change of political sub-culture is only in its formative stage. It seems we are witnessing a transition to a new socialist political sub-culture, one in which democratic values and pragmatism play a central role.

CONCLUSION

National political cultures are only abstractions that often do not correspond to reality. We tried to demonstrate this point by depicting a different image of Iran's "national culture"; one characterized by conflict, competition and the struggle for hegemony among various political forces associated with various political (sub-)cultures. In the past fifty years, Islamic, monarchist liberal–democratic, and socialist political sub-cultures have been the most noticeable in Iranian history. The 1978–9 revolution not only expressed the direct victory of the Islamic forces and political culture over the Pahlavi monarchy, but also implied an indirect success *vis-à-vis* the liberal–democratic and socialist forces and sub-cultures.

This new [Islamic] ideology . . . substituted for the secular and nationalist ideas of earlier decades a new ideology, that of Islamic revolution. The legitimacy of the Islamic Republic therefore required a depreciation of these other trends.[70]

The defeat of socialists in the revolutionary process of the 1980s cannot be analyzed solely on political and military grounds. By defeat we do not necessarily imply inability in conquest of political power; rather, what is meant here is the ineffective, undefined, and confused nature of political behavior that was pursued during the 1971–83 period. This by no means is a denial of harsh political and cultural repression that faced socialists both before and after the 1978–9 revolution. Nonetheless, in this defeat, a major role was played by socialists themselves specifically their underdeveloped political sub-culture. Their economistic interpretation of "super-structure" manifested in their disregard for cultural ideological, and democratic issues, their anti-intellectualism, their populistic admiration for the folk culture, their over-emphasis on the dependency perspective, their resort to violence and finally their ignoring of Islamic values and attitudes among their own ranks are clear examples of socialists' responsibility for their cultural underdevelopment.

These internal features contributed to the socialist movement's defeat in two major ways: first, preoccupation with the radical nationalistic dependency perspective prevented the socialist movement from seeing and valuing fundamental democratic demands, needs, and interests of the modern urban strata; and second, common cultural beliefs, values and attitudes within the Islamic political culture created a wedge between the socialist movement and its potential secular new middle-class sympathizers.

Perhaps the left's anti-imperialist agenda was different from the Islamicists' outright rejection of Western civilization. But this was not quite clear to the participants in the revolution. They heard similar anti-American slogans and observed anti-imperialist demonstrations organized in unity with the occupation of the American embassy in Tehran. And they found other symbols and values resonating in the Islamic political culture: populism, anti-intellectualism, sacredness of martyrdom, violence, cult of personality, sectarianism, etc. In the summer of

1979, when socialists focused their attacks on *liberals* as the "road-rollers of imperialism," the *hezbollahi* supporters of the Islamic regime chanted "Democratic and *melli* [patriotic] are both deception of the masses." In competition for the mass support, however, the Islamicists enjoyed a threefold advantage over the socialists. First, the Islamic political culture was organically linked to a deeply-held and familiar 1,400 year-old popular Islamic culture; second, the post-revolutionary government enjoyed a virtual monopoly over the mass media (perhaps with the exception of the first six months of the revolution); and third, whereas the Islamic thinkers constantly challenged the philosophical, political and cultural foundations of the socialist movement, the latter hardly engaged in a critical evaluation of Islamic thought and its political foundations.

Politically, the dominant socialist strategy sought to prove that socialists were the most sincere, radical, and authentic anti-imperialist force in Iran. That is, they were the best defenders of Iran's national sovereignty and interests in the face of imperialist inroads. The early Islamic universalist tendency (pan-Islamicism echoed in themes such as the export of the revolution and denunciation of Persian nationalism) contributed to the Islamicists' vulnerability regarding patriotic values. Nevertheless, twelve years' experience of running a complex modern state and coming to terms with a wide range of domestic and foreign issues, especially the eight-year war against Iraq, strengthened the regime's other coexisting political tendency, namely its nationalism, albeit mixed with Shi'ite fervor; the Islamic Republic increasingly adapted its universalist Islamic ideology to the national context. This was not totally new to the Islamicists. In fact, as mentioned earlier, nationalistic elements within the Islamic political culture were deeply integrated and, at least since the 1881 Tobacco Movement, had manifested themselves on various occasions. Among the political leaders and the intellectual architects of the Islamic Republic one can even identify major pre-revolutionary writings and speeches that had a strong nationalistic echo. It is no surprise then that the majority of Islamic thinkers speak of an "Islamo-Iranian" culture and identity; they find a symbiotic relation between Islam and Iran; "We possess both religious Islamic sentiments as well as patriotic [*mihani*] Iranian sentiments."[71]

Ayatollah Khomeini's reference to Persian as the "language of the revolution"; the regime's defence of the Persian language in its confrontations with ethnic minorities; its sensitivity on "Persian Gulf" rather than the more neutral term "the Gulf"; its war-time invocation of Persian nationalistic themes and images and finally its promotion of Persian language and culture in Afghanistan and Tajikestan, all testify to the strong presence of a nationalistic element, albeit cloaked in Islamic guise, in the Islamic political culture. President Rafsanjani's letter of August 8, 1990, to President Saddam Hussein of Iraq best captures this spirit:

> we decided that except whatever concerns the legitimate and definite rights of *mellat-e Iran* [Iranian nation], nothing else should prevent us from progressing toward peace and thus we have acted.[72]

Doesn't this indicate that the post-revolutionary socialist project of Third Worldist nationalism never stood on firm ground?

NOTES

1 For example, see: Manochehr Dorraj, *From Zaratustra to Khomeini: Populism and Dissent in Iran* (Lynne Rienner Publishers, Boulder, CO 1990); Fred Halliday, "The Iranian Revolution; Uneven Development and Religious Populism" in F. Halliday and H. Alavi (eds), *State and Ideology in the Middle East and Pakistan* (Monthly Review Press, New York, 1988), pp. 31–63; "Populist Movements in the Underdeveloped Countries", *Nazm-e Novin*, no. 4, 1981.

2 Alister Hennessy, "Latin America" in G. Ionescu and E. Gellner (eds), *Populism: Its Meaning and National Characteristics* (Macmillian, New York, 1969), p. 30.

3 Misagh Parsa, *Social Origins of the Iranian Revolution*, (Rutgers University Press, New Brunswick, NJ 1989), pp. 8–11.

4 Michael M. J. Fischer, *Iran: From Religious Dispute to Revolution* (Harvard University Press, Cambridge, MA 1980), p. 185.

5 Lucian Pye and Sidney Verba (eds), *Political Culture and Political Development* (Princeton University Press, Princeton, NJ 1965), p. 513.

6 Ervand Abrahamian, *Iran Between Two Revolutions* (Princeton University Press, Princeton, NJ 1982), p. 51.

7 Homa Katouzian, *The Political Economy of Modern Iran* (New York University Press, New York, 1981), p. 85; Richard W. Cottam, *Nationalism in Iran* (University of Pittsburgh Press, Pittsburgh, PA 1979), p. 249.

8 Sussan Siavoshi, *Liberal Nationalism in Iran* (Westview Press, Boulder, CO 1990).

9 *Ibid.*, pp. 68–74.

10 See: Nikki Keddie, *Sayyid Jamal ad-Din "al-Afghani"* (Berkeley University Press, Berkeley, CA 1972).

11 See: Bizhan Jazani, *Capitalim and Revolution in Iran* (Zed Press, London, 1980); Homayoun Katouzian (ed.) *Khaterat-e Siasi-e Khalil Maleki*, 3rd edn (Jebheh Publishers, London, 1983).

12 For a discussion on Third Worldism see: Ronaldo Munck, *The Difficult Dialogue: Marxism and Nationalism* (Zed Press, London, 1986) pp. 144–6; Gerard Chaliand, *Revolution in the Third World* (Viking, New York, 1977), pp. 17–24.

13 Abdallah Laroui, *The Crisis of the Arab Intellectual* (University of California Press, Berkeley, CA 1976), p. 129.

14 One can refer to a number of publications by Ayatollah Mahmoud Taleqani during the 1960s; formation of the *Monthly Religious Society* in early Fall 1960 by a group of clergy led by Ayatollah Morteza Motahhari; Dr Ali Shari'ati's politicization of Islamic discourse during his (1967–73) public lectures in the Husseinieh Ershad Center in Tehran. For a more detailed analysis see: Shahrough Akhavi, *Religion and Politics in Contemporary Iran* (State University of New York Press, Albany, 1980).

15 Bizhan Jazani, *Tarikh-e Si Saleh-e Iran* (2 vols, Tehran, 1979), vol. 2. pp. 65–80.

16 James Bill, *The Politics of Iran* (Charles Merrill Publishing, Columbus, OH 1972), pp. 69–70.

17 *Salnameh-e Amari-e Keshvar (Annual Statistics for the State)* (The Plan and Budget Organization of Iran, Tehran, 1980), pp. 56–7.

18 *Ibid.*, p. 138.

19 Parichehr Navai, "A Comparison of Perception of Iranian Educators and Students", unpublished PhD thesis, George Washington University, 1983, p. 47.

20 Franz Fanon, *The Wretched of the Earth* (Grove Press, New York, 1966), especially pp. 29–163.

21 Regis Debray, *Revolution in the Revolution?* (Grove Press, New York, 1967), pp. 68–9.

22 Amir-Parviz Pouyan, *Zarurat-e Mobarezeh-e Mossallahaneh Va Radd-e Teori-e Baqa* (OIPFG Publications, Tehran, 1979), p. 42.

23 Fedaiyan-e Khalq (OIPFG) *Payam-e Daneshjoo*, no. 1 (1975). pp. 9–14.

24 *Ibid.*

25 Abrahamian, *Iran Between Two Revolutions*, pp. 480–2.

26 Compiled by the author from various OIPFG publications particularly *19th Bahman* Publications.

27 Louis Althusser and Etienne Balibar, *Reading Capital* (New Left Books, London, 1970); Miriam Glucksmann, *Structuralist Analysis* (Routledge & Kegan Paul, London, 1974), p. 8.

28 Marvin Zonis, *The Political Elite of Iran* (Princeton University Press, Princeton, NJ 1971), p. 304.

29 Daryush Homayoun, *Dirooz Va Farda* (USA, 1981), p. 47.

30 Assef Bayat, "Ravand-e Proleterizeh Shodan Kargaran-e Karkha-nejat-e Tehran," *Alefba*, new series, no. 4 (1983), p. 101.

31 Hamid Nafici, "Cinema as a Political Instrument" in M. Bonine and N. Keddie (eds), *Modern Iran* (State University of New York Press, Albany, 1981), pp. 349–51.

32 One can refer to such satirical stories in magazines such as *Jahan-e Now*, *Ferdowsi*, and *Tehran Mosavvar* paricularly during the 1960s.

33 Jalal Al-e Ahmad, *Gharbzadegi [Weststruckness]* translated by J. Green and A. Alizadeh (Mazda Publishers, Lexington, MA 1982) pp. 115–23.

34 Ali Shariati, *Khod-sazi-e Enqelabi* cited in Ali-Mohammad Naqavi, *Jame'eh-Shenasi Gharbgerai* (2 vols, Amirkabir Publishers, Tehran, 1984), vol. 2, p. 75.

35 Cited in Ehsan Tabari, *Forupashi-e Nezam-e Sonnati Va Zayesh-e Sarmayeh-dari Dar Iran* (Tudeh Publishing Center, Stockholm, 1975), p. 125.

36 Mass'oud Ahmadzadeh, *Mobarezeh-e Mossallahaneh, Ham Estrateji, Ham Taktik* (OIPFG Publications, Tehran, 1972), pp. 43–4.

37 Ali-Akbar Safaii-Farahani, *Ancheh Yek Enqelabi Bayad Bedanad* (Ahang Publishers, Tehran, 1979), p. 50.

38 Reza Baraheni, *Tarikh-e Mozakkar* (Nashr-e Avval, Tehran, 1984).

39 Samad Behrangi, *Kand-o-Kav Dar Massayel-e Tarbiati-e Iran* (Shabgir Publications, Tehran, 1979), p. 7.

40 Mostafa Rahimi, *Didgahha* (Amirkabir Publishers, Tehran, 1977), p. 101.

41 Mohammad-Ali Sepanloo, *Nevisandegan-e Pishrow-e Iran* (Iranzamin Publishing, Irvine, 1986), p. 82.

42 Safaii-Farahani, *Ancheh Yek Engelabi*, p. 36.

43 Bizhan Jazani, *The Socio-Economic Analysis of a Dependent Capitalist State*, translated by Iran Committee (Iran Committee, London, 1978), p. 17.

44 *Ibid.*, pp. 19–110.

45 Mohammad Mokhtari, "Barrasi-e Sho'arhay-e Dowran-e Qiam" *Aghazi No*, no. 3 and 4 (1987–8), pp. 40–52.

46 Feda'iyan-e Khalq, *Elamieha Va Bayanieha* (OIPFG Publications, Tehran, 1979), p. 199.

47 A. Bani, "Chag-e enqelabi-e Iran va mass'aleh-e raha'i' " *Akhtar*, no. 6 (1988), p. 5.

48 *Ibid.*, p. 39.

49 Maurice Meisner, *Marxism, Maoism, and Utopianism* (University of Wisconsin Press, Madison, 1982), p. 112.

50 Dorraj, *From Zarathustra*, p. 120.

51 Bayat, "Ravand-e Proleterizah Shodan," p. 103.

52 Richard Hofstadter, *Anti-Intellectualism in American Life* (Vintage Books, New York, 1963), p. 7.

53 An example of Mao's populistic thinking is echoed in the following statement: "I have spent much time in the rural areas with the peasants and was deeply moved by the many things they knew."

He continued: "Their knowledge was rich. I was no match for them." Cited in Meisner, *Marxism, Maoism, and Utopianism*, p. 99.

54 *Qanun-e Assasi-e Iran*, p. 13.
55 Babak Bamdadan, "Emtena'e tafakkor dar farhang-e deeni" *Alefba*, new series, no. 2 (1965), p. 26.
56 Akhavi, *Religion and Politics*, p. 121.
57 Paykar Organization, *Rowshanfekran Va Jonbesh-e Kommonisti* (Paykar Supporters in Washington DC, 1981).
58 Ahmadzadeh, *Mobarezeh-e Mossallahaneh*, p. 96.
59 Mostafa Rejai, *The Comparative Study of Revolutionary Strategy*, (David McKay Company, New York, 1977), p. 9.
60 Fanon, *The Wretched of the Earth*, p. 93.
61 B Mortez Motahhari, *Qiam Va Enqelab-e Mahdi* in F. San'atgar, "Khomeinism" *Nazm-e Novin*, new series, no. 7 (1985), p. 73.
62 Roqieh Daneshgary, "Shekanjeh" *Asr-e Amal*, no. 6 (1976), p. 142.
63 Mehdi Rezaii, *Matn-e Kamel-e Defa'iyat* (Organization of Iranian Students, New York, 1975), pp. 38–9.
64 *Mardom*, Fall 1979.
65 *Khalq*, no. 3, Summer, 1979.
66 Younes Parsa-Benab, *Esteqlal Va Vabastegy* (2 vols, Azar Publishing Co., New York, 1982), vol. 1, p. J.
67 *Kar*, no. 59, Spring 1980.
68 *Kar (Minority)*, no. 142, Summer 1981.
69 For example, we can cite bloody conflicts within the Fedaiyan (Minority) in Winter 1986 in Kurdestan.
70 Fred Halliday, "Iranian Foreign Policy Since 1979" in J. R. Cole and N. Keddie (eds), *Shi'ism and Social Protest* (Yale University Press, New Haven, CT 1986), p. 92.
71 Morteza Motahhari, *Khadamat-e Moteqabel-e Eslam Va Iran* (Sadre Publishing Co., Tehran, 1988), p. 13.
72 *Iran Times*, August 24, 1990.

5

ISLAMIC MAN AND SOCIETY IN THE ISLAMIC REPUBLIC OF IRAN

Manoucher Parvin and Mostafa Vaziri

INTRODUCTION

The ideology of the Iranian Islamic Revolution provides an occasion to examine the Islamic Republic's stated purposes in light of its policies, actions and intentions. This revolution has profoundly influenced Shi'i and Sunni communities everywhere, and has had a significant impact on world affairs. This chapter is a critical review of the Islamic ideology with respect to two aspects of that ideology: the creation of a new Islamic human being under divine rule, and the restoration of Islamic economic justice. In Iran, the Islamic Republic has sought to attain four important goals. These are, first, the establishment of an ideal divine rule; second, the creation of true Islamic society and person; third, restoration of Islamic economic justice; and fourth, the restoration of the independence of Iran and other Muslim nations – through export of revolution if necessary. Here we shall address the first three goals of the Islamic Republic. The last is a question that is beyond the scope of our study.

The three goals were articulated in the context of the Islamic Revolution but actually confirmed after the victory of the Islamic revolutionary faction of the coalition that toppled the regime of Mohammad Reza Shah. Each of the victorious coalition partners envisioned a different form of government. These ranged from a secular socialist republic to an Islamic theocracy, the Islamic Republic of Iran. We shall assess the theory and practice of the Islamic Republic in regard to its stated goals. One possible approach is to examine and probe the historical origin of the Islamic revolutionary ideology with an eye to identifying its class interest, its purposes, and its internal conceptual logic and then compare it to competing ideologies, especially those that it distances itself from: Eastern socialism and Western capitalism. Another is to juxtapose the regime's ideals to its own policies and actions in order to assess its capacity to realize its own stated objectives and to test its sincerity. However, we shall rely to some extent on both approaches, especially as the scope of our inquiry is limited to basic issues.

DIVINE RULE, ISLAMIC SOCIETY AND PERSON

The establishment of divine rule on earth, perhaps more specifically in Iran, was possible only as a consequence of the success of the Islamic Revolution and the founding of the Islamic Republic. Islamic rule is based on and justified by the fundamental notion of faith in the inseparable *Umma* (community) founded by Mohammad in this world (on earth) and promised as well in the other world (in heaven).

Mohammad articulated this prophecy: "that a community under God was more meaningful and thus of greater political promise than a community under tribal law."[1]

Thus the seed of theocratic rule was planted by Mohammad in the seventh century. But the unmistakably pristine divine rule of the Prophet was modified and elaborated during the subsequent stages of the Islamic empires: the Umayyad and Abbasid. The Sunni–Shi'i split, early in Islamic history, also modified the pristine character of the early Islamic *Umma*. Thus, as a result of the religio-political controversies, not only was Islam as a religion split into orthodox (Sunni) and heterodox (Shi'i) sects but also the ideology and practice of governance differed between these sects. Contrary to the Sunni Umayyads and Abbasids, the Shi'a established their own distinct theology and system of leadership. One of the principal controversies that served to distinguish the Shi'a from the Sunni mainstream was the denial by the Sunnis of the rights of Ali's descendants or *Imams*, as they became known. Perhaps most relevant for Shi'i rule, the twelfth Imam is believed to have gone into occultation by the will of God. His return, according to Shi'i belief, will signal the end of the world and the establishment of ideal divine rule on earth. He will be the *Mahdi*, the Messiah, of deliverance and justice. In the intervening period, between his

117

occultation and return, that is in the absence of a living, ruling Imam, theologians (*Faqihs*) have a prominant role in guidance and leadership of the Islamic *Umma*.

According to Shi'i theology, the *Mahdi* is not dead; he is living in occultation and will reappear only in response to divine order. Shi'i theology asserts that the Islamic community cannot or should not ever be deprived of the leadership of the Imam. In such an event, human beings would lose contact with heaven.[2] The twelfth *Imam* has been considered, at least by this faction of the Shi'a, to be the only true and legitimate living leader, although invisible. His absence has not, in reality, served to promote and achieve Islamic goals. Such a visible void brought on a theological controversy, protracted and divisive, that reached crisis proportions in eighteenth-century Iran. Since then this controversy was pressed by two opposing schools of theological Shi'i thought, the *Usulis* and the *Akhbaris*.[3] In the absence of the living *Imam*, the *Usulis* argued for the active participation of the theologians (*Faqihs*) in the affairs of the community in contradistinction with the quietist attitude urged by the *Akhbaris*. In this controversy, the *Usulis* came out victorious as the religious clerics – theologians (*Mojtaheds* or *Faqihs*) legitimated their position through actual intervention in social, economic, and political matters. Ever since, Shi'a theologians have arrogated to themselves an activist role and shadow legitimacy in the absence of the twelfth Imam, the *Mahdi*.

The *Velayet*, the guardianship of the Community, in *Usuli* Shi'i theology is thus traced from the Prophet, through the twelve *Imams*, and eventually, after the occultation of the last (twelfth) *Imam*, to the learned theologians, the *Faqihs*. This conclusion was reached by the *Usulis* on the basis of the same sources that the *Akhbaris* also used. These sources, four in number, have been the legal and theological bases in terms of which *faqihs* not only decide on their communal role but also solve everyday social problems. The four sources, in order of importance are: (1) the Holy Quran, a speculative interpretation of the words and will of God in the process of *Ta'wil* (spiritual interpretation) and *Tafsir* (technical interpretation) to systematize a convincing explanation for a concrete situation; (2) *Sunna*, the body of Islamic custom and practices based on the words and deeds of the prophet Mohammad (e.g., the works of *Sahih* by Bukhari and Muslem) and those of the Shi'i *Imams* (early Shi'ite traditions - e.g., Koleyni, Tusi, Ebn-Babuya); (3) *Shar'ia*, derived from sources (1) and (2) as a result of further interpretation by the clergy through the art of *Kalam*, extending and specifying the appropriate Islamic behavioral code; finally (4) the individual's conscience, whenever a clear path is not delineated by consultation with sources (1) through (3). Note that the fourth source is by its nature controversial and so is often contested in political and legal areas. Where the boundary of the first three sources ends and that of the individual's free reasoning begins is not clear.

Modern Islamic scholars may use any of three approaches to applying the Islamic sources to solve everyday social problems: (a) adhering to the Quran but updating *Sunna* by means of radical *Hadith* criticism; (b) interpreting the Quran and *Sunna* radically to discern the deeper and broader moral principles inherent in specific doctrinal prescriptions; or (c) claiming that certain modern ideologies (e.g., socialism) are anticipated by (or even derived from) Islam and incorporating them into Islam by a democratic process called *Shora*.[4] Of course, radical interpretations produced by (a) and (b) and apologetic adoptions of modern ideologies provided by (c) are not independent processes; they feed into one another and can occur jointly. Thus the absorption of evolving, social ideologies and economic systems into Islam is nearly limitless. It is not, therefore, surprising that Islamic ideology and practice regarding relations between person and person, person and state, and person and God have changed over time and adjusted to various political and economic forms and systems.

Islamic person

The influence of dogma on social norms, behavior and relationships is very strong, pervading all Islamic societies.[5] What sort of Islamic person does the actual and potential Islamic society produce, and what kind of person already culturally formed would be willing to live under the rule of the Islamic Republic voluntarily? To discuss this question, we must first subdivide the Islamic population according to gender, since people are appraised differentially and treated preferentially on the basis of gender in the Islamic society as prescribed by divine law and rule. A summary of the attributes of the new Islamic persons whom the Islamic Republic is attempting to create at the present time is given in Table 5.1. This table is based on material reported from various sources of official dogma, pronouncements, policies and actions of the Islamic Republic.[6]

The essentials of what we call clerical culture, such as absolute submission to the will of God as communicated by the *Velayat-e Faqih*, fractured individualism, spiritual materialism, dogmatic philistinism, and Islamic unidimensionalism, are imposed on citizens – differentially according to gender – through monopoly of schooling, media, and mosque.

In an Islamic society, the socio-political role of the individual with free reasoning (as opposed to absolute submission to the unchangeable will of God as interpreted by the clergy) remains yet unclear. This ambiguity has been the subject of Islamic debate for centuries, as disputants clash over the question of whether God's final destination for man has been fully determined or whether man still has a right to reason out things without undermining the power of God. In one Quranic verse the determinism of God is explicitly asserted as conclusive, and man is said to have no power or right to change it. "It is not for any soul to believe save by the permission of *Allah*. He had set uncleanness upon those who have no sense" (10: 101). This Quranic verse categorically contradicts the sayings of the fifth and sixth *Imams* (Mohammed Baqer and Ja'far Sadeiq who proclaimed, "God loves His creation so much that He will not force it to commit sin, then punish it."[7] Nevertheless, this contradiction and those arising from interpretation of the other sources cumulatively produce a fuzzy conceptual area that has not been clarified in the history of Islamic debates to the satisfaction of all Muslims. Nonetheless, according to one account, Muslims are not fatalists and belief in *Kismet* (fate) is not a tenet in the theology.[8] In the Shi'i *Ithna Ashari* (twelvers) theology, influences exerted from the *Mo'tazelite* (free thinkers) gave rise to a speculative theology that permits the limited free reasoning of a designated theologian by referring to the sources of law (e.g., Quran and *Shar'ia*); however, here the right of free reasoning, significantly, continues to be reserved to the clergy, not to laymen.

In the Islamic Republic of Iran, the supreme spiritual, judicial, and political authority is vested in the *Velayat-e Faqih* (the

Table 5.1 Islamic society and the Islamic person: the imposition of the clerical ideology

General attributes of clerical ideology promoted by the Islamic Republic	Specific attributes promoted for men	Specific attributes promoted for women
Absolute submission	Internalization of submissiveness: submission to the interpretation of Islam according to the existing ruling political faction. (Absolute submission to rule of *Velayat-e Faqih*.)	Absolute submission to Islam in social life and submission to the rule of men at home.
Fractured individualism	Internalization of individualism in sharply limited social spaces. Conformity of private and public life to isolated enclosures of Islamic prescriptions.	Greater constraint for women on individualism, including severe limitations on private and professional choice.
Spiritual materialism	Internalization of legitimacy of Islamic wealth accumulation driven through profit, rent and wage (not interest). Internalization of quasi-feudalism at home, capitalism in the market and socialism in government as divine is considered the essence of evolving public Islamic man.	Same as for men, except for differential treatment in laws (e.g. inheritance and professions, prohibition of a woman to become a judge).
Islamic philistinism	Internalization of supreme value of conformity to clerical ideology.	Same as for men except for additional constrictions for female gender in most cultural affairs, work and leisure.
Islamic unidimensionalism	Islam as the only appropriate dimension of being for capitalist, worker, peasant, intellectual, scientist, and artist.	Same as men except the Islamic dimension is more confined for women.

guardianship of jurisconsult), signifying a person (e.g., the late Ayatollah Khomeini) or a divine office. He is the ultimate adjudicator of all secular conflicts and spiritual questions.[9] The *Velayat-e Faqih* is not elected by universal suffrage – in a direct or indirect democratic process – but by the discretion of a council of experts who have risen to prominence within the domain of the clergy. By means of this office, the clergy can perpetuate its absolute rule, violating democracy even in theory according to Western precepts that stipulate the free expression of the will of the people as a prerequisite. In this regard Ali Shariati, an influential Iranian sociologist of Islam, views the Western idea of democracy as expressing a directionless and irresponsible liberalism. He states that to obtain brotherhood and harmony (*Umma*: an ideal society), emphasis must be placed on the "purity of leadership, committed and revolutionary leadership, responsible for the movement and growth of society on the basis of its world-view and ideology and for the realization of the divine destiny of man in the plan of Creation."[10] The notion of *Velayat-e Faqih* fits such explanation – even though Shariati was known to be a staunch critic of the traditional clergy!

Traditionally the clergy has enjoyed an unparalleled level of respect from the practicing Shi'i community in Iran – a tradition whose roots lie in the pre-Islamic period, when people always had a particularly high regard for the *Mo'bed* (clergy).[11] Of course, the notion of *Marja-e Taqlid* in a quasi-secular system of Pahlavi, Iran, had already had psychological and cultural impacts on those who followed it. This type of religious authority promoted what we call here "fractured individualism" and unquestioned submissionism *vis-à-vis* the divine laws as interpreted by the designated theologians. It is not possible to weigh the psychological and spiritual dependency of the citizens on the religious orders and the judgements of the clergy, but one can assert that the moral consciousness of the masses alone by and large challenged the system's non-Islamic practices. Although the emerging groups of skeptics – educated and Marxist – were opponents of the clergy and of Islamic norms, they were nonetheless marginal in an already indoctrinated society. The clear example of this can be seen in events and the pronouncements of people between the years of 1977 and 1979, when the channels of expression for the socio-religious morality of the masses were opened. The religious leaders were viewed by some as ignorant and reactionary, but they came to represent such socio-religious morality. The structure of communal relations of the clergy and its followers was transformed into a nationwide paradigm regarding religious, spiritual, and political affairs. To establish firmly its newly gained status, the clergy pressed for absolute submission to Islam as a supreme divine religio-political duty and for rigid conformity with Islamic values and laws.

To promote the goals of Islamic society and to create Islamic man, the clergy began to articulate Iranian society as a whole. The attributes of clerical ideology in the Islamic Republic of Iran are as follows:

1 *Absolute submission*: the unquestioned acceptance of Islam, as interpreted by *Velayat-e Faqih*, as an all-encompassing guideline to life. To oppose or criticize a law (*Shar'ia*) or an opinion of the clergy (notably that of the *Velayat-e Faqih*) would mean to obstruct God's will and therefore to be repudiated and maybe even assigned punishment for defiance.

2 *Fractured individualism*: tolerance of individualism only within sharply limited and discrete economic, political, scientific, and artistic spaces. The lack of social (non-governmental) institutions for promoting newly emerging ideas on the one hand and the absence of any political parties on the other have restricted the new life of the masses under the Islamic regime to the narrow range of what is permitted by the government.

3 *Spiritual materialism*: divine sanctioning of exploitation and private wealth accumulation. Commissioning of profit by the clergy (*Khoms*) had, by religious means, legitimated the accumulation of wealth. Consequently, those who are not certain about the sources of their profit or who know that the source may not be in accordance with Islamic order name a prominent clergyman to handle the assignment of giving away part of that profit for a good cause (*Sadaqeh*), in order to "purify" their gain or wealth.[12]

4 *Islamic philistinism*: produced by ideological monopoly relations and subdivided into three components:
   (a) Little or no interest in individualized spontaneous artistic and literary development, appreciation, and expression; elimination of appreciation for a large part of traditional

Persian culture and for modern human cultural development and heritage through self-censorship or ruler-
imposed censorship.
  (b) Subjugation of science to dogma whenever a conflict –
real or apparent – arises between the two realms.
  (c) Unquestioned acceptance of clerical culture (e.g., art as a
state propaganda tool and not as a means for freely
expressing human understanding, aesthetics, and
creativity).
5 *Islamic unidimensionalism*: the wholesale promotion of a new
dogma by rejecting the existing world economic, social, and
political order (that is to say, neither East nor West).

Although the clergy made attempts to put all of the above
mentioned features of an Islamic system into practice, internal
and external pressures forced the clergy to introduce some
minor adjustments which in fact did not change the nature of
their view about a puritan Islamic system and an Islamic
person. Integration of women into low-ranking government
positions and tolerance of certain artistic activities in the fields
of music, cinema and other forms of art (which Islamic tradition
expresses mixed feelings toward) are examples of the government's learning to adjust. However, facile generalizations
should be avoided in assessing the extent to which imposition
of the clerical culture has been absorbed by the masses or,
alternatively, that it is possible that the masses harbor a great
deal of hidden resistance to these policies. At present no
empirical study exists that explores the nature of the relationship between the citizens and the authorities, whose role as
statesmen obscures their religious and spiritual role. A par-
adoxical attitude may be noted in this regard. The massive
funeral of Ayatollah Khomeini came as a surprise to those who
believed that opposition against the government and its policies
would keep people away from mourning demonstrations. It
may be true that opposition to the government's policies has
been increasing, but it is important to bear in mind that the
paramount spiritual role of Ayatollah Khomeini as the sole
promoter of the Islamic policies exerted an emotional influence
over the masses as well.

Thus the revolution for the clergy was a stage and an
opportunity to consciously apply Islamic norms. In such an

environment, men and women found themselves divided: to obey divine norms according to theologians, or to disobey and thus be labelled anti-Islamic (even anti-religious) and risk incurring severe punishment. The entire purpose of the clergy was to rehabilitate an Islamically ill society whose men and women had been contaminated with Western values.

Consequently the influence of members of the clergy – through their previous role as *Marja-e Taqlid* among the less educated and traditional classes – guaranteed their subsequent role as statesmen. The very same people who followed the clergy in its previous religious role followed it in its political direction, as well; they also became the agents of the Islamization process and imposed the norms upon their fellow neighbors by inspiration from the clergy.

Islamism in Iran did not only emerge since the Islamic political revolution, it had already long been rooted in the folk culture and the psycho-spiritual realm of the society. It should be added however, that aside from those who followed the traditional ritual of *Marja-e Taqlid*, many opportunists emerged who exploited the situation to personal advantage. But realization of the dream of creating an Islamic person and society in the present Iranian Republic has, as one important prerequisite, success in the struggle to impose the clerical ideology forcefully on non-conformist individuals. For example, it led to the imprisonment, execution, and suppression of many opponents of Islamic rule. Others fled into exile.

As a consequence of the imposition of clerical ideology and the constriction of artistic, scientific and political freedom, an untold number of professional, scientific and artistic personnel have left Iran. This massive migration of human capital has occurred not just for the benefit of the adult immigrants politically or economically, but for the future of the children. Some parents seem to accept any cost to avoid bringing their offspring up as Islamic men and women. However, it is not Islam that the exiles are running from but the clerical culture and rule which have wrapped themselves in Islamic verses as the divine and only choice.

The spirit of Islamism in Iran is in turmoil. In our time it is the spirit of quasi-feudalism in the household, spiritual materialism in the market, and chaotic and marginal socialism in the government due to haphazard nationalization and confiscations.[13] It is claimed by the Islamic Republic ideology that these conflicting social structures and their related functions have an Islamic identity. More accurately put, however, they indicate an Islamic identity crisis. Symbolic "taking of poison," as Khomeini put it in reference to the ceasefire with Iraq and granting of certain artistic freedoms – to save the regime – are manifestations of the crisis. The demotion of the heir-apparent Ayatollah Montazeri graphically demonstrated how political factions of the ruling regime were devouring one another during Khomeini's last months. Meanwhile, from a purely economic viewpoint, as inequalities in income distribution increase,[14] Islamic political rule by necessity must become more exclusive and authoritarian in order to maintain control, especially over the working classes and dissenting intellectuals.

Finally, there exists a dichotomy today between the Islamic ideology of the regime, by which it seeks overall unity of the populace under Islam, and true Islamic policies and actions. Attempts by the clergy to achieve cultural hegemony are not succeeding except among the least educated, most economically disadvantaged, and most culturally impoverished citizens. But other groups' compliance with Islamic rule and the clerical cultural hegemony is involuntary, transitory, and volatile for those who are unable to leave the country.

RESTORATION OF ISLAMIC ECONOMIC JUSTICE

In addition to the creation of an Islamic society and person in Iran, the Islamic Republic promised the populace restoration of economic justice. This was especially important to the masses of Iranians who over the years were dispossessed economically and disenfranchised socially and politically. The Shah's Iran had become socio-economically polarized with a tiny minority – especially the court, associated retainers, and the advantaged landlord class and mercantile bourgeoisie – accumulating vast wealth and the large masses increasingly depeasantized, proletarianized and pauperized. The fact that a modern "middle class" of professionals and bureaucrats also emerged did not negate or moderate the wrenching socio-economic transformations and social polarization of Pahlavi Iran. More so, culturally speaking, as the Court and the ruling political-economic power bloc became Westernized, they increasingly alienated the vast disenfranchised and/or pauperized masses, both urban and rural. Similarly, large sectors of the traditional middle strata, both urban (especially the bazaars) and rural, were also alienated culturally, politically and socially. Hence, the promise of the Islamic Revolution and the Islamic Republic to restore both Islamic society and economic justice had enormous appeal to the disenfranchised and dispossessed of Iranian society under the Shah.

Above, we have analyzed the ideology and, to a lesser extent, the practice of re-establishing Islamic society and creating the Islamic person. Here we shall address the question of social economic justice. The question of restoring economic justice in the Islamic Republic is a difficult matter to assess. To begin with, Islam has never been antithetical to capitalism and private property although some Islamic ideologues have argued for "Islamic socialism." Ayatollah Khomeini's position regarding the two systems of socialism and capitalism was ambiguous. He has said that he "approves both and neither."[15]

Islam as an ideology cannot resolve the issue of private ownership, because the sources mentioned above are contradictory, and current evidence and practice are inconsistent at best.[16] So theocratically it is possible that two regimes, both adhering to the divine rule of Islam, may choose opposite paths of socio-economic development and justice. For example, Libya has adopted a number of socialist measures while Saudi Arabia has adopted a mixed capitalist economy, and yet both regimes claim strict obedience to the Divine Rule of Islam. It has also been established that Islamic rule allows and legitimates gender exploitation and class exploitation.[17]

The ideology of Islamic economic justice

Arguments about what are or should be the elements of Islamic economic justice stretch back to the time of the Prophet Mohammad. Here, we will try to summarize the current interpretation of Islamic economic justice according to Hashemi Rafsanjani, the President, commander of the armed forces, and the Friday *Imam* of Tehran – in short, the most important voice in Iran. Rafsanjani indicates that God is the ultimate creator of all wealth – tangible and intangible.[18] Tangible wealth is made up of financial assets, real property, and even physical appearance. Intangible assets are attributes such as intelligence and status. Wealth is distributed according to God's will; hence class and gender differentiation in society is of God's making. Thus people are divided into two God-created groups of advantaged and disadvantaged, although through hard work and God's will one can elevate oneself materially.

However, class and gender exploitation and economic injustice stem not from such divinely imposed differentiations but from non-divine relations that may arise between advantaged and disadvantaged individuals. If the advantaged is a greedy, self-righteous, conspicuous consumer and is exploitative, he becomes arrogant in his behavior and thus unjust. But if the advantaged individual is religious and humble, not arrogant, then justice is preserved in harmony with God's will. Indeed, if the advantaged is not arrogant, then the disadvantaged must resign himself to his station in life and be obedient to the Islamic rule which sanctions private ownership of productive property, unearned income, limitless profit, and thus, the accumulation of private wealth.[19] In short, the disadvantaged must accept exploitation if it is devoid of arrogance, but God will punish the arrogant in the day of judgement. From such analysis it is clear that Islamic thought among the leaders of the Islamic regime in Iran is not conscious of, and ignores, the existence of classes, class conflict, and the necessity for class analysis, and it follows that economic justice in the Islamic Republic is more a problem of public relations rather than elimination of exploitative relationships.

As noted above, such interpretation of Islam defines the appropriate relationships between the individual and God and specifies only a few reciprocal responsibilities between an individual and the state. Thus, by implication, if the advantaged individual is not arrogant then the disadvantaged violates God's will if he is disobedient to the existing rule or condition. Social conflict and social harmony both arise from individual actions and relations, and not from clashes of class interests. Table 5.2 exhibits four possible outcomes derived from the relationship between the advantaged and the disadvantaged, according to the words of Hashemi Rafsanjani. Note that Rafsanjani is explicit about conditions I and IV in the table, while the other two conditions (II and III) are implicit in his argument.

According to Table 5.2, the injustice does not arise from

Table 5.2 Four possible Islamic conditions of human relations and economic justice

Advantaged	Disadvantaged	
	Devout; not arrogant	*Arrogant*
	I	II
Devout; not arrogant	Just and peaceful relations. God's will manifested on earth.	Just but unstable relations. God's will violated by the disadvantaged.
Arrogant	III	IV
	Unjust but peaceful relations. God's will violated by the advantaged.	Unjust, unstable relations. God's will violated by both.

existing exploitative social relations but from individuals' public relations. Moreover, whenever social or economic conflict arises between advantaged and disadvantaged persons, the *Velayat-e Faqih* will be the ultimate adjudicator because he is the representative of God on earth. And, as it happens, the ultimate adjudicator believes in the legitimacy of private ownership of productive property and thus unearned income from profit and the accumulation of wealth and rent. Interest is prohibited in Islam. Consequently, capitalism is sanctioned without interest. However, note that interest collected from a non-Muslim by a Muslim is sanctioned.[20]

The Islamic Republic, accordingly, did not institute fundamental programs of economic reform, nor, specifically, agrarian reform. Nor has the republic developed a comprehensive welfare program. To the contrary, it has relied on traditional Muslim institutions of philanthropy.

High hopes of the Islamic state in Iran to promote an extensive welfare program in order to fill the socio-economic gaps on the one hand, and to link the low strata of the society to the state on the other, have not yet been fully achieved for its capitalist economy. The private sectors have continued to absorb wealth and have subsequently enjoyed the fruits of high inflation without heavy government control, although modifications in the tax system were proposed to prevent the accumulation of wealth in the hands of a few.[21] The state, despite its control over the influx of major revenue from oil and other resources, proved to be inadvertent toward the problems and crucial policies of an already socio-economically ill society: notably, nationwide health insurance, social security and unemployment benefits.[22] The state organizations were set up to respond to certain needs of the society, and in fact carried out tasks of building roads, bridges, providing drinking water and electricity in various rural areas of the country. The agencies created by the Islamic regime to assist the population in educational, urban, economic and regional development, ended up being preoccupied with the damages brought about by the nine-year war with Iraq. Many organizations of the government such as *setadha* (headquarters), *nahadha* (institutions), *bonyadha* (foundations), *shoraha* (councils), *gorouhha-ye kar* (work groups) and *comiteha* (committees),[23] by and large took measures in responding to immediate symptoms of the war and reconstruction rather than introducing sophisticated long-term platforms including comprehensive welfare programs.

CONCLUSION

The Islamic Republic has in twelve years subverted the purposes of the revolution as understood by secular intellectuals who rose against the Shah and also as stated by the current leaders before they took power. Such promises were related to democracy, divine rule, justice, and national independence. Today, even the traditional and policy debates among or within the clergy itself are constrained. A number of ayatollahs were put under surveillance, notable examples being the late Grand Ayatollah Shariatmadari and Ayatollah Montazeri, whose spiritual and political authorities were substantially reduced.

Islam, according to the ideology of the Islamic Republic, is divine *a priori*, so the truth and validity of basic Islamic tenets are not to be doubted and questioned – especially the brand introduced by Ayatollah Khomeini after the revolution of 1979. Existing contradictions and conflicts in the household between male and female, due to Islamic gender differentiation, in the market between capitalist and worker, in national government between ruler and that portion of the ruled whose compliance is not voluntary, and on the international scene between the regime and the West remain unresolved and consume great quantities of economic, political and emotional resources. Class and gender exploitation are maintained and in fact heightened, and due process in upholding human rights as understood universally is violated. Islamic ideology of the clergy is dominant in schools, media and mosques. The Islamic man or woman of the Islamic Republic is a very culturally limited individual. He or she will have a fractured individuality, will be materialistic with spiritual trappings, and will be submissive but intolerant of competing thoughts and dogmatic in regard to human affairs both public and private, uncritically obedient to a theocratic state, suspicious of international contact, and fearful of the supernatural.

In sum, clerical Islamic ideology is an incoherent mixture of various ideologies and is an attempt to create men and women obedient to Islam with the purpose of perpetuating clerical rule in Iran. At this point in time, it is not possible to estimate to what extent, in which direction, and in whom clerical Islamic ideology will take self-sustaining roots. It appears, in conclusion, that the Islamic Republic is marching forward while staring fixedly into the past for guidance.

NOTES

1 G. von Grunebaum, *Medieval Islam*, (University of Chicago Press, Chicago, 1966), p. 72.
2 H. Corbin, *En Islam Iranien*, I, (Edition Gallimard, Paris, 1971), p. 59.
3 G. Scarcia, "Intorno Alle Controversie Tra Akhbari e Usuli Presso gli Imamati de Persia" in *Rivista degli Studi Orientali*, XXXIII (1956), pp. 211–50.
4 W. Shepard, "Islam and Ideology: Towards a Typology" in *International Journal of Middle East Studies*, vol. 19, no. 3, (1987), pp. 307–35.
5 M. M. Pickthall, *Cultural Side of Islam*, (S. M. Ashraf, Lahore, 1979).
6 H. Amirahmadi and M. Parvin, *Post-Revolutionary Iran*, (Westview Press, Boulder, CO, 1988).
7 A. Tabatabai, *Shi'ite Islam*, (State University of New York Press, Albany, 1975), p. 135.
8 H. Kung and Josef Van Ess, *Christianity and the World Religions*, (Doubleday & Co., New York, 1986), p. 76.
9 *Vellayat-e Faqih* (primarily an articulation of Ayatollah Khomeini) and its legitimacy is a current Islamic ideological controversy even among Grand Ayatollahs. See Dabashi (1988) for a discussion of the concept in relation to Islamic ideology.
10 A. Shar'iati, *On the Sociology of Islam*, (Mizan Press, Berkeley, 1979).
11 B. Spuler, "Iran: The Persistent Heritage," in *In Unity and Variety in Muslim Civilization*, G. E. Von Grunebaum, ed., (University of Chicago Press, p. 192) p. 172.

12 Ayatollah Khomeini, *Tozih al-Masa'el*, (Tehran: Islamieh Bookstore, n.d.) pp. 364–6.

13 M. Parvin, *The Political Economy of Divine Unity: A Critique of Islamic Theory and Practice*, (Darwin Press, N. J, forthcoming).

14 *Ibid.*

15 *New York Times*, 2 Jan. 1989.

16 H. Housseini, "Notions of Property in Islamic Economics in Iran: A Review of Literature," paper presented at the annual meeting of the American Economic Association, December, 1987; Maxime Rodinson, *Islam and Capitalism*, (University of Texas Press, Texas, 1981); S. M. Taleqani, *Islam and Ownership*, (Mazda Publishers, Kentucky, 1983).

17 Class exploitation refers to appropriation of surplus labor and in capitalism it refers to unpaid labor, while gender exploitation signifies unpaid labor beyond that of class exploitation and is specific to the female gender. The degree of exploitation is the ratio of unpaid to paid labor (Marx 1965) and is greater for gender exploitation. It means that, in a marketplace where capitalist exploitation exists, women are paid less for the same work as compared to exploited male workers, if the job is legally or traditionally open to women. Of course, some jobs are simply foreclosed to them. For example, women under Islamic jurisprudence are not allowed to become judges. The Quran is explicit about the inherent superiority of men and inferiority of women. Quran, verse 34, Sura 4.

18 See *Keyhan Hava-i*, July 1 and July 22, 1987, for the Friday Imam speeches.

19 Taleqani (1983, p. 114) states that no limit should be put on profit. He also argues (p. 111) against amassing wealth beyond need, but he does not indicate who determines the boundaries of need and how. Also, he does not refer in his argument to scriptures, but only to secondary (lesser) sources and reinterpretations.

20 We call the dogma's legitimation of exploitation "spiritual materialism." See Khomeini (1978, pp. 417, 590). In questions 2080 and 2854 he distinguishes between a loan to a Muslim by a Muslim and a loan from a Muslim to a non-Muslim. Only in the second case are interest charges permitted.

21 Hooshang Amirahmadi, "Middle Class Revolutions in the Third World," in *Post-Revolutionary Iran*, H. Amirahmadi and M. Parvin (eds), (Westview Press, Boulder, CO, 1988), p. 237.

22 H. Amirahmadi, "Economic Reconstruction of Iran: Costing the War Damage", *TWQ*, vol. 12, no. 1 (1990), pp. 42–3.

23 H. Amirahmadi, "Destruction and Reconstruction: A Strategy for the War Damaged Areas of Iran," in *Disasters*, vol. 2, no. 2 (1987), p. 143.

6

SHI'ISM AND THE STATE IN THE CONSTITUTION OF THE ISLAMIC REPUBLIC OF IRAN[1]

Mohsen Milani

Then he [Imam Ali] said: The people are of three kinds: the divine scholars, those who seek knowledge and tread the path of salvation, and the rabble who follow every crowing creature, never partaking of the light of knowledge, never relying on a solid base.

(Sheikh Tusi, *al-Amali*)[2]

If 100 million people, if all the people of the world, stand on one side and you [the *ulama*] see that they say something which is against the Quranic principles, stand up against them and repeat God's words, even if they rebel against you.

(Ayatollah Khomeini, *Sahefey-e Nur*)

Broadly defined, constitutionalism, a modern and Western-originated phenomenon, aims at legitimizing a limited government based on separation of powers and protection of certain civil liberties, usually with a written constitution as its symbol. Among its most conspicuous features are the twin pillars of popular sovereignty and separation of the state from religion. This is essential because popular sovereignty implies that people, as masters of their destiny, enjoy unconditional discretion to promulgate laws that may contradict religious edicts.[3]

This chapter examines how the Islamic Constitution of 1979 and its 1989 revised edition respond to the issues of popular sovereignty and the separation of the state from religion. Their response can be better appreciated when compared with that of the 1906–7 constitution.

133

The architects of the Islamic Constitution, unlike those of the 1906-7 constitution, did not suffer from an inferiority complex toward the West or from intellectual confusion. With decisive language but without ambivalence or compunction, they translated their well-articulated religious goals into constitutional principles.

The Islamic constitution created a republic that repudiates popular sovereignty. Like its predecessor, it is founded on what I call "limited popular sovereignty." But unlike the first constitution, it unambiguously subordinates the state to Shi'ism, terminating the prolonged conflict between the *urfi* (secular) and *shar'i* (Islamic) laws.

In this study, I make extensive use of the recently released deliberations of the Assembly of Experts (AOE) which produced the Constitution. Born out of the people's deep anger, the Islamic Revolution popularized egalitarian, romantic and utopian ideas that mesmerized the masses. Many of these ideas found expression in the deliberations, which reflect the mood of a nation in the throes of a revolution. In interesting ways, the study of the Islamic constitution is also an investigation of the intricacies of the political culture of Shi'ism.

THE DOUBLE PERSONALITY OF THE 1906-7 CONSTITUTION

Whereas in the West constitutionalism developed after the Reformation and acceptance of separation of the state from religion, in the Islamic nations it took a different shape as it harmonized itself with a set of Islamic laws that had permeated every facet of life. The cases of Ottoman Empire and Iran are illustrative of this point.

The Medhat constitution of 1876, so named after the Ottoman's Grand Vazir Medhat Pasha (1822-84), was the first constitution in the Islamic world. It was based neither on popular sovereignty nor on separation of the state from religion. Islam was declared the state religion, and sovereignty resided in the sacred soltan, the caliph and the promoter of Islam who was unaccountable for his pacts.[4] It curtailed some of the soltan's powers, and this may be why it survived only until February 1877, when Medhat was exiled by Soltan

Abdolhamid. But constitutionalism in the Islamic world did not wane, as Iran carried its torch to a temporary success in 1906.

In the symbiotic relationship between the monarchy and Shi'ism, which began with the Safavids' ascendance in 1501, there always existed an uneasy tension between the *shar'i* and *urf'i* laws, which the kings deftly kept manageable, using the combined strategies of force and divide-and-rule. By the turn of this century, a new element, the people's power, made it much harder to manage this tension. The constitutional movement, which reflected this force, sought to loosen the shackles of foreign domination, to reform Iran's archaic political and economic systems, and to restrain the king's arbitrary power. Toward these objectives, a *Majles* was created and a constitution, most of it translated from the Belgian constitution of 1831 by two secular reformers, the Pirniya brothers, was signed by Mozaffar ad-Din Shah Qajar on his deathbed in 1906.[5] The 51-article constitution made the *Majles* the creator and abrogator of law and elaborated its powers and limitations. Except for those laws dealing with finance, all *Majles* legislation required royal sanction and approval by the Senate, half of whose members were to be appointed by the king (arts 17, 43 and 45).

The driving force of this urban movement was the *ulama* and the intelligentsia, whose tenuous alliance was based on convenience, not on ideological compatibility. The intelligentsia, hoping to create a European-style constitutional monarchy founded on secular laws, manipulated the *ulama* for objectives they could not have achieved alone: "Because the Iranian people need fanaticism," Mirza Aqa Khan Kermani admitted, "if we receive assistance from the half-alive group of the *ulama*, we probably will achieve our goal much sooner."[6] The *ulama*, determined to protect the integrity of Shi'ism, participated in the movement because of their myopic vision of constitutionalism and their desire to be recognized as promoters of progressive ideas. The eminent Ayatollah Tabataba'i frankly acknowledged that he scarcely understood constitutionalism; he could only say "he had heard" it would bring security and prosperity.[7]

These two forces' opposing visions for the future, coupled with Mohammad-Ali Shah's reluctance to relinquish power and his unceasing intrigues, created an atmosphere of tension and mistrust. The Supplementary Laws were drafted by five secular reformers to create harmony between the court, the *ulama*, and the intelligentsia by defining their powers and limitations. They were signed reluctantly by Mohammad-Ali Shah late in 1907. But they only accentuated the conflict between the antagonists and created a rift within the *ulama's* ranks. The divisive issue was the *Majles'* legislative prerogatives. For the first time, the *urfi* laws were to be promulgated by a body that represented all the people. In that age of mass politics, the *ulama* developed two distinct approaches to constitutionalism.

The sagacious Mirza Mohammad-Hossein Gharavi-Na'ini, influenced by Efendi's *Constitutional Government*, which was published in Turkey in 1876 to defend constitutionalism, considered Islam essentially constitutional because of its reliance on religious and civil laws. Regarding all temporal authorities as illegitimate in the absence of the Hidden *Imam*, he argued that a constitutional form of government that limits the rulers' arbitrary power and grants people limited sovereignty was less abhorrent than other forms.[8]

But a small faction of the *ulama*, represented by Ayatollah Fazlollah Nuri, opposed constitutionalism. For Nuri, sovereignty belonged to God, the Prophet and his family, and after the Greater Occultation, to the *ulama*. He declared that laws written by "drapers and grocers," in reference to some *Majles* deputies, were inferior to those in the Quran, respected as the ultimate constitution.[9] He favored creating a *shar'i* government based on the fusion of Shi'ism with monarchy in which the *Majles* was an extension of the *ulama*.[10]

Even if the Supplementary Laws granted many concessions to the *ulama*, Nuri called them a "Book of Error." Article 1 recognized Shi'ism as the state religion. Article 2, allegedly written by Nuri, created an "ecclesiastical committee", consisting of five *ulama*, to examine the compatibility of all *Majles* legislation with Islam. Articles 20 and 21 made all publications and associations free, except those inimical to Islam. And article 27 created the *ulama*-controlled ecclesiastical tribunals for matters connected with religious laws, and the civil tribunals to deal with issues of secular law.

Because it addressed the contradictory needs of different constituencies, the constitution contained a host of inconsistencies. It generated a dual power structure by simultaneously creating a *Majles* and an ecclesiastical committee. Either the function of the ecclesiastical committee had to be suspended or the *Majles* had to be turned into an impotent legislative power, both of which defied the spirit of the constitutional movement.

The constitution's approach to popular sovereignty was equally ambiguous. Although it never mentioned popular or national sovereignty, people's powers and their limitations were explicitly recognized. First, the constitution came close to accepting popular sovereignty by declaring that "the powers of the realm are derived from the people" (art. 26). The *Majles'* powers, however, were restrained by the ecclesiastical committee, the king, and the Senate. Second, in the Introduction to the Constitution, Mozaffar ad-Din Shah accepted the "fundamental principle" that people have the "right to participate in approving and superintending the affairs of the country."[11] Third, people were granted various freedoms, including freedom of association and speech. But these freedoms were to end if they came into conflict with Islamic principles or threatened the system's tranquility. And, finally, article 35 stated that "Royalty [*saltanat*] is a trust confided, by the Grace of God, to the person of the King by the nation [*mellat*]." Here, it attempted in vain to reconcile royalty, an Iranian tradition, divine trust (*moohebat-e elahi*), a providential Islamic concept, and the nation (*mellat*).[12] The constitution was silent on the source of the Shah's power: did it emanate from God or from the people? It appears that power emanated from both the people and God: The *ulama* represented God, the *Majles* symbolized the people, and in the Shah these two sources were combined. Ultimately, God's power was supreme because of the *ulama's* veto right over the *Majles*. .

Despite these ambiguities, the constitution popularized elections and granted people rights and powers they hitherto had not enjoyed, such as equality before the law. In a political culture oblivious to the role of the masses, this was an auspicious victory.

But for a good part of the Pahlavi rule (1926–79), the constitution was blatantly violated, as the ugly face of autocracy once again resurfaced: the *Majles* was turned into a submissive body, the *ulama* were suppressed, the ecclesiastical committee was never convened, and the principle that the people can participate in politics was mocked.

THE ASSEMBLY OF EXPERTS AND THE ISLAMIC CONSTITUTION OF 1979

Upon his triumphant return to Iran in February 1979, Ayatollah Khomeini was determined not to allow the intelligentsia to push aside the *ulama*, as they had done in the constitutional movement. He was alert not to repeat "Kerensky's mistake of not using the weapons of the revolution against allies of convenience who would seize the moment for their own deed".[13] He used his immense popularity to create a theocracy, whose attributes the Islamic constitution articulates.[14]

The struggle over the constitution began with the altercations over naming the new order. Ayatollah Khomeini insisted on an "Islamic Republic," arguing that the addition of adjectives such as democratic or progressive to Islamic Republic, as advocated by some groups, implied that Islam was neither.[15] Hojjatoleslam Rafsanjani quotes Ayatollah Khomeini as saying: "These people . . . want Islam. From these people of Iran, 98 per cent cannot even pronounce the word 'democratic.' Say something that the people understand and have made a revolution for."[16] Ayatollah Khomeini had it his way when in a referendum the voters were asked to choose between an Islamic Republic and a monarchy. Ayatollah Kazem Shariatmadari, one of the leaders of the revolution, argued that the referendum gave a Hobson's choice to the voters because the revolution had already rejected the monarchy. Despite this opposition, on May 1, 1979, an overwhelming majority of the electorate voted for what Ayatollah Khomeini called the "Government of Allah" on the earth.

But the republic people had so enthusiastically voted for remained obscure. True, in his writings, Ayatollah Khomeini had urged creating an Islamic government. But he had not discussed its nature or structural configuration.[17] This is perhaps why the draft constitution, prepared by six secular members of Mehdi Bazargan's government, had little resemblance to what Khomeini had written about. The 151-article document had a strong democratic propensity. It proposed a presidential system and made voting the basis of governance. Although it left no privileged status for the *ulama*, it created a twelve-member Council of Guardians to assure the compatibility of all legislation with Islam, contradicting its advocacy of popular sovereignty.

The left slandered the draft. The Fadai'yan complained that it did not address "dependent capitalism and imperialism," and the Mojahedeen were outraged because it was not based on workers' and peasants' councils.[18] But the nationalists, like the National Front, and Ayatollah Shariatmadari supported the draft. Even Ayatollah Khomeini gave his approbation, demanding the retraction of the provisions granting women the right to judgeship and the presidency.[19] He suggested that it be put to a referendum without review by a constituent assembly, perhaps fearing that his forces might not strike a victory. But the nationalists and leftists demanded the formation of a constituent assembly. Because of Shariatmadari's intervention, an Assembly of Experts (AOE) rather than a constituent assembly was formed. Hojjatoleslam Ali Akbar Hashemi Rafsanjani admonished the nationalists and the leftists that should the *ulama* win the majority, they would doctor the draft so fundamentally that "you will regret your own decision."[20] Right he was.

Of the seventy-three seats in the AOE, the *ulama* won the overwhelming majority (with only one woman elected). Of course, prominent nationalists boycotted the elections because they were allegedly denied sufficient time in the media and harassed by the *hezbollah*. Before the AOE convened, the government passed new laws, prescribing harsh penalties for insulting the *ulama* or denigrating Islam, harboring suspicion that it intended to suppress the opposition during the drafting of the constitution.

Mandated to review the draft, the AOE was convened exactly on the day when twenty-six years earlier Dr Mohammad Mosaddeq was overthrown and the Shah's throne was restored in a CIA/MI-6 coup. It took some 560 hours of deliberation to produce a constitution fundamentally different from the draft. (A somewhat similar situation had occurred in the United States. The Philadelphia convention of 1776 was asked by the Continental Congress to revise the Articles of Confederation. But in a move some scholars call a "coup," it wrote a new constitution that was ratified by each of the states and has survived until today.)

Ayatollah Khomeini's opening message to the AOE unambiguously outlined the task ahead. Without mentioning the *Velayat-e Faqih* (rule of jurisconsult), it stated that the constitution must be inspired neither by the West nor the East but must be "one hundred per cent Islamic."[21] Further, the constitution's conformity with Islam was to be determined exclusively by the *ulama* in the AOE, which placed them, without the voters' consent, in a more powerful position than others.

The fundamentalists (meant here as the supporters of the *Velayat-e Faqih*), emboldened by Khomeini's message, envisioned creating a theocracy. Massive popular support, especially from the lower classes, contributed to their self-confidence, reflected in Ayatollah Hossein-Ali Montazeri's statement: "We have self-confidence, we know what our Islamic and religious duties are; we act upon them in full confidence and we do not care whether they [Westerners] like it or not."[22]

In writing the constitution, the fundamentalists pursued a three-pronged strategy. First, they captured the leadership position and determined the AOE's protocols. Although Ayatollah Montazeri was elected chair, it was Ayatollah-Mohammad-Hossain Beheshti, the vice-chair, who ran the AOE. They also determined the composition of the seven closed-door committees that studied the draft. Second, controlling the committees, they disregarded provisions deemed incompatible with Islam and wrote new ones. Bazargan's assertion that the draft was inspired by Islam landed on deaf ears.[23] Kazem Akrami argued that "all our aspirations must be Islamic."[24] Attacking the draft as Western-inspired, he proposed making Islamic laws the foundation of the constitution. Mohammad Keyavosh declared that all principles should be documented in the "holy Quran, or in the tradition of the Prophet . . . and the infallible *Imams*."[25] In fact, the constitution's major articles are substantiated by a Quranic verse or a *hadith*.[26]

The third pillar of the fundamentalists' strategy was to vote on every article separately, requiring a two-thirds majority for passage, thus depriving the deputies of the chance to vote for the entire constitution and taking advantage of the fact that in the beginning few deputies had a clear vision of the whole constitution. First the principles that made Islam the foundation of the constitution were approved and then the controversial provisions, such as articles 2 through 5, were introduced. Article 2 elaborated the five tenets of the government's belief system, such as the belief in one God, which are precisely those the Shi'ites must accept. This was to produce ideological harmony between the state and *Shi'ism*. Originally, article 4, prepared by one of the committees, indicated that all laws and regulations must be promulgated with "full consideration of the Islamic principles."[27] Rahmatollah Moqaddam Maraqeh'i, a secular–liberal nationalist, pleaded for its deletion, arguing that article 66 of the draft contained the same provision when it gave the Council of Guardians a veto power over the *Majles*.[28] But most deputies supported the article's content, only modifying its language. Article 4, in its final version, proclaimed that all laws and regulations must be based on Islamic principles and that "this principle applies absolutely and generally to all articles of the Constitution as well as to all laws and regulations, and the *foqaha* on the Council of Guardians have the duty of supervising its implementation."[29] Only seven opposed an article that made Islamic law the foundation of the republic, limited the power of the *Majles* and the president, and granted the *foqaha* of the Council of Guardians the exclusive right to examine the compatibility of all laws with Islam.

FUSION OF THE STATE WITH SHI'ISM

Having established Islamic laws as the foundation of the new order, the fundamentalists introduced the *Velayat-e Faqih* article. It was during the campaign for the AOE that the concept had first been introduced on the national level. Abol Hassan Bani Sadr, the republic's first president, suggests that the *ulama* introduced it in a defensive reaction against their opponents, fearing that they might be pushed aside again. Montazeri believed that it was designed to end the dualism between the *shar'i* and *urfi* laws.[30] Whatever the reasons for its introduction, Beheshti wrote article 5.[31] It stipulates that during the occultation, "the governance and leadership of the nation devolve

141

upon the just and pious *faqih* who is acquainted with the circumstances of his age; courageous, resourceful, and possessed of administrative ability; and recognized and accepted as leader by the majority of the people."[32]

Only two deputies spoke about the controversy. Moqaddam eloquently argued that the *Velayat-e Faqih* was contradictory to popular sovereignty. Its inclusion would mean that "we must change many other provisions," and rewrite the constitution, which the "AOE cannot legally do."[33] It would bestow upon the *ulama* extraordinary privileges which "will not be accepted by the society," he lamented. He pointed out that after Khomeini's death, it would be difficult to find someone who meets all the qualifications mentioned in the article.

Beheshti defended the article. He accepted Islam's incompatibility with popular sovereignty. Popular sovereignty, which he insisted is not practiced anywhere, is the foundation of democratic orders, where people reign supreme without limitations. But Iran is no democracy. The selection of the *maktab* (ideology) was unequivocally made by the majority of the people when they overthrew the monarchy and subsequently voted for an Islamic Republic, he declared. And "with their first selection, they [people] will limit their future selections within the boundaries of the *maktab* [Islam]."[34] Simply, once people freely embrace Islam, they must obey its laws and limitations. Hassan Ayat used a Rousseauian analogy to justify such limitations: to leave the unhappy state of nature and enter into the tranquil and happy civil society, people forfeit certain freedoms.[35]

The *Velayat-e Faqih* does not repudiate popular voting because the people must "recognize and accept the *faqih*," nor does it inspire despotism because the *faqih's* actions are limited by Islamic laws and traditions, Beheshti reasoned. But Islamic laws cannot prevent a *faqih* from abusing and manipulating his immense power, for the constitution grants him unlimited discretion to interpret them. Moreover, article 5 is reticent on the precise mechanism for measuring the *faqih's* popularity. Neither does the constitution identify the authority responsible for determining the *faqih's* popularity. Direct voting was definitely not intended because the *faqih* must first be accepted by senior clerics and then chosen and emulated by the people.

Only eight deputies voted against an article that gave the *faqih* a special mystique and an aura of infallibility, made obedience to him a religious and political responsibility, and sanctified politics.[36] Ghorshi argued that because of the *Velayat-e Faqih* "governmental laws and decrees are transformed as Allah's decrees, and obeying such decrees becomes religiously necessary."[37] Taheri Esfahani stated that the *faqih* "in the absence of the Hidden *Imam* . . . has authority from the Leader of the Age to rule."[38] Abdul-Hossein Dastqaib was convinced that God will never leave humanity without a *faqih*, who appears when the majority of the people express their desire to "obey" him.[39]

Once the *faqih* was made the soul of the republic, the deputies specified his powers. The most critical of such powers was the commandership of the armed forces which the draft had delegated to the president. According to Ayat, the *faqih* must be the commander to prevent any *coup d'état* by counter-revolutionaries and to position the faithful in all strategic posts.[40] Farsi argued that the Muslim people of Iran will never form an alliance [*bay'at*] with a president whose only qualification is administrative skill and not necessarily an immaculate moral outlook. They will do so exclusively, he added, with the *foqaha* who have proven their impeccable moral values and unfaltering conviction to Islam in long years of service.[41]

Naser Makarem-Shirazi contended that "we should not give so much power to one man."[42] By depriving the popularly elected president from the commandership of the armed forces, he argued, the foundation of the republic will be undermined. Because a presidential candidate needs the people's confidence to win, any fear of a counter-revolutionary coup by the president is a mockery of the wisdom of the electorate, he added. He warned that if "the *foqaha* would like to both appoint a person to the presidency but would also like to have all the responsibilities," people would accuse them of "creating a despotic system based on our rule" and would eventually defy the constitution.[43]

But advocates of maximum power for the *faqih* won readily. Consequently, article 110 granted comprehensive powers to the *faqih*, greater than those given the king in the 1906-7 constitution. Regarding the military, the *faqih* is the supreme commander of the armed forces. He appoints and dismisses the chiefs of the general staff and the *Pasdaran* (the Revolutionary Guards), and four of the seven members of the Supreme National Defense Council; he also appoints the commanders of the three branches of the armed forces, and declares peace and war.

With little opposition from the deputies, the *faqih's* power was extended to the judiciary. Unlike its predecessor which created two distinct tribunals for religious and temporal affairs, the Islamic constitution constructed a unified judiciary controlled by the *ulama* and based exclusively on Islamic principles. It created the Supreme Judicial Council, the highest judicial body, which among other things appoints and dismisses judges whose rulings must be based either on Islamic law or on the *fatvas* of reputable ayatollahs. Its five members must be *mojtahed* (one who is sanctioned to make independent judgment on religious matters). Of these, the head of the Supreme Court and the Prosecutor-General are appointed by the *faqih* and the rest are chosen by all the country's judges. If the *Velayat-e Faqih* legitimized the fusion of the state with Shi'ism, the articles on the judiciary strengthened it.

To complete the fusion of the state with Shi'ism and to end the conflict between the *shar'i* and *urfi* laws, the constitution created the Council of Guardians, whose twelve members, serving for six years, must assure that Majles legislation is harmonious with Islam and the constitution. There was actually little disagreement over the powers of this body, since a somewhat similar provision existed in the 1906–7 constitution and in the draft. The *faqih* appoints six of the *foqaha* of the council, who alone can examine the conformity of *Majles* legislation with Islam. The other six members, who must be jurists, are chosen by the *Majles* from a list prepared by the Supreme Judicial Council. Together, the jurists and the *foqaha* will examine the congruence of all legislation with the constitution. The Council of Guardians, whose members are not elected, must be in session to give legitimacy to the *Majles*, the elected representative of the people.

Thus, unlike its predecessor which advocated a peaceful coexistence between the *urfi* and *shar'i* laws, the Islamic constitution made Islam the basis of law and of the state.

THE *VELAYAT-E FAQIH* AND LIMITED POPULAR SOVEREIGNTY

Are the *Velayat-e Faqih* and popular sovereignty compatible? While Tehrani regarded the *Velayat-e Faqih* as complementary to popular sovereignty, Musavi-Tabrizi compared it with a *melli* [nationalist] government because they both supposedly rely on majority support.[44] Most deputies, however, recognized the incongruity of the *Velayat-e Faqih* with popular sovereignty, creating a profound predicament for which they really found no solution.

They had to satisfy the growing demands of millions of people for political participation. After all, the revolution was precipitated by the Shah's pertinacious refusal to allow such participation. The framers' response to the popular demand for democracy was the inclusion of articles 6 through 8. Article 6 states that the "affairs of the country" must be administered on the basis of public opinion expressed by means of elections or referenda. Article 7 stipulates that elected councils, like the provincial councils, belong to the decision-making and administrative organs of the country. And article 7 declares that "summoning men to good by enjoining good and forbidding evil is a universal . . . duty that must be fulfilled by the people . . . with respect to the government."[45] For many deputies, the combination of the *Velayat-e Faqih* and these articles was equivalent to popular sovereignty.

But it was not. Hamidollah Mir Maradzehi argued that the *Velayat-e Faqih* blatantly violates article 6 because the *faqih* is not elected.[46] And Sahabi argued that unless the popular vote is explicitly declared to be the basis of governance, which the constitution avoids doing, the term republic is devoid of real meaning.[47]

In fact, a provision in the draft had granted the people sovereignty. Although its language was changed in one of the committees, it still retained its democratic propensity: "National sovereignty, which is the same as the right to determine social destiny, is a public right that God has given to all the people so that it can be exercised directly or through selection and election of the qualified individuals."[48] Sahabi, in line with Na'ini, pleaded that the least illegitimate government is that which relies on national sovereignty.[49]

But defined as such, national sovereignty contradicts the *Velayat-e Faqih*. Opposing the provision, Beheshti argued that people's freedoms are limited by God's laws: a priori, sovereignty must be limited, but such limitation is not included in the provision. Some deputies considered the provision superfluous because articles 6 through 8 supposedly grant the people sovereignty. Farsi opposed national sovereignty because it has a Western origin, has no basis in the Quran or the Traditions, and contradicts the *Velayat-e Faqih*.[50]

There were a few attempts to offer a compromise between the proponents and opponents of the provision. Fouzi argued that because both the people and the *ulama* can exercise sovereignty, and because the *ulama* are not elected but are chosen by the fellow *ulama* and then recognized by the masses, the provision must not state that "sovereignty is expressed directly or through election of qualified individuals". It must indicate that sovereignty is exercised "directly and through recognition of the qualified individuals."[51] The critical words are "and" and "recognition" which together add up to acceptance of a dual sovereignty exercised by the people and the *ulama*, and rejection of the *ulama's* sovereignty based on popular voting.

In its final form, article 56 states: "Absolute sovereignty over the world belongs to God, and it is He who has placed man in charge of his social destiny. No one can deprive man of this God-given right," which the people exercise through their government.[52]

Read in isolation from the rest of the constitution, the provision makes the people sovereign, which in turn contradicts the *Velayat-e Faqih*. But a diligent reading of the entire constitution reveals the repudiation of popular sovereignty, even if the people do enjoy certain powers and rights that are conditional.

First, the constitution is lucid about the sources of power. Power emanates, by sequence of priority, from God, the *faqih*, the *foqaha*, and the people. Since God is not directly involved, and the non-elected *faqih* is, by definition, one of the *ulama*, there are only two actual players in the power equation: the people and the *ulama*.

Second, the constitution unambiguously stipulates that absolute sovereignty belongs to God. God has placed man in charge

146

of his social destiny, but has also created laws that only the qualified *ulama* can interpret. Moreover, the highest and most sacred authority is not the president, the people, or the Majles but the *faqih*.

Third, the people's capacity to determine their social destiny, symbolized in the institutions of the presidency and the *Majles*, is, through various constitutional mechanisms, restrained by the *faqih* and the Council of Guardians. These mechanisms include the veto right exercised by the Council of Guardians over the *Majles* and its interference in the *Majles* and the presidential elections (arts 110d, 118 and 99). For example, the suitability of the presidential and Majles candidates must be approved by the Council of Guardians. (In 1980, Ayatollah Khomeini exercised this power when he disqualified Massoud Rajavi, the leader of the Mojahedeen organization, from running.) Keyavosh regarded such intervention as indispensable; it would eliminate the chances that a "demagogic leader" might arise, as if the electorate were incapable of making rational and self-serving choices.[53] This was indeed extraordinary power given to a non-elected body. To end the suspicion that the *ulama* were creating a dictatorship, Rouhani, like Makaram Shirazi and Sahabi, insisted that while the clerics must have their own candidates, all candidates should freely run for the presidency and the *Majles* without supervision by any power.[54] But the AOE was not receptive to such proposals. The fourth element of limited popular sovereignty is the *faqih*'s lack of accountability to the people. Article 84 makes the *Majles* deputies responsible to the entire nation, but no such a provision is designed for the *faqih*. Under the 1906–7 constitution, the king, in a symbolic gesture of respect to the will of the people, must appear before the *Majles* to take the oath of office, declaring his unconditional support for the constitution. Although the king was also declared non-accountable, there was a reciprocity of sorts between the king and the people, as loyalty was a gift given to the king by the people. Abuse of this divine gift, which the *Majles* was to judge, could justify the king's dismissal, as was the case when Mohammad Ali Shah was dethroned. But there is no such a reciprocity between the *faqih* and the people since the *faqih* is primarily accountable to God. The *faqih*, who does not have to be Iranian or of Iranian descent, takes no oath of office before the *Majles* or any other authority, nor must he respond to, or appear in, the *Majles*.

Of course, Article 111 elaborates the procedure for the *Faqih's* dismissal. He may be dismissed should he fail to fulfill his legal responsibility or lose one of the attributes mentioned in article 5. But determination of this failing is granted not to the *Majles* but to a small Council of Experts, whose members, all clerics, are elected by the people. Their qualifications and the internal protocols of the council are determined by the *foqaha* of the Council of Guardians, half of whose members are chosen by the *faqih* himself. Still, as Shaybani argued, the constitution does not indicate what happens if the *faqih* makes a military mistake. Nor does it identify, as Nurbakhsh insisted it should, to whom the *faqih* is accountable.[55]

Finally, Chapter III of the constitution grants considerable civil and political rights and freedoms to the people, but they end, as they do in the 1906–7 constitution, when they violate Islamic laws or threaten the order. Political parties, for example, can freely operate on condition that they do not "violate the criteria of Islam, or the basis of the Islamic Republic." In short, people's powers and rights, which include popular voting, end if they come into conflict with Islamic precepts, and can be modified and limited by the intervention of the *faqih* and the Council of Guardians, justifying the coining of the term "limited popular sovereignty."

CHALLENGING THE CONSTITUTION

The most vehement opposition to the *Velayat-e Faqih* stemmed from three sources outside the AOE. The first source was the moderates and the leftists. Bazargan attempted in vain to convince Ayatollah Khomeini to terminate the AOE on the procedural excuse of having failed to complete its mission according to the original schedule.[56] The National Front declared that the "turban-wearers", were "determined to create a theocratic order in which the *ulama* enjoyed a privileged status."[57] The Fada'iyan condemned it as a camouflaged effort to replace the monarchy with a "Khomeini-styled *caliphate* system."[58]

The second source was the ethnic and religious minorities,

such as the Turks and the Sunnis, who were annoyed by the constitution's favoritism toward the Persians and Shi'ism.

The third and most potent opposition was crystallized by the *ulama* who questioned the constitution from the perspective of Shi'i jurisprudence. Before his assassination in 1979, Ayatollah Morteza Mottahari explicitly stated that the *Velayat-e Faqih* does not mean that "the *faqih* himself heads the government . . . or the *foqaha* should rule and manage the administration of the state."[59] For him, the *faqih* should primarily be the ideologue of the system. In the same vein, Ayatollah Shariatmadari argued that the primary roles of the *faqih* include teaching and guiding the faithful, acting as the state's ideological supervisor, and providing guardianship over the orphans, widows, and so forth. For him, only under emergency conditions can the *faqih* directly intervene in politics, as Ayatollah Khomeini did when he appointed Bazargan to head the transitional government in February 1979.[60]

Ayatollah Shariatmadari rejected the *Velayat-e Faqih* because "the foundation of the dissolution of the former regime was a popular referendum; [thus] the will of the people should also be the foundation of the new government."[61] He saw an irreconcilable contradiction in the constitution: on the one hand it adheres to a vague notion of popular sovereignty (art. 56), and on the other hand it contains the *Velayat-e Faqih* which denies the supremacy of the will of the people.

Opposition to the *Velayat-e Faqih* could have unified the opponents of the fundamentalists, but it did not, and the fundamentalists continued to rise to the pinnacles of power. The November 1979 seizure of the American Embassy by the Students Following the Line of the Imam contributed immeasurably to this consolidation of power. The anti-American hysteria of the hostage crisis provided the fundamentalists with a golden opportunity to suppress their opponents. With Hojjatoleslam Kho'iniha as the Imam's representative on the state's radio and television network, the fundamentalists deftly made opposition to the constitution tantamount to collaboration with the United States and a treasonous betrayal of the revolution. They also selectively released the documents captured from the American Embassy to defame the opposition. Hundreds of people were thus accused of being enemies of the revolution and American spies.

Some leftists and the Mojahedeen joined the bandwagon of anti-Americanism, often embellishing them. Without convincing evidence, the Fada'iyan condemned Shariatmadari and the Muslim People's Republican Party, two of the main bastions of opposition to the *Velayat-e Faqih*, for having received financial assistance from the SAVAK. Rumors were spread about Shariatmadari's alleged collaboration with the CIA.[62] The leftists and the Mojahedeen went one step further and attacked the pro-Shariatmadari forces. They prematurely celebrated Ayatollah Shariatmadari's defeat, unaware that soon they would become the victims of the fundamentalists' wrath.

Nor did the National Front and the Freedom Movement fully support Shariatmadari, who had issued a *fatwa* against the constitution.

The constitution was put to a plebiscite in December 1979, in the midst of the hostage crisis. It was approved, and soon the moderates and the leftists were either pushed to oblivion or were silenced.

REVISING THE ISLAMIC CONSTITUTION

Before becoming a decade old, the Islamic constitution was revised. In April 1989, Ayatollah Khomeini admitted that for many years he had been aware of the constitution's dire deficiencies, but had kept silent in order to focus on the war with Iraq. He therefore ordered the creation of the Council of Reconsideration to revise the constitution.[63] He appointed fifteen deputies and the *Majles* appointed the remaining five. The council had two months to study eight topics, all selected by Khomeini himself. The council selected Ali Meshkini and Rafsanjani as chair and vice-chair, respectively.

The council faced difficult predicaments: what to do with the institution of the *Velayat-e Faqih* in the absence of Ayatollah Khomeini, and how to centralize power without altering the structural configuration of the Republic? President Khamene'i, a member of the Council, traced the roots of the latter problem to the lack of "administrative skills among the original framers" of the constitution, of which he was one.[64]

The updated version, which includes substantial changes in forty-nine areas, was approved in a national referendum in 1989. It gives more power to the *faqih* while altering the meaning of the *Velayat-e Faqih*, centralizes political power by strengthening the presidency and demolishing the post of prime minister, destroys the collective leadership of the judiciary by centralizing all power in the hands of a man appointed by the Leader, establishes a mechanism for future revision of the Constitution, solidifies the fusion of the state with Shi'ism, and takes a few steps further away from popular sovereignty.

The concept of the *Velayat-e Faqih* is somewhat changed, giving credence to Bazargan's assertion that it was an *'aba* (robe) exclusively tailored for Ayatollah Khomeini. In the 1979 version, the *faqih* was to enjoy the support of the decisive majority of the people. In fact, some AOE deputies relied on this "majority support" to equate the *Velayat-e Faqih* with popular sovereignty. In this vein, the 1979 constitution emphatically stipulates that when no *faqih* enjoys massive popular support, the Assembly of Experts, whose members are elected, should appoint three or five recognized *faqihs* to the Leadership Council which then becomes the country's supreme authority. This stress on collective leadership, or power sharing, was probably designed to appease various factions within the clerical establishment and to pave the way for a smooth transition of power in the post-Khomeini era. But the revised constitution is insensitive to massive popular support for the *faqih* and to collective leadership.[65] Now, the Leader need not enjoy even simple majority support, undermining the republican foundation of the order. Moreover, the new constitution has eliminated the Leadership Council, moving away from collective to single leadership. Should the Leader die, resign, or be dismissed, a council, consisting of the President, the Head of the Judiciary, and one of the *foqaha* of the Assembly of Experts, will perform the Leader's responsibilities. This council, which must be controlled by the *ulama*, will lead the country until the Assembly of Experts selects a new leader (art. 111).

Nor do the qualifications of the *faqih* remain the same. It was the intention of the original framers of the constitution to place the *faqih*, who was to be a nationally accepted and respected leader and a religious source of imitation with massive popular support, at the helm of the state to protect Islam and the republic. In the new version, the Leader need not be a *marja* (a source of imitation with a considerable following who renders independent judgment over a variety of issues) or enjoy the support of the majority; he need only be well-informed about *feqh*, or about socio-political problems, or have popular legitimacy (art. 107), and must be "just and pious." Article 109 states that the Leader does not have to be a *marja*.[66] What happens if the people follow a *marja* not selected as the Leader? What are the implications of allowing such a Leader to appoint religious figures to strategic posts? The constitution is silent about these questions.

Despite these drastic changes in the qualifications of, and the level of popular support for, the Leader, his powers were extended beyond those of Ayatollah Khomeini's. Most significantly, Article 110 grants the Leader the extraordinary power to "determine the general policies of the Islamic Republic." That he must do after consultation with the newly created Council of Determination of the Interests of the Republic, which was designed to resolve the outstanding differences between the *Majles* and the Council of Guardians. The Leader will single-handedly determine the composition of this new Council (art. 112). This provision reduces the power of the *Majles*, and seems incompatible with articles 6 and 56, which respectively make voting the basis of the administration of the country's affairs, and place man in charge of his destiny. Furthermore, the provision grants legislative power to the Council for Determination of the Interests of the Republic, all of whose members are non-elected. Therefore, the power of the *Majles*, an important symbol of the people's power, is restrained by two non-elected bodies, the Council of Guardians and the Council for Determination of the Interests of the Republic.

The Leader can also order referenda, delegate some of his duties and responsibilities to others, and decide when to revise the Constitution, powers Ayatollah Khomeini did not constitutionally enjoy. Ayatollah Khomeini could only appoint the members of the Council of Guardians, while the Leader can now appoint and dismiss them. In the 1979 version, the Judicial Council was the highest judicial authority, with two of its members appointed by Ayatollah Khomeini and the other three elected by all the judges. In the new version, that body has been demolished and its responsibilities and powers given to a "just and pious *mojtahed*", the Head of the Judicial branch, who is appointed by the Leader for five years (art. 157). This provision increases the *faqih's* power within the judiciary, reduces the president's power, undermines the autonomy of the branch, and deprives the judges of the power to elect their leadership. The people's power is, therefore, diminished.

The Leader's power is also strengthened within the Council of Guardian. The *faqih* would appoint six of the *foqaha* of the Council and the Head of the Judiciary, appointed by the Leader, would propose the names of six jurists to the *Majles* for confirmation.

In addition, the updated version contains an entirely new chapter. In it, the Leader is given the power to determine that the constitution needs further revision and to order the convening of the Reconsideration Council. Again he is required only to consult with the Council of Determination of the Interests of the Republic to decide what must be revised or amended. The constitution limits what the Reconsideration Council can accomplish: it cannot change the republican form of government, violate Islamic principles, or alter the *Velayat-e Faqih* provision. It is ironic that the Reconsideration Council must first submit its final product for approval to the Leader and then put it to a plebiscite. The constitution does not specify what happens if the voters reject what the Leader has already approved (art. 177). One thing is clear: the people's power to revise and amend the constitution is jeopardized because they are devoid of the power even to elect those who are empowered to revise the constitution.

The constitution has also given substantial powers to the president. These new powers do not seem to reduce the people's power, as the president is the elected representative of all the people.

SHI'I POLITICAL CULTURE AND THE ISLAMIC CONSTITUTION

Some of the Islamic constitution's main characteristics are congruent with the spirit of Shi'ism and reflect the vicissitudes in the *ulama's* fortunes in the twentieth century.

Social groups, like nations and individuals, possess a collective consciousness, a reservoir of the history of memories about allies and antagonists, defeats and glories. This collective consciousness vigorously influences any group's behavior toward the outside world, often in accordance with its collective interests. The Islamic constitution was written by a group whose corporate fortunes were adversely affected by the Pahlavis' secularization and modernization and the West's cultural encroachment into Iran.

The *ulama* experienced rapid downward mobility, losing their elite status. Nor were they any luckier in their political activities. Three times in this century, the *ulama* formed an alliance of convenience with the secularists. They were twice pushed aside, in the constitutional movement and in the early years of Reza Khan's ascendance to power. And, they once broke away unilaterally, but under pressure, during the struggle to nationalize the oil industry in 1951–3. A combination of these two experiences – downward mobility and futile coalition formation – created within the *ulama* establishment a sense of insecurity and a determination to defend their interests against a hostile world.

That hostile world suddenly and unexpectedly became hospitable, as the Islamic Revolution gave the *ulama* a new lease on life. With the collapse of the monarchy in 1979 and Ayatollah Khomeini's immense popularity, the *ulama* became a formidable force, with a popular base of support encompassing the bazaar, the traditional middle class, the working class, and especially the rural immigrants to the city. With such massive support and a unique capacity to communicate with the masses, they readily won the elections for the Assembly of Experts that produced the constitution. This time, the *ulama* wrote a constitution that in some ways reflected their collective feeling of insecurity and determination to defend their interests. It contains built-in mechanisms to guarantee the privileged status of the *ulama* as new rulers.

But the delegation of privileged roles to the *ulama* and the acceptance of limited popular sovereignty are harmonious with the Shi'i hermeneutics, temperament and history. Shi'ism was born as a minoritarian and esoteric movement with, as Hamid Enayat perceptively observed, "an attitude of mind which refuses to admit that majority opinion is necessarily right." The history of Shi'ism is replete with episodes in which a minuscule minority opposed a large majority. Thus, despite the consensus among the majority of the Prophet's companions to select Abu Bakr the caliph, a handful favored the succession of Ali. And,

Hossain defied all odds and confronted Yazid's intimidating army in Karbala with only seventy-two confidants. In these cases, the Shi'ites insist, Imams Ali and Hossein were right because their message was divine.

In Shi'ism, the truth is independent of the perception or belief of the masses. Moreover, the affairs of the state and religion are too exquisite to be delegated to those incapable of comprehending the real meaning of the Quran or the *hadith*, even if they enjoy majority support. This elitism in hermeneutics is manifest in the prevalent view that only the best of the best of the *ulama* can surmise the *baten* (secret meaning) of the Quran and the *hadith*, while the masses can only digest their *zaher* (apparent meaning). In the religious realm, this elitism has long been established since all the faithful must emulate a living ayatollah.

The *Velayat-e Faqih* has only extended this deep-rooted tendency into the political domain. This mistrust of the wisdom of the masses and their perceived tendency to, in Imam Ali's words, "follow every crowing," justifies the existence of a powerful authority, a shepherd, a religious superman of sorts to protect and spread Shi'ism. The same mistrust is the underlying reason why the Council of Guardians has the responsibility to examine the suitability of all candidates running for the *Majles* or the presidency so that, in the words of one AOE deputy, the chances for the emergence of demagogic leaders are eliminated. The implicit assumption is that the people are often incapable of distinguishing good from evil, truth from falsehood, a view that a host of Western thinkers, ranging from Plato to Machiavelli, shared with the framers of the Islamic constitution.

The other side of this coin of cynicism about the wisdom of the masses is the total trust placed in a gifted leader, an *imam* or a *faqih*. After decades of autocracy by the two Pahlavi shahs, why did the framers of the constitution design no institutional mechanism, similar to the checks and balances in the democratic constitutions, to prevent the potential abuse of power by the *faqih*? A major part of the answer to this puzzle lies in the framers' conviction that by the time a man becomes a *faqih*, he is simply immune to evil temptations and manipulation of power.[67]

Therefore, it is not surprising that the Islamic constitution rejects popular sovereignty. However dubious the wisdom of excercising it, popular sovereignty can be attained when, among other things, the boundaries between the state and religion are defined. This is perhaps why in Western Europe popular sovereignty gained acceptance when the boundaries between Christianity and the state were explicitly drawn. In Iran this process has yet to occur.

Now that after centuries of waiting the *ulama* are directly ruling, now that for survival they must adjust to the morality of *realpolitik*, there is the possibility of a renaissance within Shi'i political thought. The signs of such a development, with its distinguished prodigy in Iran, are already apparent. What will distinguish this possible renaissance from all earlier attempts is that, until the Islamic Revolution, the *ulama* were in the periphery of power but they now are in direct control of the state. Shi'ism, therefore, is now confronted with new dilemmas it has never faced before. The abstract theorizing of the past must now be replaced with concrete plans. This is why there are those, like President Rafsanjani, who support a dynamic Shi'i jurisprudence in which the Shi'i decrees and principles are to be made compatible with the exigencies of our time and needs. Either the *ulama* must champion such reforms or they will face insurmountable difficulties. The alternatives are then clear.

The most challenging task is to create favorable conditions conducive to the blossoming of this possible Shi'i renaissance. Too many times, impatient Iranian intellectuals/secularists have imported to Iran Western ideas that the people neither accepted nor understood. Too many times, they have tried to weaken Shi'ism by ignoring it or denigrating it. They all have failed, not only because Shi'ism can easily thrive and grow in hostile environments, as it did for centuries, but also because Shi'ism is an inseparable component of the Iranian psyche and political culture. Substantial change in Shi'ism cannot be initiated or completed exclusively by secular intellectuals, nor can it be achieved by force and intimidation, as the sad story of the Pahlavis indicates. The painstakingly slow process of reform must be championed by the erudite *ulama*, or by intellectuals well-informed about the intricacies of Shi'ism. After all, Martin Luther was a devout Christian priest and a once loyal supporter of the Pope.

NOTES

1 I wrote most of this article during my trip to Los Angeles in December 1989. My appreciation to Hussein and Hassan Milani and to "Uncle" Hussein Alagheband for their hospitality. My thanks to Abbas Milani and Adnan Mazar'ei, Jr, who read an early version of the article and made constructive suggestions.

2 Quoted in H. Enayat, *Modern Islamic Political Thought* (University of Texas Press, Texas, 1982), p. 20. Unless otherwise stated, all translations from the Persian are the author's.

3 On constitutionalism, see F. Wormuth, *The Origins of Modern Constitutionalism* (Harper, NY, 1949). On sovereignty, see C. Merriam, *History of the Sovereignty since Rousseau* (Columbia University Press, NY, 1900).

4 See R. Devereux, *The First Ottoman Constitutional Period: A Study of the Midhat Constitution and Parliament* (John Hopkins University Press, Baltimore, MD, 1963).

5 See A. Kasravi, *Tarikh-e Mashrute-ye Iran* (The History of the Constitutional Movement in Iran) (Amir Kabir, Tehran, 1954), p. 80.

6 Quoted in F. Adamiyat, *Ideoloji-ye Enqelab-e Mashruteh* (The Ideology of the Constitutional Revolution) (Payam, Tehran, 1976), p. 30.

7 *Ibid.*, p. 226.

8 A. Hairi, *Shi'ism and Constitutionalism in Iran* (Brill, Leiden, 1977), pp. 165–97 and Enayat *op. cit.*, pp. 160–74.

9 A. Hairi, "Shaykh Fazl Allah Nuri's Refutation of the Idea of Constitutionalism," *Middle East Studies*, vol. 13, no. 3 (1979), pp. 333–4.

10 Kasravi *op. cit.*, p. 385. Some of the mullas believed that the Quran is the ultimate constitution for all Islamic nations. See M. Malekzadeh, *Tarikh-e Enqelab-e Mashruteh* (The History of the Constitutional Revolution), vol. 2 (Soqrat Tehran, 1949), p. 413.

11 Translation by E. G. Browne, *The Persian Revolution of 1905–1909* (Cambridge University Press, Cambridge, 1966), p. 353.

12 C. Mozafari, *Authority in Islam* (M. E. Sharpe, New York, 1988). For a different interpretation, one which emphasizes the democratic tendencies of the constitution, see Mostafa Rahimi, *Qanun-e Asasi-ye Iran and Osul-e Demokracy* (Iran's Constitutional Law and the Principles of Democracy) (Abu Sina, Tehran, 1957). The word *"saltanat"* has often been wrongly translated as sovereignty. *Saltanat* means royalty.

13 *Asnad-e Lane-ye Jasusi*, vol. 16, September 4, 1979, p. 4.

14 On the ascendancy of the fundamentalists, see Mohsen Milani, *The Making of Iran's Islamic Revolution* (Westview Press, Boulder, CO, 1988).

15 R. Khomeini, *Kalam-e Imam: Enqelab-e Eslami* (The Imam's Words: The Islamic Revolution) (Amir Kabir, Tehran, 1984), p. 175.

16 A. A. Rafsanjani, *Enqelab Ya Be'sat-e Jadid* (Revolution or a New Mission) (Yaser, Teheran, n.d.), p. 162.

17 R. Khomeini, *Hokumat-e Eslami Ya Velayat-e Faqih* (Islamic Government or the Velayat-e Faqih) (Adab Press, Najaf, 1969).
18 *Mojahed*, no. 6, Mehr 23, 1358 (October 15, 1979); *Kar*, no. 17, Tir 7, 1358 (June 29, 1979).
19 Quoted in S. Bakhash, *The Reign of the Ayatollahs* (Basic Books, New York, 1984), p. 74.
20 Quoted in A. H. Bani-Sadr, *Khiyanat Behi Omid* (Betrayal of Hope) (Paris, 1982), p. 61.
21 *Surat-e Mashruh-ye Mozakerat-e Majles-e Baresi-ye Nahai'e-ye Qanun-e Asasi-ye Jomhuri-ye Eslami-ye Iran* (The Detailed Deliberations of the Proceedings of the Council on the Final Review of the Constitution of the Islamic Republic of Iran; henceforth as *Surat*) (*Majles-e* Eslami-ye Iran, Tehran, 1986), vol. 1, p. 5.
22 *Ibid.*, vol. 2, p. 1182.
23 *Ibid.*, vol. 1, p. 7.
24 *Ibid.*, vol. 1, p. 53.
25 *Ibid.*, vol. 1, p. 49.
26 The AOE produced a short bibliography called "Parts of the Quranic Verses and the Hadiths that Form the Basis of the Constitution," *ibid.*, vol. 3, pp. 1877–83.
27 *Ibid.*, vol. 1, p. 313.
28 *Ibid.*, vol. 1, p. 314.
29 Translation by Hamid Algar, *Constitution of the Islamic Republic of Iran* (Mizan Press, CA, 1980), p. 29.
30 *Surat*, vol. 2, 1066.
31 *Ibid.*, vol. 1, p. 376.
32 Algar, *op. cit.*, p. 29.
33 *Surat*, vol. 1, p. 375.
34 *Ibid.*, vol. 1, p. 380.
35 *Ibid.*, vol. 2, pp. 1092–3.
36 Ezatollah Sahabi declared that "a nefarious but secular government can be dismantled by the people, but a critical blunder by the *faqih*, even if inadvertent, would anathematize the ulama and calumniate Shi'ism," *Asnad-e Laneh-ye Jasusi*, September 20, 1979, p. 118. It is not clear how Ayatollah Taleqani, who died before the approval of art. 5, would have voted. One newspaper claimed that he had decided to oppose it. Quoted in *Asand-e Lane-ye Jasusi*, September 18, 1979, p. 107.
37 *Ibid.*, vol. 1, p. 73.
38 *Ibid.*, vol. 2, p. 1090.
39 *Ibid.*, vol. 2, p. 1158.
40 *Ibid.*, vol. 2, pp. 1112–13.
41 *Ibid.*, vol. 2, pp. 1135–36.
42 *Ibid.*, vol. 2, p. 1110.
43 *Ibid.*, vol. 2, p. 1115–16.
44 *Ibid.*, vol. 1, p. 510; vol. 2, pp. 1101–2 and 1127.
45 Algar, *op. cit.*, pp. 30–1.
46 *Surat*, vol. 1, pp. 403–4.
47 *Ibid.*, vol. 1, p. 389.

48 *Ibid.*, vol. 1, p. 510.
49 *Ibid.*, vol. 1, pp. 388 and 514–15.
50 *Ibid.*, vol. 1, p. 524.
51 *Ibid.*, vol. 1, pp. 510–13.
52 Algar, *op. cit.*, p. 49.
53 *Ibid.*, vol. 2, pp. 1194–5.
54 *Ibid.*, vol. 2, p. 1192–3
55 *Ibid.*, vol. 2, pp. 1132 and 1080.
56 Mehdi Bazargon, *Avalin Sal-e Enqelab-e Iran* (The First Year of the Iranian Revolution) (Daftar-e Azadi, Iran, 1981), p. 295.
57 FBIS, September 25, 1979.
58 *Kar*, no. 33, Mehr 30, 1358 (October 2, 1979).
59 Morteza Motahhari, *Piramun-e Enqelab-e Eslami* (On the Islamic Revolution) (Tehran, n.d), pp. 85–6.
60 *Ettela'at*, Shahrivar 29, 1357, p. 2 (September 20, 1978).
61 *Ibid.*, Mehr 19, 1358, p. 2 (October 11, 1979).
62 *Kar*, no. 40, Day 12, 1358 (Jan. 2, 1980); *Kar*, no. 41, Day 19, 1358 (Jan. 9, 1980).
63 *Iran Times*, April 20, 1989, pp. 1 and 12.
64 *Ibid.*, April 28, 1989, pp. 1 and 12.
65 For a critical interpretation of the new changes in the constitution, see the paper by the Society for Defense of Freedom and Sovereignty of the Iranian Nation. Part of this paper has appeared in Kayhan (London), August 10, 1989, p. 5.
66 *Qanun-e Asasi-ye Jomhuri-ye Eslami-ye Iran*, 1368 (The Constitution of the Islamic-Republic of Iran) (Tehran, 1989), p. 63.
67 See, for example, Abassali Zanjani, who makes this explicit in his *Mabani'ye Feqhi-ye Qanun-e Asasi-ye Jomhuri-ye Islami-ye Iran* (The Jurisprudential Basis of the Constitution of the Islamic Republic of Iran) (Daftar-e Markaziy-e Jehad-e Daneshgahi, Tehran, 1984), p. 79. This is a required book for many universities.

7

EDUCATION AND THE CULTURE OF POLITICS IN THE ISLAMIC REPUBLIC OF IRAN

Rasool Nafisi

INTRODUCTION

Political systems are often studied in the context of their institutions, pronounced plans and goals, ideologies, and the similarities and differences between them. In this framework, political culture is discussed as a psychological process of individuals taking political action.[1] Cognitive, affective and evaluative components of the national attitudes toward political objects are studied under the rubric of political culture.

Defining political culture as a collective psychological phenomenon can help us understand the political climate. However, in studying political changes in the traditional societies, an emphasis on the ideological devices of the political culture, or the culture of politics, may help the student of Third World political sociology form a broader comprehension of the idiosyncrasies of these political systems. Research into the symbolic interaction at the political level or the influences of the political–cultural practices of the past on the present political action, and the shaping of the political attitude of the elite by their traditional beliefs would shed light on some aspects of the political practices of Third World societies which otherwise may look anachronistic and incomprehensible.

There are a number of studies on the nexus between traditions and politics in the Third World, such as Clifford Geertz's work on Indonesia.[2] He argues that the experiences, rituals, habits and beliefs (or "politics past" as he calls it) are essential elements in the politics of the present. During transitional periods, the new states search even more for modes of operation. A new symbolic framework to equip the newly seated government to formulate

160

and react to political dilemmas is on the top of the agenda. The new statesman now more than ever looks for something to hold on to, something from the past. The culture, the past experiences of the nation, the web of meaning through which a nation interprets existence, all provide the necessary framework of symbols which becomes the beacon by which the new states navigate in the troubled waters of the modern world. Although Geertz's study is on Indonesia with an emphasis on Bali, using his concept will further our understanding of the political culture in equally traditional Iran where revitalization has taken place in the form of a complete revolution.

THE IRANIAN POLITICAL CULTURE

Iran, before and after the Islamic Revolution will be discussed based on Geertz's concept. In order to study the elements of these cultures, we will investigate the educational institution as a major subsystem of the ideological apparatus and as a key to understanding the larger political culture.[3]

Education and ideology

Education is primarily perceived in its functional capacity as a producer of skilled manpower and an important agent of socialization. The political–ideological aspect of educational practice has received more attention lately by political sociologists. The size of educational institutions in the Third World often comes only second to military size. As a result, educational institutions occupy a major position in the political life of those countries.

Education as a state sub-system is widely used to legitimate the system. Education in this context turns into an ideology. Geertz's definition of ideology in this paper is used to connote the schematic images that cover the lack of cultural orientation or pragmatic solutions available to provide an adequate image of political process. Ideology, Geertz argues, is used to remedy social, psychological, and cultural maladjustments and strains.[4]

This argument ties well into the Habermasian concept of legitimacy. He defines legitimacy as the third factor of social structure, after the forces of production and organization. A legitimacy crisis arises when the legitimation system does not succeed in maintaining the requisite level of mass loyalty. A legitimation system is a state's action for securing its legitimacy through the cultural sub-system. This sub-system functions by providing motivation which is produced by the educational system and mass media. The legitimizing system, according to Habermas, compensates for the crisis of legitimacy of the state which is caused by unequal distribution of economic resources.[5]

Based on the preceding argument, education in the Third World countries corresponds well with the concept of ideology. On the one hand, education is presumed to develop the country and create the proper milieu and standards for further industrialization and democratization of the country. On the other hand, the inadequate legitimacy of the state is caused by the same underdeveloped economic and political institutions. Education is therefore perceived as a panacea, an ideology which can at least temporarily postpone the immediate demands for political and economic development (the process called "delayed effects" by Buck).[6] Moreover, the political socialization of the younger generation in Third World societies (which at times resembles political indoctrination) is mainly undertaken by schools. A further study of the relationship between ideology and education in pre- and post-Islamic regimes in Iran would help provide more support for this argument.

Ideology and education in two regimes

The former regime in Iran, the Pahlavi family, ascended to power through the backing of the military, unlike previous rulers and dynasties who had established their rules upon tribal origins and direct participation and support of clerical hierarchy. This, and other elements such as involvement of foreign powers in the maintenance of the Pahlavi rule and the autocratic command of the dynasty, were delegitimizing factors of that regime. The Pahlavi state's major claim to legitimacy in the face of its continuing legitimacy crisis was its avowal of modernization. For example, Reza Shah, the founder of the dynasty, was titled "the father of modern Iran." Later, reforms under the second Pahlavi, which were named "The White Revolution", also were a series of modernizing reforms – assumed or real – although basically limited to the countryside.

Education was used as the main agent of legitimation under the Pahlavis. They established the new system of schooling. The second Pahlavi liked to identify his rule with educational expansion, and on the occasion of celebrating the 2,500 years of the Persian monarchy, promised construction of 2,500 schools. In the meantime, education was used as a vehicle for "delayed effects." A full democracy was postponed until full literacy was achieved. As early as 1944, the Shah was quoted as saying that the "truly democratic country" he desired was only possible by educating the nation.[7] But this was a circular argument because even by the end of the reign of the Shah more than half of the nation was still illiterate.

On the other hand, in the nascent ideology of the Islamic Republic (which had been elaborated already in Ayatollah Khomeini's works) the Shah's educational system was received with disdain and indignation. For Khomeini, the modern educational system was the fulcrum of a cultural dependency which was ruining the Islamic tradition of the country. In fact, he consistently deplored the educational system for being devoid of moral exaltations. In his first published work, *Kashfol Asrar*, Khomeini discredited modern schools as being the hub of immorality and corrupt attitudes, and for infusing innocent Muslim youth with alien and unsound ideas imported from the decadent West.[8] Up to the 1979 Revolution, Khomeini's works and declarations were congruous.[9] We can classify these messages into two categories: first, messages addressing students and educationists; second, messages criticizing a cultural dependency allegedly caused mainly by modern schooling.

In the first category, Khomeini admonished students to look into "true Islam" as a force which embraces all the necessary rules for social, economic, and political life of a society. He invited students to adhere to the "strong rope" of faith, seek unity with the *Ulama* (clergy) and the *Madrasa* (the theological school), pay no attention to mundane pleasures of flesh, and repel the foreign influences corrupting youth.

Unity between modern schools and the *Madrasa* was a plan which was never elaborated on by Khomeini, although always preached. In essence, he alluded to the emerging power of modern schools which were the most popular at the time, while the *Madrasa*, as well as the clergy itself, were rapidly losing ground. A unity between the modern school and the *Madrasa*, therefore, was meant to promote understanding and cooperation between old and new. The *Madrasa*, established around the tenth century, was progressively losing ground to the modern schools. For example by 1975, all six *Madrasas* (dispersed in major Iranian cities) contained only 10,350 students, while modern schools enrolled 6,609,771 students.[10]

In the second category, the culture (which traditionally means the same as education in the Persian language) was condemned by Khomeini for being convoluted and degenerated by foreign influences. Self-sufficiency for him meant not only full utilization of the present resources, but more avowedly, a return to pristine Islam, to the time of glory. A purification – not updating – was needed to attain the true faith. Students and educationists should publicize the true Islam, and stay away from Westernized culture.[11]

After the successful Islamic Revolution of 1979, Ayatollah Khomeini's messages entertained the same ideas but with some additions. For example, for a period of time, universities were labelled as the hub of "Westoxicated"[12] individuals, or producers of "SAVAKi–communists". Sometimes these communists were labeled as "American-inspired communists," and a purge was seen as being needed to cleanse the system. When universities evolved into centers for the further gathering of more disillusioned students and disgruntled intellectuals, the new Islamic call was for their total closure.[13] Meanwhile, the *Madrasa* assumed a major role in rewriting texts for educational institutions. The advocated unity of modern schools and the *Madrasa* ended in the hegemony of the traditional.

Education, therefore, was a major article of the ideological discourse between the Pahlavi regime and its religious opposition. A content analysis of elementary textbooks as a major element in schooling may help us understand the ideological content of this education and serve as a key to better understanding of the educational component of political culture.

METHOD OF CONTENT ANALYSIS

Iranian primary and secondary education are divided into three stages: a five-year primary school, a three-year guidance program, and a third stage which is a four-year period with more emphasis on specialization. To conduct the content analysis, two series of Farsi texts from primary schools (second to fifth grade) of the two different regimes were selected. The first grade Farsi was omitted because of lack of political themes. The Farsi text is used for the reading comprehension and grammar of the Persian language. Other subjects taught in the primary school include the Quran, religion and ethics, dictation, social studies, natural sciences and hygiene, arithmetic and geometry, art, calligraphy and physical education.

In order to study the textbooks as a major element in the schooling process, we need to elaborate on the socializing role of the textbooks in the schools, which is one of the ongoing issues in the sociology of education. Unlike other socializing agencies such as family,[14] the extent of the effects of curriculum, school climate, teachers and peer group is not clearly measured.[15] However, as the findings of Langton and Jennings show, the curriculum has different effects on different groups of students. While white students are less affected by the civic curriculum, black students show more susceptibility. They argue that such an effect could be attributed to the lower level of information exposure for blacks.[16]

The same argument could be extended to Iranian students. Unlike more modern societies, the majority of Iranian students are not exposed to massive information from the media, and may be more inclined to receive the bulk of their political socialization from the schools and curriculum. In fact, based on her field research in the Iranian schools in 1975, Jakubielski concluded that schools were the main agent in political socialization of the students.[17] Another researcher, Golnar Mehran, has studied the socialization of schoolchildren in post-revolutionary Iran. She concluded that the political socialization efforts of the schools have had different effects among different students due to the existence of conflicting messages conveyed by different socializing agents. Children from more traditional/religious families respond more to political socialization in schools than students from secular/Westernized families.[18]

Although ideological matters are directly addressed in courses such as social studies and religious studies, the Farsi text, however, contains more hidden curricula. The Farsi text reveals the type and frequency of political themes and the method of indirect inculcation of ideological themes. For example, the second grade Farsi book of the Pahlavi period shows less ideological themes than the later period, and the fifth grade Farsi text unexpectedly has no praise of the Shah. On the other hand, religious studies and social studies texts of both regimes show more or less the same frequency. The Farsi text thus was selected as a source to show the type and frequency of the themes, as well as the pursuance of the latent ideological themes in a text which is supposedly purely instructional and apolitical.

In order to explain the themes used in Iranian texts, research was done by studying and evaluating lessons from those books. Themes comprised of stories, poems, or lessons addressing an issue were classified and the more ideological/political ones were selected. Thereupon tables containing the most frequent political–ideological themes were formed. There are some other important themes which do not enjoy high frequencies and therefore are not included in the tables. Notwithstanding, in the discussions their role is explored.

THE POLITICAL CULTURE AND TEXTBOOKS IN THE PAHLAVI PERIOD

Paging through the Pahlavi period texts, one would notice two features highly accentuated. One is the emphasis on the Shah's image, and the second is an optimistic presentation of materials. The first four pages of the texts are filled with pictures of the Shah, his son, his wife and his sister. In fact, as Table 7.1 shows, the second most highly emphasized theme in the texts is about the Shah or praising his efforts to modernize the country (18 per cent). The optimistic presentations are elaborated in gleeful messages and pretty drawings which often embrace nature or display fanciful designs. Another 14 per cent of the themes are devoted to direct governmental propaganda, wherein again the centrality of the Shah's role in modernizing the country is stressed.

The first priority, however, goes to Persian (pre-Islamic) mythology (39 per cent). This area covers the Persian legacy prior to the Muslim Arab invasion in the seventh century. More than thirteen centuries of Islamic Iran do not receive much attention. Razi, the chemist, and Avicenna the philoso-

Table 7.1 The highest frequencies and percentages of political/ideological themes in Pahlavi textbooks (2nd through 5th grades)

Theme	G.2	G.3	G.4	G.5	Total	%
Persian (pre-Islamic) myths/traditions	7	9	4	5	25	39
The Shah's praise	0	8	3	0	11	18
Government propaganda (modernization efforts)	0	6	3	0	9	14
Patriotism	1	2	4	2	9	14
Benign ruler	0	2	3	1	6	9
Extreme patriotism	0	0	0	4	4	6
Total	8	27	17	12	64	100

pher–physicist – two major medieval Iranian Muslim personalities – are introduced, but emphasis is on them being Persian, and facts such as them writing their books in Arabic are not discussed. Pre-Islamic Iran is envisaged as an idyllic empire with no contradictions, in which benign rulers like *Kasra* are admonished by a peasant, and festivities are almost year round.

Patriotic themes occupy 23 per cent of the total. While 14 per cent of the themes are on the love for one's country, another 9 per cent explicate extreme patriotism. In this category, one can find allusions to shedding one's blood for the country, like the legendary *Arash*, who by sacrificing his life empowered the arrow which determined Iran's boundary with its enemy.

The image of a benign ruler is a hidden message which is supposed to project a good image of the Shah. This theme is inherent in stories such as the popular legend of *Kaveh the Blacksmith*. An ordinary man, Kaveh suffers greatly under the rule of Zah'hak, the serpent-man, the imposter, who is a *Tazi* (Arab) as well. He starts an uprising and helps Fereydoon, the benign, legitimate and Persian ruler, to dethrone Zah'hak the imposter and claim his reign. Fereydoon ascends the throne and the world calms down and all types of oppression disappear.

TEXTBOOKS OF THE ISLAMIC REPUBLIC

Unlike the Pahlavi textbooks, the Islamic Republic of Iran has not emphasized pictures of Khomeini and his family. Direct

Table 7.2 The highest frequencies and percentages of political/ideological themes in the Islamic Republic's textbooks (2nd through 5th grades)

Theme	G.2	G.3	G.4	G.5	Total	%
Islamic faith	4	6	9	13	32	40
Allah	7	6	4	12	19	24
Anti-authority messages	2	1	4	12	19	24
Martyrdom	0	2	0	6	8	10
Khomeini	0	0	0	2	2	2
Total	13	15	17	35	80	100

references to Khomeini, as it is shown in Table 7.2, also are minimal (2 per cent). The textbooks' overall design and content is gloomy, serious and deliberately doctrinaire. It is not unusual to find illustrations of graveyards on the pages, such as in the third grade Farsi text. Matini notices that the pictures of little boys and girls which are transferred from the Pahlavi texts are now refashioned with Islamic attire. He also points to the curious fact that the majority of the people illustrated in the texts now appear with the old Arabic garments.[19] Matini adds that the Arabization of the texts went so far as to change the famous verse from the *Shahnameh*, the book of Persian epic, that was the motto of the old Ministry of Education, "who is wise is powerful," to the Arabic words and Persian copula *"ta'leem va ta'allom ebadat ast"* – "education is worship." Pre-Islamic heritage now disappears from the texts. Iran starts from the time of its fall into the hands of Arab Muslims. It is no wonder then to see Arab personalities, rather than Persians, dominating the texts. In some cases, even a story in the old texts featuring a Persian, now features an Arab. In the Farsi text of the Pahlavi period, in the history of flight, a story from *Shahnameh* is mentioned. According to this story, King Kavoos used eagles to fly his throne. In the Islamic Republic's text, however, a Muslim Arab's attempt to fly with artificial wings is referenced. Concentration here is on the Islamic faith with high emphasis (39 per cent), a subject non-existent in the Farsi text of the previous regime. Expectedly, the second highest featured theme is *Allah* (24 per cent).

Another dramatic change from the old to the new is an

elaboration on anti-authority themes (24 per cent). While the undercurrent in the ancient regime's texts is a love of and submission to the authority of the Shah and the state, here in the new regime, themes such as revolution, uprising against unjust rulers, sympathizing with the poor and oppressed, and fighting inequality all abound. Empathy for the people of Palestine in the third grade Farsi text is a part of general concern for the oppressed. Violent action as a means toward attaining one's rights is suggested. Themes reflecting rage, bloodshed and torture are also found in the texts.

The crux of the violent action for making the wrong right is martyrdom (10 per cent). Martyrdom is what made the Islamic Republic feasible; the way of moral exaltation and of reaching to *Allah*. Martyrdom is the path taken by the chosen people of *Allah* to bring down the unjust world.

Nature studies, which are otherwise ideologically neutral in most other texts, in the Islamic Republic change form. Every act of nature is just another manifestation of the power of the Almighty. In order to make sure that no point is missed, in the exercise section of the lessons, students are supposed to relate any natural and most social phenomenon to the will of Allah. Texts are geared towards moral purification as advocated by Ayatollah Khomeini. Mehran correctly argues that the final goal of political socialization in the schools is a revolution in values and a moral–political transformation.[20]

Although the effects of the 1979 revolution and the Iran–Iraq war would have contributed to the sullen themes of the texts, further study may show the functionality of somber themes in the texts. The following discussion about the political culture is intended to analyze the overall cultural tendencies of the two regimes, and it may enable us to have a better understanding of the context in which the texts are developed.

THE PAHLAVI REGIME AND THE "PERSIAN" CULTURE

The history of the modern Iranian state begins with the Safavid dynasty (1501–1722) which revitalized the Iranian state and reunited the country. More importantly, this dynasty chose Shi'ite Islam as the state religion. Prior to this, Shi'ism had been an obscure sect only known to a few Muslims in Lebanon, Iraq and Iran. The shift to Shi'ism was partly made to fend off the Sunni (mainstream Muslim) Ottomans who claimed the caliphdom of Islam and were eyeing the north-western part of Iran.

Shi'ism depends highly on the religious guidance of the *ulama*. Another element contributing to the aggrandizement of the role of the religious authority was due to the fact that the majority of the Islamic texts were available only in Arabic and the *ulama* were about the only authority who could interpret those sources for the Farsi speaking Iranians.

The importance of the *ulama* ebbed after the defeat of Safavids by the Sunni Afghans. The later defeat of Afghans by Nader Shah did not help the cause of Shi'ism either, because he again tried to re-establish Sunnism as the state religion. However, the emergence of the Qajar Dynasty (1796–1925) brought the *ulama* back to the arena of religious and political power. During this period, the religious authority shared power with the court and was exclusively in charge of judiciary and education.

The coup staged by Reza Khan Pahlavi in 1925 terminated the rule of Qajars and the *ulama* simultaneously. Impressed by modernization efforts in Turkey which had denigrated the role and power of the *ulama*, Reza Khan Pahlavi tried to establish an autocratic, centralized, and secular state in Iran in which there was no room for the religious authority. A new military dictatorship replaced the traditional alliance between the court and the *ulama*. The source of legitimacy was no longer the blessings of the *ulama*, but the shining boots of the new army men, modernity, and the pre-Islamic kingly traditions of Persia. Appeal to the pre-Islamic traditions was supposed to help the new regime's image to present itself as the new force destined to bring the old glories back. Moreover, a new ideology based on pristine Persia would have discreetly associated the clergy – now the rival of the state – with the years of decline of the dwindling Persian state. Pre-Islamic Persian history was generally known in the form of an epic which was registered in *Shahnameh* until the late nineteenth century when European and American archaeologists' findings in Iran made a systematic writing of that country's history possible. The second half of the twentieth century also witnessed the relative decline of the established European hegemony after two international wars, which contributed to an overflow of patriotism and national independence movements in the Third World.

The Pahlavi state based its legitimacy on an amalgam of the ideology of modernization, and the glorification of the ancient Persian empire (the two subjects comprised 14 per cent and 39 per cent of the themes in the textbooks respectively). That amalgam was useful at the time but it also created limitations. The ideology of modernity was an economic approach, apolitical in nature. Textbooks of this period testify to a system of education disinterested in politics, except the legitimation of the Shah (14 per cent of the themes) and the economic progress made under his auspices. This was a major factor in the gradual depoliticization of the society.

The kingly tradition of ancient Persia also imposed certain restrictions. The perceived glories of the past may have brought home comparisons for some Iranians who judged the present disfavorably, and the splendor of the past might have come into contrast with the inefficiencies of the existing state. On the other hand, if the past remained illusive and unattainable, the image of the Persian emperor reincarnated itself in the modern Shah. He became as aloof and haughty as the old emperors, and managed to place himself above the society. The art of communication with the populace – an art in which the clergy were masters – was totally abandoned. Notwithstanding, here was an emperor with no empire, ruling over subjects who strongly desired to be citizens.[21]

Imitation of the old Persian emperors by the Shah led to more centralization of power in his hands. One may argue that his tendency to monopolize power may have caused the utilization of the myths of ancient Iranian culture. Nevertheless, during his reign the Shah became unavoidably the embodiment of the entire politics of Iran.

Unlike the Pahlavi regime, which looked back towards the pre-Islamic tradition of Persian culture as something to be resurrected, the Islamic clergy's history, as the textbooks show, starts right from the demise of that culture. If the Pahlavis adhered to modernity, the clergy in power cherished the assumed simplicity and purity once associated with pristine Islam at its inception. It was argued that economics was mundane and it was the Faith which was sublime, and that was what the nation made a revolution for; this is the logic of the new regime.

THE ISLAMIC REPUBLIC AND THE CENTRALITY OF THE PULPIT

After ascending to power, the clergy hastened to establish a symbolic framework and a workable model for the Iranian state. Khomeini argued that in Islamic tradition there was no separation of church and state. Since it was virtually impossible for the clergy to recreate a caliphdom after the model of the Abassids and Ottomans, the new government adopted the patronage system that was already used by the *ulama* and their followers. The symbolic interaction of the nation and its new rulers also was patterned after the practice of *rawda* (pronounced "rowzeh"). The *rawda* is the preaching from the pulpit, it is used in death memorials, religious commemorations and some other social gatherings. It basically draws on the martyrs of Karbala, the revered Shi'i *Imam* and his followers in the seventh century (61 AH)[22]

The preacher warms up with religious chants in Arabic, takes on social issues, then reaches a climax when he dramatically recites the sufferings and innocence of the martyrs. The volume of crying, chest beating and lamenting is the measure of the preacher's success. At these moments, the preacher immediately assumes the role of the mediator between God and his people, and prays for them to be forgiven. A captive audience, fascinated with the stern images of death and martyrdom, becomes highly susceptible to suggestions from the pulpit.

Ayatollah Khomeini was always aware of the symbolic power and political capacity of *rawda*. From his early work *Kashfol Asrar* in 1944, until the establishment of the Islamic Republic in 1979 and after, he stressed the centrality and the unifying power of *rawda*, and realized the potential and catalytic role of tears and grief for Islam (Shi'ism). He asserted that the existence of Islam (Shi'ism) has been dependent upon the continuity of the *rawda* tradition.[23]

Death and martyrdom, as illustrated in the children's texts (10 per cent of the themes), is also the main theme of the Islamic Republic's political culture. The clergy, aware of the numbing effects of death, and the fear and fascination evinced by martyrdom, uses this psychological game quite effectively. In this context, death becomes the rule, while life, as stated frequently by the clergy, is just a transitory stage, meant for purification of the soul. A new phenomenon which may be called "the politics of the corpse" is another aspect of the obsession of the draconian Islamic state with death. Not only does the clergy adore cemeteries and treat them as national parks, it also overtly utilizes corpses for its political purposes. While some corpses are monuments to the faith elevating the cause of Islam, others might be simply disposed in ditches like "dogs," the impurest of the impure. Ayatollah Khomeini's burial was skillfully used for another show of the unity and popularity of the Islamic Republic. On the other hand, bodies of the executed members of the opposition were not even allowed to be buried in public cemeteries. Public hanging was abandoned for years, but now again is a frequent show. Multiple hanging is preferred; and in political cases, construction cranes are used to hang the victim in the proximity of his house.

Unlike the old regime's politics which was woven around the person of the Shah, the new center of politics now is the pulpit, not any personality. The ideology and power are mainly disseminated from the pulpit. The move from the cult of the individual, as practiced in the Shah's time (14 per cent of the themes in the text books), to revering pure ideology (*Allah* themes, comprising 24 per cent) may have two reasons. First, the Islamic faith has an emphasis on worshipping *Allah* rather than any earthly entity. The high frequency of religious themes and praise of *Allah* in the textbooks of the new regime might have been caused by the same fact. Second, one may conjecture that this move means the Islamic regime has learnt a few lessons from its predecessor: a high stress on the Shah's personality did not help the old regime once it faced crisis.

The aloof and alienated state of the Shah is now replaced by an intimately engrossing populist state of the clergy. The politics of the new state is face to face. Encounters with the populace are no more through public ceremonies, ordered articles in the papers or the foreign media. The new state meets the people in Friday prayers, mosques, graveyards and ceremonies for the newly-born and newly-dead. This new state, reaching to the populace through grief and fear, differentiates the nation into insiders and outsiders. The insiders have proved their allegiance through sacrifice and shedding of their blood (martyrdom makes 10 per cent of the themes in the texts). The rest of the nation is comprised of outsiders. Unlike the old regime which would require one's acquiescence, the new regime asks for an allegiance proved by activism and ritualistic sacrifice. Real and imaginary often become the same. The first circle of insiders of the new regime consist of the Guardians of Revolution whose loyalty is tested in the Iran–Iraq war and elsewhere, and "the martyrs' families," those whose relatives have come out triumphant in the test of fire and blood.

The lethargic, dishonest, and ostentatious political culture of the past is now replaced by a virile, dramatic, ever-demanding, and aggressive one. The concept of mission, also entertained by the Shah's regime, now finds its real meaning. The new regime is not only for one nation, but for the world. It is the unfulfilled, the oppressed, the betrayed Shi'ite truth, suppressed by tyrants, now back for revenge. The state deals not with the ephemeral, but with the eternal. The state is not ruling the populace because they desire so, but because they deserve so; the state is not there to reward but to punish. People indulged in opulence and have rebelled; now is the time to repent: *Va low basatalla hol rez ghal ibadehi labaghow felarzi* (And if *Allah* were to increase his worshippers' provisions, they would rebel on earth) (Quran, *Shura*, verse 27). Moreover, the clerical state is the precursor to the re-emergence of the *Mahdi*, the Imam in occultation, and upon his appearance comes the all-embracing rule of justice.

While cherishing the insiders, the regime deals with the opposition as they dealt with those modern-minded youth who despised *rawda*. They ridicule them as a bunch of gigolos, *Westoxicated*, and ungodly. The underground opposition is portrayed as promiscuous groups that lure innocent women into their dens for sexual iniquity.

The masculine, dominant culture, never a secret, now culminates to a new phase. Translated into political action, the suppressed sexual instinct manifests itself in a game ritual. Fully armed and driving in cars, the guardians of chastity chase "improperly dressed" women, arrest them and haunt them for ever. This primordial game of sex and aggression disguised in the form of a morality play goes on in the streets which are not public places any more; the same goes on at home which holds no privacy from intruders looking for improper pictures in the family albums. Justification for this street game is the necessity of chastity, to keep the young away from carnal temptations, to let them attend their spiritual needs, and strengthen them through self-denial.[24]

The preacher, on the other hand, sermonizing from the pulpit, the impresario of the ceremony of grief, is the focus of audience's attention. Like any other stage actor, the preacher becomes accustomed to this attention. While the audience is at the height of its grief, the preacher masterfully sets up the tent of fear and awe, then unpegs it, and assures the believers of their deliverance. He, the stage master, commands attention and thrives upon it. This may explain the dramatic behaviors of the clergy in power: the global chase after the Shah, their getting involved in highly publicized events such as hostage taking, inviting Gorbachev to Islam, and last but not least, the order to murder Salman Rushdie. All these may fall into the category of drama for political purposes.

CONCLUSION

The pre- and post-Islamic regimes in Iran have used two different periods of the historic legacy to legitimize their rule. While the Pahlavi regime emphasized the pre-Islamic Persian heritage, the Islamic Republic initiated its history from the time of the demise of that culture and the inception of Islamic Iran. The Pahlavi regime utilized the Persian emperor's image as a model of kingly conduct, while the Islamic Republic emphasized the faith itself, and defended a retrieval of pristine Islam. In the Pahlavi regime, however, ritual was superseded by the ideology of modernization. In the Islamic Republic, the ritual becomes the central part of political action. *Rawda*, the traditional preaching of the clergy, becomes a model for the new state. Symbols such as martyrdom employed in *rawda* become the working paradigm for the newly established regime. Some aspects of the political behaviors of the new officials are also explained in terms of the drama of *rawda*.

The model of the Persian empire utilized by the Pahlavis embraced limitations and an anachronism; so does the Islamic model. Notwithstanding, the new model might prove to be more enduring under similar circumstances due to its emphasis on ideology rather than on the individual ruler.

NOTES

1　See, for example, Almond and Powell, "Political Culture" in Gabriel Almond and G. Bingham Powell, Jr (eds), *Comparative Politics* (Little, Brown & Co., Boston, 1976), pp. 52–77.

2　C. Geertz, *The Interpretation of Cultures*, (Basic Books, New York, 1973).

3　The educational system, according to Althusser, is the ideological apparatus in modern societies replacing church. In Iran, however, one may argue that during the Pahlavi regime the educational system was close to such an ideological status. Later developments and the occurrence of Islamic fundamentalism might have brought the church (mosque) back as another competing institution in inculcation of the ideology of the state. For Althusser's argument see L. Althusser, "Ideology and Ideological Apparatuses," in B. R. Cosin (ed.), *Education, Structure and Society* (Penguin, London, 1972), pp. 37–49.

4　Geertz, *op. cit.*, pp. 218–19.

5　J. Habermas, *Legitimation Crisis* (Beacon, Boston, 1973).

6　John Buck argues that education in the Third World is used for what he calls "delayed effect." This means that the governments of the Third World consciously promote an image of education which appears as the only vehicle for overhauling the backwardness of the country in the long run. Any promise for the betterment of the system, accordingly, is postponed and conditioned upon the full literacy. See J. C. Buck, "Education and Development; a Conflict of Meaning," in P. Altbach, R. Arnov and G. P. Kelly (eds), *Comparative Education* (Macmillan, New York, 1982), pp. 78–101.

7　H. Ladjevardi, "The Origins of US Support for an Autocratic Iran," *International Journal of Middle East Studies*, vol. 15, (1983), pp. 223–4.

8　R. Khomeini, *Kashfol Asrar* (unknown publisher, 1944).

9　See R. Khomeini, *Farhang va taleem o tarbiat*, in *Dar jostojooy-e rah az kalam e Imam*, vol. 22 (Amir Kabir, Tehran, 1987); and R. Khomeini, *Islam and Revolution* (Mizan, Berkeley, 1981).

10　For more information on *Madrasa* see M. J. Fischer, *Iran: from Religious Dispute to Revolution* (Harvard University Press, Cambridge, 1980), pp. 12–60, and for statistics on modern schools see *Unesco's Statistical Yearbook* (Unesco, Paris, 1979–80), pp. AZ–771, AI–58.

11　R. Khomeini, *Daneshgah va enqelab-e farhangi*, in *Dar jostojooy-e rah az kalam e Imam*, vol. 21 (Amir Kabir, Tehran, 1983).

12　"Westoxication" is the translation of *Gharbzadegi*, a term popularized by the Iranian writer and social critique Al-e Ahmad. Westoxication meant the state of mind of an Iranian who was totally absorbed by Western ideas and values.

13　R. Khomeini, *Kalam e Imam*, vol. 21, pp. 182–266.

14 M. Kent Jennings and Richard G. Neimi, "The Transmission of Family Values from Parents to Child," in J. Dennis (ed.), *Socialization to Politics* (Wiley, New York, 1973) pp. 323–48.
15 Kenneth P. Langton and M. Kent Jennings, "Political Socialization and High School Civics Curriculum in the United States," in J. Dennis, *Socialization*, pp. 365–90.
16 Kenneth P. Langton and M. Kent Jennings, *op. cit.*, p. 390.
17 L. Jakubielski, "The Political Socialization of Elementary School Children in Iran," Unpublished PhD thesis, Michigan State University, 1975.
18 G. Mehran, "The Socialization of Schoolchildren in the Islamic Republic of Iran: a Study of the Revolution in Values in Iranian Education," unpublished Ph.D thesis, University of California, Los Angeles, 1988.
19 J. Matini, "Textbooks in the Islamic Republic of Iran," *Iran Nameh*, vol. 3, no. 1 (1984), pp. 1–26. He also refers to the high emphasis placed on Khomeini. Since he omits the Pahlavi textbooks, his claim seems valid. But a comparative content analysis of the textbooks in both periods, as being conducted in this paper, shows a much higher stress on the Shah, which makes no comparison possible with the later period, at least in Farsi texts.
20 Mehran, *op. cit.*, p. xix.
21 For an analysis of contradiction between the perceived role of Iranians as subjects and their desire to become citizens see D. Yankovich, Statement, in J. Jacqs (ed.), *Iran, Past, Present and Future* (Aspen Institute, New York, 1976), pp. 1–13.
22 For a more detailed description of the *karbala* tragedy see Michael M. J. Fischer, *Iran: from Religious Dispute to Revolution* (Harvard University Press, Cambridge, 1980), pp. 13–27.
23 R. Khomeini, *Rouhaniat*, in *Kalam-e Imam*, vol. 8, p. 70 and p. 301.
24 Ayatollah Khomeini had maintained that the co-ed colleges were designed by foreigners to propagate promiscuity, and weaken the Muslim youth's determination, see: Imam Khomeini, *Daneshgah va enqelab-e farhangi*, in *Kalam-e Imam*, vol. 21.

8

ISLAMIZING FILM CULTURE IN IRAN[1]

Hamid Naficy

INTRODUCTION

On a hot day on August 10, 1978, during the last year of the reign of Mohammad Reza Shah Pahlavi, Hossein Takab'alizadeh and his two friends, Farajollah and Hayat, walked into Rex theater in the city of Abadan, the site of one of the largest oil refineries in the world. They were each carrying a brown bag containing a bottle of high octane airplane fuel and matches. They joined the audience, which was engrossed in *Gavaznha* (*Deers*), a film about an anti-government smuggler. Half way through, Hossein and Farajollah left the hall, doused the three closed exit doors with gasoline, set the doors on fire, and fled from the scene.

The fire quickly spread, engulfing the entire building. Unable to escape or quell the flames, Hayat along with over 300 others trapped inside, burned to death in the inferno.[2] Anti-Shah revolutionary fervor found its rallying point, and the city of Abadan, which up to that time had remained relatively calm, was galvanized into action and joined the protest movement. Although government sources attempted to place the blame for the incident on religious factions, the overwhelming public consensus held the by now discredited government responsible. Testimonies and documents compiled after the fall of the Shah, however, established a clear link between the arsonists and the anti-Shah clerical leaders.[3]

From then on, destroying cinemas became a key symbolic act against the government of the Shah, during whose time cinema was considered, especially by clerics and religious folks, to be filled with Western mores of sex and violence and part of the imperialist strategy to "spray poison" and corrupt people's

178

thoughts and ethics.[4] Although some among the opposition accused the Shah's government of setting cinemas on fire, the leaflets and *samizdats* they themselves issued clearly shows that they either urged destruction of cinemas and banks as representation of the Pahlavi cultural and economic system, or reported such action in glowing terms.[5]

Anti-cinema feelings run deep in Iran. Historically, religious attitudes, intensified by activist clerical leaders since the introduction of films into Iran in 1900, have consistently condemned cinema as a morally offensive and an ethically corrupting Western influence. The "influence" was seen to be direct and unidirectional. In fact, the clerical elite seem to have subscribed to a "hypodermic theory" of ideology, whereby, similar to the Althusserian formulation, the mere injection of ideology transforms an autonomous and ethical "individual" into a dependent, corrupt "subject."[6] Cinema as a Western import is condemned consistently in the religious literature on account of its hegemonic and interpellative power, which is seen to be irreversible and total. For instance, there is a report that in 1904 a major clerical figure, Sheikh Fazlollah Nuri, attended Iran's first public moviehouse in Tehran and proscribed it, causing it to shut down only after one month of operation.[7] We do not know for sure his reasons for this, but this action fits his general paradigm of Westernization as either a drug ("sleeping potion")[8] that puts believers in a stupor or a "fatal, killer disease"[9] which annihilates its victims.

Mojtaba Navab-Safavi, one of the leaders of *Feda'iyan-e Eslam* in Iran, a fundamentalist group operating in the 1940s, selects a different but equally powerful and graphic metaphor to talk about cinema and its supposedly direct effect on society. He calls cinema, along with other Western imports (romantic novels and music), a "smelting furnace," which melts away all the wholesome values and virtues of a Muslim society.[10]

Ayatollah Ruhollah Khomeini, too, in two of his important works prior to the revolution, links cinema directly with the onset of corruption, licentiousness, prostitution, moral cowardice and cultural dependence. If the metaphor of Nuri is medical and Navab-Safavi's industrial, that of Khomeini's in *Kashf-ol Asrar* is sexual. According to him, cinema, as well as other manifestations of Westernization (theater, dancing and mixed sex swimming), "rape the youth of our country and stifle in them the spirit of virtue and bravery."[11] In *Velayat-e Faqih*, written many years later, Khomeini hammers on this theme of cinema and entertainment as the direct cause of prostitution, corruption and political dependence. Indeed, he is a proponent of the hypodermic theory of ideology, using the term "injection" (*tazriq*) to describe the ill effects of Westernization. For example, he posits that Reza Shah's policy of removing the veil from women and imposing hats and Western clothing on men "injects" immorality, vice and dishonesty;[12] while religious education "injects self-sacrifice and service to the country and to the people."[13]

It is significant to note that despite the hypodermic and unmediated formulation of the effect of motion pictures, none of these leaders seem to have considered cinema's ideological "work" alone but in the context of over-determination of Westernization in Iran. Cinema is seen as one of the ideological apparatuses, imported from the West by a despotic regime, which in tandem with other media and leisure activities such as theater, radio, popular music, dancing, mixed swimming pools, and gambling is said to produce its ideological work of interpellation. This is a significant formulation in that it considers, however crudely and without self-reflexivity, the intertextuality and cross-fertilization of the signifying institutions of the society, such as the mass media. The drawbacks to this formulation, however, are that unlike Michel Foucault's polysemic cultural analysis,[14] that of Khomeini's elides the possibility of resistance, ignores the local conditions and the contradictions existing among the media, and effaces the specificity of their unique ideological work, all of which can undermine and *mediate* the effects of the "injection" of Westernization. Without taking into consideration these contradictory structurations, we can discuss neither what Horkheimer and Adorno pessimistically have called the "ruthless unity" of the culture,[15] nor what Khomeini and others have called the "society of idolatry," or the "culture of idolatry."[16]

It is also significant to note that both Navab-Safavi and Khomeini are willing to entertain the idea of adopting cinema only if it is done "properly" and "ethically." In rare passages they talk about this. Here is what Navab-Safavi says:

Moviehouses, theaters, novels, and popular songs must be

completely removed and their middleman punished according to the holy Islamic law. And if the use of motion picture industry is deemed necessary for society, [then] the history of Islam and Iran and useful material such as medical, agricultural, and industrial lessons should be produced under the supervision of chaste professors and Islamic scholars observing the principles and criteria of the holy religion of Islam and then shown [to the public] for education, reform, and socially wholesome entertainment.[17]

Khomeini spells out a similar theme, only years later, upon his triumphant return to Iran after the fall of the Shah. In *Behesht-e Zahra* cemetery, he announced:

We are not opposed to cinema, to radio, or to television [. . .] The cinema is a modern invention that ought to be used for the sake of educating the people, but as you know, it was used instead to corrupt our youth. It is the misuse of cinema that we are opposed to, a misuse caused by the treacherous policies of our rulers.[18]

In these passages, the clerical leaders are not speaking of removal and proscription of cinema; instead, they both are advocating its adoption as an ideological apparatus to combat the Pahlavi culture and usher in an Islamic culture.

The major concepts frequently pronounced by authorities when speaking of "Islamic culture" can be classified under the following categories: nativism (return to traditional values and mores), populism (justice; defense of *mostaz'afan*, the disinherited); monotheism (*towhid*); anti-idolatry (anti-*taqut*); theocracy (*Velayat-e Faqih*, rule of the supreme jurisprudent); ethicalism and puritanism (*Amr-e beh Ma'ruf va Nah-ye az Monkar*); political and economic independence (*esteqlal*); and combatting *estekbar-e jahani* (arrogant world imperialism), a concept often condensed in the slogan "neither East nor West."

To appreciate the process of its development, in what follows, I will present a more or less chronological history of cinema since the revolution of 1978–9, making references to these cultural categories when it is warranted.

More than ten years after the establishment of the Islamic government, a new cinema is emerging which is markedly different from the one existing during the preceding regime. Periods of transition and social turmoil seem to produce some of the most innovative cineastes and cinematic movements.[19] Thus, there is good cause to expect the Islamic Revolution in Iran, and its preconditions have helped create a new, "Islamic" cinema. This expectation is marred, however, by the perception, almost universal in the West, that Shi'i Islam as practiced in Iran today, is anti-modern and backward. The widely reported curtailment by the Islamic Republic of Western-style performing arts and entertainment and its maltreatment of entertainers, have certainly reinforced such impressions.

Nonetheless, it is the thesis of this chapter that the Islamic Revolution has led to the emergence of a new, vital cinema, with its own special industrial and financial structure, and unique ideological, thematic and production values. This is, of course, part of a more general transformation in the political culture of Iran. However, Iranian post-revolutionary cinema is not a fully developed "Islamic" cinema in the sense that it is not by any means a monolithic, propagandistic cinema in support of a ruling ideology. In fact, two cinemas seem to be developing side by side. The "populist cinema" affirms post-revolutionary Islamic values more fully at the level of plot, theme, characterization, portrayal of women and *mise-en-scène*. The "quality cinema," on the other hand, engages with those values and tends to critique social conditions under the Islamic government. There are many variations and cracks in the hegemony of the post-revolutionary cinema, which in this overview cannot be fully considered; only passing references must suffice.

FROM "*TAQUT* CINEMA" TO AN "ISLAMIC CINEMA" (1978-82)

Purification process

The moviehouse

The first stage in transforming the Pahlavi's cinema (dubbed by Islamists "cinema of *taqut*") into an Islamic cinema, was the cleansing of the Pahlavi moviehouses by means of what in retrospect turned out to be a baptism by fire of sorts. By the time the Islamic government was established less than a year after the Rex theater event, up to 180 cinemas nationwide (32 in Tehran alone) had been burnt, demolished, or shut down, leaving only a total of 256 cinemas extant.[20] Fortunately, with the exception of the Rex theater, no casualties were reported since most of the theaters were empty at the time of the attacks.[21]

Those theaters which remained had their names changed, usually from Western names popular during the Pahlavi period to Islamic, Third World ones. For example, in Tehran, Atlantic was changed to *Efriqa* (Africa,) Empire to *Esteqlal* (Independence,) Royal to *Enqelab* (Revolution), Panorama to *Azadi* (Freedom), *Taj* (Crown) to *Shahr-e Honar* (City of Art), Golden City to *Felestin* (Palestine), Polidor to *Qods* (Jerusalem), and Cine Monde to *Qiam* (Uprising).[22]

The imports

Immediately after the revolution the volatile and uncertain economic and political conditions discouraged investment in the production of new films, but encouraged exhibition of old and importation of new films. Thus, foreign-made films flooded the market. Comedies and "spaghetti" Westerns came from Italy and karate films from Japan. US imports covered a broad range from comedy to political and from classical to current, with such films as *It's a Mad, Mad, Mad, Mad World, Modern Times, Three Days of the Condor, The Cassandra Crossing, The Great Escape, Cinderella, The Jungle Book*, and *Papillon*.

Russian and Eastern bloc films – inexpensive to import – also flourished to the point of taking precedence over the American, Italian, and Japanese films. For example, 74, or more than a third, of the 213 foreign films licensed by the Ministry of Islamic Guidance for 1981 came from the Soviet bloc. Sixty-nine of these were produced in the Soviet Union alone. Italy ranked second with 38 films, and surprisingly the United States came third with 27 movies.[23] Of the new imports those that catered to the revolutionary spirit of the time clearly dominated. The best known of these, banned during the Shah's era, include such films as Costa Gavras' Z and *State of Siege*, Guzman's *Battle of Chile*, Kurosawa's *The Seven Samurai*, Akad's *Mohammad the Messenger*, and Pontecorvo's *Battle of Algiers*. The latter was so popular that it was shown simultaneously in 12 Tehran cinemas and in 10 theaters in provincial towns.[24]

The clerical establishment was concerned but divided on the issue of film imports. Some praised these so-called "revolutionary films" because, they felt, such films show "the struggle of people oppressed by colonialism and imperialism."[25] Others condemned these films by characterizing them as made-in Hollywood films with only a "revolutionary mask."[26] Likewise, Hojjatoleslam Ahmad Sadeqi-Ardestani, a leading clergyman in charge of supervising the film industry in 1981, invoking the Islamic values mentioned earlier, wrote that Iran has "continued its cultural dependence on imperialists" by importing American (Western) and Russian (Eastern) films into the country, where "millions of people are mentally and culturally nourished by cinema." Updating the language of Navab-Safavi and Khomeini, he predicted that continued "acceptance of Western and Eastern films will lead us to cultural colonization and economic exploitation."[27]

The secular intellectuals, too, worried about the influx of the so-called revolutionary foreign films for different reasons. For example, Gholam Hossein Sa'edi, a leading dissident writer and editor of the literary monthly *Alefba*, would later offer, from exile, the following definition for the "revolutionary" films shown in Iran: Films "full of cannons, tanks, rifles, weapons, and corpses, without regard to quality or artistic merit."[28]

As early as July 1979, efforts to purify the imports, by lowering their inflow, began. First the importation of B grade Turkish, Indian and Japanese films was curtailed followed closely by a ban on all "imperialist" and "anti-revolutionary" films.[29] American films were the next group to be excluded as the political relationship between the two countries deteriorated. In fact, corroborating the link made between films produced in the West and moral corruption of the indigenous population, a larger percentage of Western films were denied exhibition permits than films from any other region. Tables 8.1 and 8.2 document this.

Thus, in the first three years of post-revolutionary government, a total of 898 foreign films were reviewed, 513 of which, the bulk of them Western imports, were rejected. The curb, however, was not hermetic, in that American films imported prior to the cut-off, such as *Airport 79* and *High Noon* continued

Table 8.1 Number of films receiving exhibition permit 1980–82

Year	Permit received	Western bloc	Eastern bloc	Third World
1980	121	56	36	2
1981	161	74	58	11
1982	85	56	18	4
Total	367	186	112	17

Source: Unpublished internal memo: "Marahel-e Mokhtalef-e Nezarat bar Sakht va Namayesh-e Film" (Tehran, Ministry of Islamic Guidance), pp. 38–9.

Table 8.2 Number of films denied exhibition permit, 1980–82

Year	Permit rejected	Western bloc	Eastern bloc	Third World
1980	182	87	18	5
1981	326	156	97	8
1982	23	75	25	4
Totals	531	318	140	17

Source: Unpublished internal memo: "Marahel-e Mokhtalef-e Nezarat bar Sakht va Namayesh-e Film" (Tehran, Ministry of Islamic Guidance), pp. 38–9.

to appear on the screens even during the "hostage crisis" episode.

Locally produced films

To purify the existing stock of films, many of the pre-revolution films were re-edited to conform to Islamic standards. Some films were cut, recut, and retitled. In this process, film producers engaged with the government in a cat-and-mouse game of resistance/submission. The most interesting of these cinematic negotiations, was the retitling process which at times led to the exhibition of the retitled films without much change in the content. When caught, however, the result was a new round of retitling. For example, the title of the film *Bi Harekat, Tekun Nakhor* (*Freeze, Don't Move*), made by Amir Shervan was changed in 1978 to *Jahel va Mohassel* (*The Thug and the Student*), and after the revolution, it changed again to the drug *Hero'in*

(*Heroin*). These changing "colors" apparently did not help the sale of the film. In general, the contradictions between changed elements and basically unchanged films were such that such films failed badly at the box office.[30]

Sensing the inevitability of Islamization of cinema, film exhibitors attempted to control the damage by voluntarily keeping sex off the screens, claiming that "our contribution to the Islamic Revolution would be made best by replacing dirty films with entertainment of an educational caliber."[31] One method for accomplishing this was the "magic marker" method of censorship, which involved painting over the naked legs and exposed body parts. When this method failed, other more drastic ones were used. The manager of Rex cinema in Tehran, for example, stated that "We have to show films in keeping with Islamic standards. When the Magic Marker doesn't work, we cut."[32]

Dissatisfied with limited changes made by producers and exhibitors, the government threatened the closure of cinemas and mandated an exhibition permit for all films.[33] The process of receiving a permit meant a review of all films made, with the end result that many indigenous films produced prior to the establishment of the Islamic Republic were banned outright. Table 8.3 shows the outcome of reviews conducted by Islamic authorities of Iranian features produced both before and immediately after the revolution. Since post-revolution films were very limited in number, one can safely construe these figures to be a decisive vote of no confidence against Pahlavi-era cinematic products and an effective end to the post-revolutionary *laissez faire* atmosphere.

Sleazy films (cheaply-produced exploitation films) were not the only type to receive the axe, many features produced by progressive "new wave" directors were also banned, some of which are: *Malakut* (*The Divine One*, 1976), *Shatranj-e Bad* (*The Chess of the Wind*, 1976), *OK Mister* (1979), *Cherikeh-ye Tara* (*Tara, the Woman Guerrilla*, 1978), and *Hayat-e Poshti-ye Madreseh-ye Adl-e Afaq* (*The Yard Behind the School*, 1980), *Aqa-ye Hiroglif* (*Mr Hieroglyphic*, 1980).[34]

While most film-makers applauded the curbing of sleazy imports, they did not condone their banning, as Bahram Baiza'i, a noted new wave film-maker whose film *Cherikeh-ye Tara* had been banned, observed, "It is the enhanced public awareness

Table 8.3 Iranian films which received or were denied exhibition permit, 1979–82

Year	Films reviewed	Permit granted	Permit denied
1979	2,000	200	1,800
1980	99	27	72
1981	83	18	65
1982	26	7	19
Total	2,208	252	1,956

Sources: Unpublished internal memo: "Marahel-e Mokhtalef-e Nezarat bar Sakht va Namayesh-e Film" (Tehran, Ministry of Islamic Guidance), pp. 38–9, and "Namayesh-e Filmha-ye Hendi va Torky Mannu' Shod," Ettela'at, (12/27/ 1358: March 18, 1980), p. 10.

which should be driving these trite films off the screens not government force." What is more, he said, the vacuum created by the absence of imports must be filled with local productions, but the regulations, mechanisms, and structures conducive to the flourishing of local films are non-existent.[35]

Entertainers and film-makers

Many entertainers and film-makers were regarded to be too closely associated either with the Westernized excesses of the Shah or with SAVAK, his national security agency. As a result, they were not immune to this purification process, which involved legal charges, incarceration, banning activities, censoring products, and, on rare occasions, execution.[36] Mehdi Misaqiyeh, a famous producer, was jailed for five years and his properties and theaters confiscated.[37] He was released apparently some time after he publicly recanted and renounced his Baha'i religion.[38] When in March 1983, new wave film-maker, Bahman Farmanara, traveled to Iran after four years of absence, he was prevented from exiting the country. His powerfully allegorical film, Sayehha-ye Boland-e Bad (Tall Shadows of the Wind, 1978), had been banned by the Forbidden Acts Bureau and he was accused of making "anti-Islamic" films. "Ironically," says Farmanara, "both the Shah and the Islamic regimes interpreted the scarecrow which in the film terrorizes a village as symbolizing their own rule and tried to ban it."[39] Some theater owners were arrested and charged with crimes such as smuggling narcotics, peddling pornographic materials and prostitution.[40]

The aforementioned purification measures and persecutions, however, are only one set of reasons for the slow revival of cinema during the transition period. Islamization was not pro forma by any means, as many other factors contributed to creating a very fluid and contentious atmosphere within the film industry. These included the financial damage that the motion picture industry suffered during the revolution, a lack of government interest in cinema during the transitional period (e.g., the first five-year budget plan in 1983 did not include any item devoted to cinema),[41] a vacuum of centralized authority and antagonistic competition over cinema among various factions (e.g., among the Ministry of Culture and Higher Education, the Foundation of the Disinherited, and the Revolution Committees),[42] unavailability of an appropriate cinematic model (no "Islamic" film genre existed),[43] heavy competition from imports, a drastic deterioration in the public image of the industry as a whole, and the haphazard application of censorship.

It was under these circumstances that in January 1980 in a letter addressed to the Minister of Culture and Higher Education, the Society of Cinema Owners could with impunity chide the government for its inaction *vis-à-vis* the state of cinema in the country, announcing that if the government *"approved the necessity of the existence of cinema"* (emphasis added), then, the private sector with government assistance can put the film industry on the track of "the revolution and the people" within five years. The letter concluded by reminding the Minister that unplanned, "spontaneous reform" in cinema is not possible.[44]

Film-makers, too, shared the concerns of theater owners and in 1981 in an open letter to the "people and government," they took the government to task. They charged that two years after the "holy and anti-dependence revolution of Iranian people" the revolution has not only failed to find a place within the film industry, but also it has fostered a kind of dependency, akin to the one existing during the Shah's time. The writers urged the government to apply the constitution "organically and comprehensively," otherwise, Iranian cinema will become a caricature of Eastern bloc solutions to cinema, and the "solution to the problem will result in the elimination of the problem."[45]

NEGOTIATING AN ISLAMIC CINEMA(1982-9)

In this period, the Islamic hardliners gradually took charge of all major institutions, and with the continuation of the Iraq–Iran war, the resolution of the American "hostage crisis," and the routing of major organized opposition, consolidated their grip on the country. Political consolidation entailed influence and often direct control of all arts, including cinema and broadcasting. However, transformation of cinema, from the Pahlavi to the Islamic, entails a major cultural and ideological shift, which cannot take place univocally, unidirectionally, monolithically or rapidly. Mohammad Beheshti, director of the Farabi Cinema Foundation, put it well in cinematic terms when he observed that "transformation in the context of cinema occurs with a 'dissolve' not a 'cut.' "[46]

The structural reorganization of the entertainment and broadcasting under the Islamic Republic in part resembles that which existed during the Shah's time, but there are major differences discussed below, which have helped to bring about an Islamized cinema.

Emergence of committed Islamic film-makers

Cronism based on shared Islamic ideology and values seems to have been a factor in the transformation from one cinema to the other. A case in point is the impact of a production company named Ayat Film, which was formed prior to the revolution, apparently in response to a call by Ali Shariati which urged the Islamic youths to turn to the arts for the expression of their beliefs and anti-Pahlavi attitudes. This company produced two films immediately after the revolution in 1979: *Jang-e Athar* (*Athar's War*), a fiction film, and *Lailat-ol Qadr* (*The Night of Power*), a documentary about the revolution.

The impact of the company, however, far exceeds its limited production output because of the manner in which its committed (*mota'ahed*) and religious (*motadayyen*) members fanned out soon after the revolution to take key positions within the government, the motion pictures industry and the allied institutions. For example, Mir-Hossein Musavi became Prime Minister, Fakhred-Din Anvar took up a number of high posts both within the Ministry of Culture and Islamic Guidance (MCIG) and Voice and Vision of the Islamic Republic (television networks), and Mohammad-Ali Najafi obtained high policy positions within MCIG and continued to direct films, Mostafa Hashemi was appointed to a high position in Khomeini's Propaganda Office, and Mohammad Beheshti became the director of the powerful Farabi Cinema Foundation. Initially after the revolution, these and other members and affiliated members of Ayat Film perhaps were among the few Islamists who could be trusted by the government both on account of their artistic abilities and their "correct" Islamic values. As a result, they became ensconced in positions that allowed them to influence from early on the direction of Islamization of cinema. Their impact is augmented by their longevity in office since by and large they retained their influential positions throughout the first decade of the Islamic regime.

Regulations governing exhibition of movies and videos

The Ministry of Culture and Islamic Guidance has the overall responsibility for overseeing the motion picture industry. The concentration of power at the Ministry to set policy, to regulate, and to enforce has helped both to reduce the confusion of the previous period and to enhance government control, thereby setting the stage for the emergence of an Islamic unity out of the revolutionary destruction and the post-revolutionary indeterminacy.

In June 1982, the Cabinet approved a set of landmark regulations governing the exhibition of movies and videos and charged MCIG with its enforcement.[47] These regulations, which codify much of the Islamic values noted earlier, are instrumental in facilitating the shift from Pahlavi to Islamic cinema. They stipulate that all films and videos shown publicly must bear an exhibition permit. Further, they ban all films and videos which:

Weaken the principle of monotheism and other Islamic principles or insult them in any manner.

Insult directly or indirectly the prophets, imams, the

Velayat-e Faqih (supreme jurisprudent), the ruling council, or the *mojtaheds* (jurisprudents).

Blaspheme the values and personalities held sacred by Islam and other religions mentioned in the constitution.

Encourage wickedness, corruption, and prostitution.

Encourage or teach dangerous addictions and earning a living from unsavory means such as smuggling.

Negate equality of all people regardless of color, race, language, ethnicity, and belief.

Encourage foreign cultural, economic, and political influence contrary to the "neither West nor East" policy of the government.

Express or disclose anything that is against the interests and policies of the country which might be exploited by foreigners.

Show details of scenes of violence and torture in such a way as to disturb or mislead the viewer.

Misrepresent historical and geographical facts.

Lower the taste of the audience through low production and artistic values.

Negate the values of self-sufficiency and economic and social independence.

The most telling of these regulations, which establishes the Islamic character of present-day Iranian cinema are the three heading the above list. Their analysis will be expanded below. Films which question, alter, or negate any of the following also are forbidden:

Monotheism and submission to God and to his laws.

Role of Revelation in expressing laws.

Resurrection and its role in evolution of man towards God.

Justness of God in creation and in law.

Continuity of religious leadership (*Imamat*).

Role of Islamic Republic of Iran under the leadership of Ayatollah Khomeini in ridding the Muslims and the downtrodden from world imperialism.

Clearly these regulations codify the Islamic values hinted at the beginning of this chapter, which during the transition period remained largely undefined and subject to local and expedient interpretations. Of course, the above regulations themselves contain many ambiguities, which the text of the regulations itself dictates must be resolved by appropriate committees.

Moviehouses and audience demography

Despite incompleteness and inconsistencies, statistics show that the number of theaters and filmgoers have increased over the last decade.[48] However, moviegoing has not reached the peak of the Shah's era – even though curtailment of previously allowed forms of entertainment has made cinema one of the few public forms of mass entertainment. An audience survey in 1983 of 1,800 Tehran high school students revealed that 78 per cent of the boys and 59 per cent of the girls said they go to the movies.[49] This figure is not high considering that this age group comprises a major share of audiences. Partial reasons for the apparent audience disinterest may be found in (1) decreased number of theaters nationwide compared to the Shah's time, (2) undesirability of theater locations, (3) bad conditions of halls and projection systems, (4) low quality of much of the films exhibited, and (5) demographics of spectators, which is predominantly young, unmarried and unemployed men who sometimes heckle women. All these factors are compounded by the highly aggressive and male-oriented genres and themes of much of the films.[50]

Film imports

The regulations governing film production and exhibition and the centralizing tendencies have given the authorities a firmer grip on the imports. After some deliberation, the government took control of all film imports. It created the non-profit Farabi Cinema Foundation in 1983 (FCF), attached it to MCIG and gave it, among other duties, a complete monopoly over the

Table 8.4 Films imported, 1983-4

	1983	1984
USSR	28	29
US	12	24
Italy	16	20
England	9	15
France	6	5
Yugoslavia	6	1
Japan	4	5
N. Korea	2	2
China (PRC)	1	3
Australia	1	2
Total	85	106

Source: From author's correspondence with Ministry of Islamic Guidance, (4/15/ 1364 (1985)).

selection and importation of films into the country based on their ideological suitability.[51] Table 8.4 shows the number of films imported in 1983-4 and the country of origin.

In the mid 1980s, the Soviet bloc countries dominated the import scene, but films from the US and its Western allies increased their percentage considerably. The anti-Western, especially anti-American rhetoric of the official mass media, would lead an observer to conclude that a limitation on American and Western imports is (or should be) in effect. That this is not so, demonstrates the tensions in cultural policy within the Islamic Republic and the pragmatism of policy makers. They seem to have issued an exhibition permit to any film, regardless of the source, as long as it lived up to the aforementioned Islamic values. For example, in 1983 the following American films were screened: *Star Wars*, *Close Encounters of the Third Kind*, *Ten Commandments*, and *A Bridge Too Far* and in 1984, *War Hunt*, *Law and Disorder*, *Black Sunday*, and *The Chase*.

Indigenous productions

All film ideas must go through a five-step process at the Ministry of Islamic Guidance (MCIG) before they are released as films and shown to the public. It is during this process that regulations codifying "Islamic values" are implemented. MCIG reviews the film's synopsis, evaluates and approves the screenplay, issues a production permit (approving the cast and crew by name), reviews the completed film, and finally issues an exhibition permit (specifying in which cinemas it will be shown). Until mid-1989, all film ideas were subject to this process, during which they underwent many changes prior to their release as films.[52] Statistics bear out the effectiveness of the review process (and perhaps the low quality of submitted scripts): of the 202 screenplays reviewed between 1980 and 1982, only 25 per cent were approved.[53]

Despite the rigor of the review process, a large number of films which were made were not released.[54] However, in April 1989, the government loosened its grip and began allowing previously censored films to be screened.[55] Barely a month later, for the first time in Iranian cinema, the requirement for approving screenplays was removed. Two chief reasons stand out for this liberalization policy: (1) confidence the authorities feel that Islamic values have been sufficiently inculcated, requiring less supervision (i.e., interpellation/injection have had their desired effect); and (2) a more self-assured government wishes to open up the cultural discourse and reduce criticism of its ironclad control, thereby boosting morale and film quality. Whatever the reason, it is likely that the black market in screenplays will disappear and film subjects will diversify.[56]

These measures are not isolated. Since 1984, film-makers have demanded and the government has introduced new regulations to encourage local production. In the first six months of 1984, for example, it took the following steps: the municipal tax for Iranian films was reduced from 20 per cent to 5 per cent and increased from 20 per cent to 25 per cent for imports. Ticket prices were increased by 25 per cent. The Farabi Cinema Foundation was exempted from paying any customs duty for its imports. And changes in the composition of the "screen committee," responsible for assigning films to theaters, allowed representatives of producers and exhibitors to partake in the proceedings.[57]

To generate funds for health, social security, and workers' compensation of entertainers and film-makers, the *Majles* passed a resolution late in 1985 which imposed a 2 per cent tax on the box office receipt of all theaters in the country.[58] To further bolster local production, the 1987 national budget passed by the *Majles* included a provision for banks to offer long-term loans for film production.[59] A year later, in June 1988, MCIG instituted a system of grading films according to which producers of highly rated films would earn increased revenues by exhibiting their films in higher classed theaters. In addition, they would be entitled to extensive publicity and advertising on tv.[60] In May 1989, MCIG announced further measures: allocation of foreign exchange funds for importing chronically scarce technical equipment and supplies; availability of interest-free credits and long-term loans; sponsorship of local films in international film festivals, and finally the inauguration of the social security system for film workers approved by parliament.[61]

Political consolidation, the centralization of imports, and the passing of regulations concerning production and exhibition, have enhanced coordination and cohesiveness within the industry, have brought cinema into line with Islamic values and criteria, and have improved overall film quality. The situation, however, is far from one in which the government entirely monopolizes the industry. Indeed, there seem to be more production centres in Islamic Iran than there were in Pahlavi Iran and they are not all concentrated in Tehran. These production centers are dispersed among three sectors: public, semi-public, and private. The following list contains the production centers under each sector, a number of which have branches in provinces.

Motion picture production sectors

Public (governmental) sectors

Office of Film, Photo and Slide Production (MCIG)
Farabi Cinema Foundation (MCIG)
Center for Developing Experimental and Semi-mature Films (MCIG)
Islamic Center for Film Instruction (MCIG)
Young Cinema Society (MCIG)
Foundation of the Disinherited
Center for Intellectual Development of Children and Young Adults
Voice and Vision of Islamic Republic (tv networks)

Ministry of Reconstruction Crusade
University Crusade
War Propaganda Command
Revolutionary Guard's Cultural Unit
Revolutionary Committees' Film Section
Traffic Organization
Iran Air

Semi-public (semi-governmental) sector

Islamic Propaganda Organization
Islamic Culture and Art Group

Private (commerical) sector

Film cooperatives
Independent producers
Commercial production companies
Film studios

Source: Ahmad Talebinezhad, "Raval-e Kar dar Nahadha-ye Filmsazi-ye Iran," *Mahnameh-ye Sinema'i-ye Film*, no. 53 (Shahrivar 1366/1987), pp. 6–11.

In 1987 the public sectors produced one-third of all films, but given government's financial contribution through loans and credits, its impact on film production exceeds the statistics.[62] At any rate, multiplicity of production centres and production sectors bolster competition not only among production companies but also among sectors, increase diversity, and enhance quality.

The figures for films produced during this period (Table 8.5) show an initial downward spiral followed by a definite pattern of increase in recent years, coinciding with the aforementioned reforms. In addition to Farabi Cinema Foundation and MCIG, other post-revolution institutions, such as the Foundation of the Disinherited and the Ministry of Reconstruction Crusade, have helped to Islamize the motion picture industry further. Considered one of the largest economic conglomerates, controlling 15 per cent of all the industry in the country and owning an estimated $10 billion worth of land,[63] the Foundation of the Disinherited was, by mid 1983, operating some 137 cinemas in 16 provinces nationwide, i.e., approximately half of all cinemas in the country.[64]

Table 8.5 Fiction feature films produced, 1979–88

Year	Films produced
1979–80	14
1980–81	16
1981–2	12
1982–3	11
1983–4	22
1984–5	56
1985–6	57
1986–7	49
1987–8	46

Sources: The statistics for all the years except 1986–8 are from: "Iranian Cinema: a Turning Point." *Mahnameh-ye Sinema'i-ye Film,* no. 41 (Mehr 1367/1988). pp. 1–2 English section. The source for 1986–8 is Omid, 1987.

Because of the large number of cinemas it operates, the foundation has a profound effect on production and exhibition of films. But it has not proven to be economically successful, since attendance in its theaters dropped by 300,000 in just one year, from 1981 to 1982,[65] and the number of theaters it owned declined to 80 by mid 1987.[66] The manager of the foundation's cultural department attributed this to a shortage of foreign imports with appropriate Islamic values. To offset the situation, the foundation began to assist Islamically "committed" local film-makers to make trend-setting "model" films inspired by the revolution and the Islamic values.

One such film, *Parvandeh* (*Dossier,* 1983), deals with the revenge of a worker unjustly accused of the death of a feudal landlord and jailed for fifteen years. *Hayula-ye Darun* (*The Monster Within,* 1984) focuses on the struggle of an ex-Savak torturer with his own sense of guilt immediately after the revolution and *Otobus* (*The Bus,* 1985) portrays a typical *Haidari-Ne'mati* family feud in a village. To adjust to the financial realities of production and exhibition and to increase the reach of its films, the foundation announced in May 1988 that (1) it would divest forty more of its theaters to obtain sufficient funds to build new theaters in poorer areas of cities, and (2) it would subtitle and export Islamic films for exhibition to Iranian expatriates.

The Ministry of Reconstruction Crusade, too, has contributed to the emergence of an Islamic cinema. The original aim of the crusade, established on June 17, 1979 by an edict from Ayatollah Khomeini, was to "repair the ruins" caused by the Shah's government and to help reconstruction and self-sufficiency of the nation's rural areas.[67] The Crusade is in charge of rural development and propagation of Islamic ideology, a mission it accomplishes by distributing appropriate films, slides, videotapes, posters, and audiocassettes through its vast nationwide network. In 1983, for instance, it held 31,024 theater, film, and video shows, distributed 74,789 audiocassettes and some 2,912,062 posters and photographs nationwide.[68] The Crusade's reach is actually wider than these statistics indicate since many of its films are shown on nationwide television, in mosques, and in theaters operated by the Foundation of the Disinherited. Such a use of audiovisual media is not new in Iran and its roots are to be found in the role model of mobile film unit program started by the United States Information Agency (Point 4 program) in Iran in the 1950s.[69] The basic difference is not operational but ideological: while the Point 4 film program emphasized Western-style modernization, technological transfer, and monarchy, the Crusade's film effort relies on indigenous, nativistic, and Islamic solutions.

Genre and themes of indigenous features

The application of Islamic regulations and the political exigencies of the time have resulted in the domination of action-adventure, war, comedies and family drama genres. But these genres embody varying themes which taken together can clue us in on both the kinds of tensions the society is undergoing and the way Islamic values are played out on the screen. These themes can be seen best in Table 8.6, taken from a study conducted by Massoud Purmohammad based on screenplays of films made in 1987. In what follows, the major themes identified in Table 8.6 will be examined.

Exposing the Pahlavi regime

Given the post-revolutionary socio-political situation, it is understandable for Islamic cinema to be concerned with exposing the moral corruption, economic dependence, subservience to the West, and political suppression of the previous regime. The rather large number of films in this category, shown seven

198

Table 8.6 Themes of films made in 1987

Themes	Number of films
Amnesia as a result of shock	5
Psychological disorders	9
Immigration or escape from the country	11
Problems and disputes within families	14
War as a principle and ancillary theme	12
Wealth does not bring happiness (Islamic values)	20
Exposing the Pahlavi regime	11
Exposing antigovernment groups ("goruhakha")	4

Source: Purmohammad, 1987.

years after the fall of the Shah, points out that this topic has not been exhausted yet. Also, not surprisingly, the operation of SAVAK, torture, and armed struggle against the Shah were early favorite themes.[70] Although some of these "Savak films" deal with social and political ills under the Shah, the majority are amateurish, superficial tracts. An exception is Khosrow Sina'i's *Zendeh Bad* (*Long Live*, 1980). It portrays political repression by depicting the way in which a professional, upscale engineer inadvertently becomes involved with anti-Shah forces. Corruption, too, is shown effectively in *Senator* (The Senator, 1984), which focuses on graft and heroin smuggling. This film became the box-office record holder for 1984 with sales of nearly one million dollars.

Islamic values

Emphasis on Islamic ethical values and on the spiritual instead of material rewards are also clearly indicated in the chart. In fact, post-revolutionary cinema can be characterized as a "moralist cinema," whose films are imbued with a generalized sense of morality and with dispensing moral advice to the point that even bad guys participate in it. Also, traditional values and conventions characteristic of rural folks are favorably compared with the consumerist ideology of urban areas. However, Iranian moralist and populist cinema, instead of concentrating on deeper Iranian and Islamic mystic values, has catered chiefly to superficial morality, characterized by easy hopes, cheap emotions and inexpensive good deeds.[71] *Khaneh-ye Doust Kojast?*

(*Where is My Friend's Home?*, 1989), directed by Abbas Kiarostami, is a film of quality in the moralist genre. This film, which was dubbed "agonizingly slow" but ultimately rewarding,[72] depicts the relentless efforts of an honest boy to find a friend's house in order to return a copybook he had taken by mistake.

Leading clerics, including Hojjatoleslam Mohammad Khatami, the Minister of Culture and Islamic Guidance since the revolution, have urged film-makers to propagate the notions of "self-sacrifice, martyrdom, and revolutionary patience."[73] Accordingly, such topics inundate the Islamic moralist cinema and find their most natural expression in films about the eight-year-old war with Iraq.

War with Iraq

Soon after Iraq invaded Iran, Khomeini ordered mobilization of all sectors. It took MCIG and the private sector quite a while to get around the twin problems of shortage of raw stock and unavailability of funds (because there were many films awaiting screening, thus not producing any income to invest in war films).[74] Although the first film about the war, *Marz* (*Border*, 1981), was made by the private sector, the lion's share of war films have been produced by the public–government sector.

During the war period, a total of fifty-six feature fiction films about the war were made, two-thirds of which focused primarily on fighting and military operations while the balance concerned themselves with the war's social and psychological impact.[75] Apparently, much of the war-front films emphasized action and violence over sensitivity and psychological depth. But, in a period in the mid 1980s, private sector producers seemed to pay more attention to the specificity of the conflict by exploring both psychological and ideological values of the war. *Diar-e Asheqan* (*The Domain of Lovers*, 1983), directed by Hasan Karbakhsh, examines the psychology of a young reserve soldier and the meaning of self-sacrifice and duty. Also *Khaneh-ye Entezar* (*A House Waiting*), broadcast on tv in 1987 is a technically polished film, which portrays a war-time society without resorting to showing trench warfare.

Although war led to an increase in the quantity of films which emphasize Islamic values of martyrdom and self-sacrifice, it negatively affected the quality of films which, by and large, have been limited to circulating clichés and slogans.[76] Clearly, war will continue to be a viable topic since, in its aftermath, issues relating to causes, management and consequences of the war will become foregrounded in the post-war Islamic cinema. Already Mohsen Makhmalbaf, the most promising and prolific new film-maker trained under the Islamic Republic, is producing films such as *Arusi-ye Khuban* (*Marriage of the Blessed*, 1989), which are using the war to critique the government and the society. In this film, the protagonist, a shell-shocked photographer, is used to explore the social symptomatology of the war: its consequences and many of its unresolved causes.

Women

The themes of shock and psychological disorders, split families, dislocation, and exile, listed in Table 8.6, are explored particularly in family melodramas which, because they involve women, bear scrutiny; for it is in the portrayal and treatment of women that the tensions surrounding Islamization of cinema crystallize.

By way of background, I will turn once again to the film and video regulations mentioned earlier and expand the section that deals with women. According to these rules, Muslim women must be shown to be chaste and to have an important role in society as well as in raising God-fearing and responsible children. In addition, women must not be treated like a commodity or used to arouse sexual desires.[77] These general and ambiguous guidelines have had a profound effect on the use and the portrayal of women in cinema. The most significant is self-censorship and the avoidance altogether of stories involving women, thus evading entanglement with the censors. As the star of *Gozaresh-e Yek Qatl* (*Report of a Death*, 1987) states, filmmakers are "afraid to turn to women [. . .] even when authorities have invited [them] to consider women."[78] Statistics compiled by Purmohammad point to the very low presence of women as "heroes" in films made in 1987: of 37 films reviewed, the chief protagonist in 25 films were men, in 3 they were women, and in seven they shared equal billing.[79]

If women are portrayed at all, they are given limited parts: reflecting the role spelled out for women in MCIG regulations, they are usually portrayed as housewives or as mothers. To use women, a new grammar of film has evolved, including these features: women actors are given static parts or are filmed in such a way as to avoid showing their bodies. A post-revolution film director underlines these practices by saying that women in Islamic performing arts should be shown seated at all times so as to avoid drawing attention to their "provocative walk," thereby allowing the audience to concentrate on the "ideologies" inherent in the work.[80] In addition, eye contact, especially those expressing "desire," and touching between men and women are discouraged.[81] All this has meant that until recently women often were filmed in long-shots, with fewer close-ups and facial expressions.

The process of filming and acting, too, was affected, especially in the first few years after the revolution. Government agents appeared during filming to ensure that no "unethical" conduct occurs on the set. In at least one case, the male and female actors playing the parts of husband and wife, are reported to have had to marry each other for the duration of the filming in order to stay within Islamic interpretations.[82]

Since women in movies have to don Islamic cover or *chador*, their portrayal appears very unrealistic, i.e., they are shown covering themselves from their next of kin (husbands, sons, brothers, fathers), while in real life they would not do so. Such intrusions into the realm of acting and filming undermines the actors' art and distorts the portrayal of family life and love relationships, and relegates women, in the words of an official, to a marginal position in the patriarchal system of Iranian cinema.[83] There is another side-effect: certain historical periods (the Pahlavi) and geographical regions (the West) have been closed off from Iranian cinema. Nasser Taqva'i, who directed *Nakhoda Khorshid (Captain Khorshid*, 1987), corroborates these points when he says, "This very same problem about the character of woman, has made it impossible [for us] to make a film about the Pahlavi era. You cannot show with ease the relationship of a husband and a wife, a sister and a brother, in the streets or at home, let alone portray other relations, of blood or marriage."[84]

Such constraints, which gradually have lessened, affect the relationship of men on the screen as well, resulting in fascinating gender reconfigurations and reinscription.[85] It must be noted that few exceptional directors, such as Bahram Baiza'i in *Bahsu, Gharibeh-ye Kuchak* (*Bahsu, the Little Stranger*, 1985), have continued to explore seriously women and women's issues.

If women have had problems appearing in front of cameras, they apparently have had little problem attending film schools and working behind the cameras in both the motion picture and television industries. There are more women feature film directors currently working in Iran than there were in all the preceding eight decades combined. Among them are the following three. Rakhshan Bani 'Etemad directed *Kharej az Mahdudeh* (*Beyond the City Limit*, 1986) about the perennial housing problems plaguing the teeming city of Tehran, and *Mahhaleh-ye Nowabad* (*Nowabad Neighborhood*, 1989) about the efforts of residents to make their neighborhood safe in face of the inability of authorities to do so. Tahmineh Ardekani directed *Golbahar* (1985) about the sad life and circumstances of a physically handicapped person. Finally, Puran Derakhshandeh has directed two features to date, *Rabeteh* (*Rapport*, 1985) and *Parandeh-ye Kuchak-e Khoshbakhti* (*The Little Bird of Happiness*, 1988), both of them focusing on the psychological crises of communication suffered by the hearing impaired.[86]

Ideological repositioning of cinema

A major complaint voiced against films made in the Islamic Republic, especially the populist variety, is their low quality and their ideological earnestness and superficiality. Even when approved ideas and screenplays turn into films, their quality is not guaranteed. In 1985, the authoritative journal, *Mahnameh-ye Sinema'i-ye Film*, rated Iranian films produced since the revolution and found them utterly wanting. It rated 35 films sleazy (*mobtazal*), 57 bad, 22 mediocre, 1 good, and none excellent.[87] Because of measures taken since then, the general quality of films has also improved as borne out by a series of merit awards received in recent international film festivals.

The general poor quality of the movies and the overall lack of variety on tv and film screens have helped to nurture a hitherto new and unused medium, as videocassette players became a popular alternative method for programming one's own leisure time. In 1983, 74 per cent of Tehran's households had a black and white tv set, 16 per cent had a color set, and 2 per cent had a VCR. The statistics for the nation as a whole was much smaller: 67 per cent, 6 per cent, and 0.5 per cent, respectively.[88] These figures, however, belie the actual size of the audience, because watching videos is a communal activity, during or after dinner. This alternative, like other aspects of society has been subjected to cultural negotiations. Throughout the years, the government and the public have played a cat-and-mouse game, with the government periodically banning and permitting importation of videos containing films and the public purchasing, renting, and/or circulating bootleg copies of videos in the black market. At any rate, the latest feature films from the West (including some pornographic material) are easily available to those who want it.[89]

The ideological earnestness and superficiality of films are related to such issues as: post-revolutionary conditions, pall of war with Iraq, timidity of film-makers unfamiliar with Islamic precepts, self-censorship, governmental censorship, and uneven application and varied interpretations of Islamic codes and regulations – all of which work to reposition cinema as a cultural production. For instance, changing interpretations of codes, often based on political expediency, would make certain allowable topics suddenly disallowed. This in turn would tend to make film-makers shy away from tackling controversial, social or political issues and would instead encourage them to seek safe topics. Barbod Taheri's feature documentary about the revolution, *Soqut-e '57* (*The Fall of '57*, 1980), is a good case in point. Once popular, the film was banned in 1984 because it dealt with topics which authorities no longer wanted discussed. He was told: "there are moments in a nation's life when people no longer need to know what has actually happened." He found out that were he to apply for a new exhibition permit, he would have to remove documentary footage of actual events showing wide participation by secular and leftist groups in the revolution, attacks of armed forces on demonstrators, and even Khomeini's first speech delivered in a Tehran cemetery in which he condemned the Shah for making cemeteries prosperous.[90]

As documented in previous sections, however, since the mid 1980s there has been a steady move towards rationalization of the film industry and encouragement of local productions. Concurrently, and equally significant, major repositionings and shifts have occurred in attitudes and perceptions toward both cinema and working in the motion picture business. Cinema, rejected in the past as part of the frivolous *superstructure*, has been adopted as part of the necessary *infrastructure* of Islamic culture. Fakhred-Din Anvar, undersecretary of Culture and Islamic Guidance in charge of the Film Affairs Department, tells how this was attempted: "Believing culture to be the structure undergirding all aspects of running a society [. . .] the Department has directed all its efforts towards ensuring that cinematic activities and film-making are included in all legislations, laws, systems and regulations."[91]

Working in film, once disdained and disparaged, has become acceptable and respectable. President Hojjatoleslam Ali Akbar Hashemi-Rafsanjani, then speaker of the *Majles*, publicly put his stamp on this shift when he declared in March 1987: "Our entertainers, male or female, did not enjoy the same esteem that today they enjoy from the lay and the religious people [. . .] This is a real revolution."[92]

Films, judged solely on their ideological purity and instructional values immediately after the revolution, have begun to be re-evaluated based on their ability to entertain and enlighten. For example, in 1985 Hashemi-Rafsanjani acknowledged the necessity of a lighter treatment of themes in cinema, stating: "It is true that a film must have a message, but this does not mean that we must deny its entertaining aspects. Society needs entertainment; lack of joy reduces one's effectiveness and involvement."[93] Hojjatoleslam Mohammad Khatami, Minister of Culture and Islamic Guidance, too, declared this shift in perception and repositioning of cinema in no uncertain terms. He said: "I believe that cinema is not the mosque. [. . .] If we remove cinema from its natural place, we no longer will have cinema. [. . .] If we transform cinema to such an extent that when one enters a moviehouse one feels imposed upon or senses that leisure time has changed to become homework time, then, we have deformed society."[94] The immense popularity and revenues (highest in the history of Iranian cinema), which Dariush Mehrju'i's social satire, *Ejareh Neshinha* (*Tenants*, 1986) generated is a testimony that the public, too, wants films to be well-made and entertaining as well as enlightening.

The morality codes which had become a straitjacket for cinema, limiting portrayal of women and use of music, were eased considerably starting in December 1987 when Khomeini issued an edict relaxing the application of the codes.[95]

Conclusion

Throughout its existence, the Islamic government has shown a surprising degree of flexibility and a great capacity for learning from its own mistakes. Film-makers and audiences, too, have demonstrated both resolve and ingenuity in face of incredible constraints. In fact, it is through a process of cultural negotiation and haggling – not just through hailing (interpellation) – that a new cinema is emerging, which embodies much of the aforementioned Islamic values, such as, nativism, populism, monotheism, theocracy, ethicalism, puritanism, and political and economic independence. In addition, a new crop of Islamically committed film-makers have been trained, at the same time that experienced "new wave" film-makers of the Shah era, such as, Bahram Baiza'i, Dariush Mehrju'i, Naser Taqva'i, and Mas'ud Kimia'i, have been resurrected and allowed to work. Film culture in general seems to be flourishing: a number of annual film festivals show a mixture of local and foreign-made products, film archives regularly offer screenings, at least half a dozen institutions offer academic degrees and training in film and television, serious film and theatre journals are being published, and film reviews appear in many periodicals.

The "Islamic" cinema is in a quandary, however. At the heart of the dilemma is the contradiction between the artists' fidelity to the state and their loyalty to the nation and to themselves. Chilean cineastes during a similar transition period in their nation's life, produced a manifesto which opted for the latter. It declared cinema a revolutionary art as long as there is a "conjunction between the artist and his people, united in a common objective: liberation."[96] It is too early to tell definitively which of the alternatives will be chosen by Iranian cineastes and how that alternative will be expressed. However, the history of the last ten years gives one cause for hope. The post-revolutionary cinema in Iran is not monolithic nor univocal. Situated in a state at war both with its neighbors and with superpowers, cinema has had to deal with many issues, among them: competition among various sectors in the industry, censorship, varied interpretations of regulations, aesthetic demands, chronic shortages of material and equipment, technical constraints, negative public and self-image, and finally economic realities of producing films which are ideologically correct and yet attractive to mass audiences. The resonances set in motion by the intertextuality of these factors tell us that we cannot consider the development of an Islamicized cinema in Iran merely as the imposition of a "ruthlessly united" ideological apparatus controlled by the state, but one that is open to considerable ideological work and negotiation.

Notes

1 An earlier version of this chapter was published in Britain in *Third World Affairs 1987*, I thank the journal for giving me permission to use portions of it. See Hamid Nafici, "The Development of an Islamic Cinema in Iran," *Third World Affairs 1987*.

2 Mostafa Abkashak, *Mossabebin-e Vaqe'i-ye Faje'eh-ye Howlnak-e Sinema Rex-e Abadan Cheh Kasani Hastand?*, (Los Angeles, 1985). This incident was a hot topic in the Iranian press after the revolution, where the proceedings of the trial of Takab'alizadeh and others accused of setting the theatre on fire were extensively reported. For more detail on the whole affair consult mass-circulation newspapers, such as, *Kayhan*, *Ettela'at*, and *Enqelab-e Eslami* and the opposition publications, such as *Mojahed*, especially vol. 1, no. 93 (31 Khordad, 1359/1980), p. 7 and *Paykar*, no. 17 (5/29/1358 1979), p. 12.

3 Homa Nateq, "Yaran-e Mottahed dar Kudeta va Enqelab," *Zaman-e Now*, no. 8, [Paris] (1987), pp. 17–19. Also: "Iran's Film Biz Nipped in the Bud by Islamic Belief," *Variety* (5/9/1979), p. 1.

4 Ruhollah Khomeini, *Velayat-e Faqih: Hokumat-e Eslami* (Amir Kabir, Tehran, 1360/1981), p. 188.

5 *Asnad va Tasaviri az Mobarezat-e Khalq-e Mosalman-e Iran*, vol. 1, part 3 (Abuzar, Tehran, 1357/1978).

6 Louis Althusser and E. Balibar, "Ideology and Ideological State Apparatuses (notes toward an Investigation)," in *Lenin and Philosophy and Other Essays*, Ben Brewster (trans.) (Monthly Review Press, New York, 1971), pp. 127–89.

7 Hamid Nafici, "Iranian Writers, the Iranian Cinema, and the Case of *Dash Akol*," *Iranian Studies*, vol. 28, nos 2–4 (Spring–Autumn, 1985), p. 237.

8 Fazlollah Nuri, *Lavayeh-e Aqa Shaikh Fazlollah Nuri* (Nashr-e Tarikh-e Iran, Tehran, 1362/1983), p. 49.

9 *Ibid.*, p. 27.

10 Mojtaba Navab-Safavi, *Jame'eh va Hokumat-e Eslami* (Entesharat-e Hejrat, Qom, 1357/1978), p. 4.

11 Ruhollah Khomeini, *Kashfol-Asrar* (n.p., n.d.), p. 194.

12 *Ibid.*, p. 292.

13 *Ibid.*, p. 276.
14 Michel Foucault, *Discipline and Punish: the Birth of the Prison*, Alan Sheridan (trans.), (Vantage, New York, 1979), pp. 209–22.
15 Max Horkheimer and Theodore Adorno, *Dialectic of Enlightenment*, John Cumming (trans.), (Herder & Herder, New York, 1972), p. 123.
16 Khomeini's concept of the "culture of idolatry" is reminiscent of Debord's formulation of "the society of the spectacle." See: Guy Debord, *Society of the Spectacle* (Black and White, Detroit, 1983).
17 Navab-Safavi, *op. cit.*, p. 11.
18 Ruhollah Khomeini, *Islam and Revolution: Writings and Declarations of Imam Khomeini*, Hamid Algar (trans.), (Mizan Press, Berkeley, CA 1981), p. 258.
19 For example, the Soviet formalist films of Eisenstein and Vertov followed the Russian revolution, the British realist documentaries immediately preceded and followed World War Two, the Italian neorealists emerged during and immediately after World War Two, and the Polish "black films" were made possible during the "spring thaw" of de-Stalinization period in the mid 1950s. Concurrent with the worldwide social turmoil of the 1960s and 1970s, too, several innovative film movements emerged. Examples are: "cinema novo" in Brazil, "new wave" in Iran, "cinema verité" in US, France, and Canada, "new German cinema" in West Germany, and "militant" and "liberationist" cinema in many parts of the Third World.
20 See the following: "Iran's Film Biz Nipped in the Bud by Islamic Belief," *Variety* (May 9, 1979), p. 91; "Sadha Sinema dar Barabar-e Atash Bidefa'and," *Kayhan* (6/15/1357: Sept. 6, 1978), p. 12; "Iran Theaters to Ban Sex on their Own," *Variety* (May 23, 1979), p. 7; "300 Sinema-ye Keshvar Fa'aliat-e Khod ra az Sar Gereftand," *Kayhan* (4/23/1358: July 14, 1979), p. 12; Hazel Guild in an article entitled "Lots of Mullah in Iran's Show Biz," which appeared in *Variety* (June 13, 1979), p. 1, estimates that 40 per cent of cinemas burned down. The figure quoted in *Kayhan* are official figures issued by the Society of Theatre Owners.
21 After the revolution, many moviehouses were converted for other purposes. For example, the sole cinema in Ferdows was converted into storage for hay, and one of the moviehouses in Gorgan was converted into a prison. See: "Tabdil-e Sinema beh Kahdani," *Iran Times* (April, 26, 1985), p. 15; *Mojahed* (13 Day, 1363: January 3, 1985), p. 4.
22 When renaming was deemed insufficient, the revolutionary zeal produced bizarre syncretic rituals. Rudaki Hall, a major cultural center on whose revolving stage many cultural performances had taken place during the Shah's era, was literally made to undergo ceremonial ablution (*ghosl*) in order to cleanse it fully, causing the stage mechanism to rust. See Gholamhosain Sa'edi, "Namayesh dar Hokumat-e Namayeshi," *Alefba* (Paris), no. 5, new edition (Winter 1363/1984), p 7.
23 "Moscow Gets Tehran's Oscar," *Iran Times* (April 2, 1982), p. 16.

24 "Salshomar-e Sinema-ye Pas az Enqelab-2," *Mahnameh-ye Sinema'i-ye Film*, no. 6, (Mehr 1362/1983), p. 43.

25 "Sokhani Kutah dar Bareh-ye Namayesh-e Filmha-ye Khareji," *Enqelab-e Eslami* (June 3, 1980: 3/13/1359), p. 6.

26 "Yaddashtha'i bar Mas'aleh-ye Sinemaha-ye Darbasteh dar Iran," *Enqelab-e Eslami* (July 2, 1980: 4/10/1359), p. 5.

27 Ahmad Sadeqi Ardekani, "Barresi va Rahyabi-ye Moshgelat-e Film va Sinema," *Ettela'at* (1/27/1360: April 16, 1981), p. 10.

28 Gholamhosain Sa'edi, "Farhang Koshi va Farhang Zada'i dar Jomhurey-ye Eslami," *Alefba*, new edition (Winter 1982), p. 7. For a translation of this piece, see: "Iran Under the Party of God," *Index on Censorship*, no. 1 (1984), pp. 16–20.

29 See the following: "Az Vorud va Kharid-e Filmha-ye Khareji Jelowgiri Mishavad," *Ayandegan* (July 8, 1979: 4/17/1358); "Vorud va Kharid-e Filmha-ye Khareji Mamnu' Shod," *Kayhan* (July 9, 1979), p. 14; "Iran's Islamic Regime Kicks Out Bruce Lee and 'Imperialist' Films," *Variety* (July 18, 1979), p. 2; "Sinema-ye Iran dar Rah-e Tazeh," *Ettela'at* (March 18, 1980: 12/28/1350), p. 10; "Dowlat Varedat-e Filmha-ye Khareji ra Beh Ohdeh Migirad," *Ettela'at* (1/20/1360: April 9, 1981).

30 "Salshomar-e Sinema-ye Pas az Enqelab-2," *Mahnameh-ye Sinema'i-ye Film*, no. 6 (Mehr 1362/1983), p. 42.

31 *Variety* "Iran Theatres Ban. . . ."

32 "Magic Marker Cinema Censor," *Iran Times* (June 29, 1979), p. 16.

33 "Nemayesh-e Film-e Bedun-e Parvaneh dar Sinemaha Mamnu' Shod," *Ettela'at*, (12/9/1358: Feb. 28, 1980), p. 3.

34 "Salshomar-e Sinema-ye Pas az Enqelab-2," *Mahnameh-ye Sinema'i-ye Film*, no. 6: (Mehr 1362/1983), p. 42. Also: "Salshomar-e Sinema-ye Pas az Enqelab-5, 1359," *Mahnameh-ye Sinema'i-ye Film*, no. 17: (Mehr 1363/1984), p. 28. For films banned in 1979 see Mas'ud Mehrabi, *Tarikh-e Sinema-ye Iran az Aghaz ta 1357* (Mahnameh-ye Sinema'i-ye Film, Tehran, 1357/1978), p. 184. In 1989, *Hayat-e Poshti-ye Madreseh-ye Adl-e Afaq*, directed by Dariush Mehrju'i, was retitled *Madreseh'i keh Miraftim* (*The School We Went To*) and released.

35 "Sinema-ye Iran dar Rah-e Tazeh," *Ettela'at* (March 18, 1980 12/28/1358), p. 10.

36 For details on maltreatment of entertainers and film-makers under the Islamic Republic, see Nafici, *op. cit.*

37 "Iran's Film Biz Nipped in the Bud by Islamic Belief," *Variety* (May 9, 1979), p. 91.

38 Author's interview with film producer Ali Mortazavi, August 1985, Los Angeles.

39 Author's telephone interview with Bahman Farmanara, July 1985, Toronto, Canada. For an extended review of this film, see Hamid Nafici, "Tall Shadows of the Wind," in *Magill's Survey of Cinema: Foreign Language Films* (Salem Press, Los Angeles, 1985), pp. 3016–20.

40 "Yek Modir-e Sinema Beh Etteham-e Dayer Kardan-e Eshratkadeh Bazdasht Shod," *Kayhan* (3/10/1358: May 31, 1979), p. 5.

41 "Ja-ye Sinema dar 'Barnameh-ye Panj Sal-e Avval' Kojast?" *Mahnameh-ye Sinema'i-ye Film*, no. 6 (1983), pp. 4–5.

42 See: "Dah Sinema-ye Tehran Ta'til Shod," *Ettela'at* (11/29/1358 (1979)), p. 1. *Iranshahr* (June 20, 1980), p. 1; *Iranshahr* (July 4, 1980), p. 2; and "Sinemaha-ye Sarasar-e Keshvar Ta'til Shod," *Kayhan-e Hava'i* (July 2, 1980), p. 8.

43 "Karnameh-ye Dowlat-e Jomhuri-ye Eslami dar Zamineh-ye Siasatha-ye Kolli-ye Keshvar va Arzeshha-ye Hakem bar An," *Sorush*, no. 252 (6/3/1363 (1984)), p. 22.

44 *Ettela'at*, (Jan. 1, 1980: 11/10/1358)), p. 20.

45 "Nameh-ye Sargoshadeh-ye Sinemagaran-e Iran beh Mellat va Dowlat," included as a flier inside *Daftarha-ye Sinema*, no. 4 (2/1360 (1981)).

46 "Degarguni dar Zamineh-ye Sinema, ba 'Dizolv' Ettefaq Mi'oftad nah ba 'Kat,' " *Mahnameh-ye Sinema'i-ye Film*, no. 46 (1987), p. 4.

47 All the regulations listed and discussed below are taken from an unpublished internal document, "Marahel-e Mokhtalef-e Nezarat bar Sakht va Namayesh-e Film," pp. 40–9, obtained by the author from the Ministry of Islamic Guidance.

48 For example, the number of theatres nationwide grew from 198 in 1979 to 277 in 1984 and the seating capacity in the same period increased from 141,399 to 170,265. Likewise, attendance at Tehran theatres alone rose from some 24 million in 1984 to nearly 28 million in 1986. For sources see: *Salnameh-ye Amari-ye Sal-e 1360* (Markaz-e Amar-e Iran, Tehran, Esfand 1361/1982), p. 203; *Iran dar A'ineh-ye Amar* (Markaz-e Amar-e Iran, Tehran, Mordad 1364/ 1985), p. 46; Sinema-ye Iran 1358–1363, (Ministry of Islamic Guidance, Tehran, 1984), p. 37, p. 295; *A Selection of Iranian Films* (Farabi Cinema Foundation, Tehran, 1987), p. 8. The attendance figure nationwide for 1984 topped 48 million. For sources see: Gholam Haidari, "Javanan va Sinema," *Mahnameh-ye Sinema'i-ye Film*, no. 44 (Day 1365/1986), p. 6. Theatres are classified into four distinct categories. For example, of 78 theatres located in Tehran in 1984, 14 were rated distinguished, 30 first class, 17 second class, and 17 third class. See: Edareh-ye Koll-e Tahqiqat va Ravabet-e Sinema'i, *Sinema-ye Iran 1358–1363* (Ministry of Islamic Guidance, Tehran, 1984), pp. 37, 295.

49 Haidari, "Javanan va Sinema," p. 7.

50 Haidari's survey of Tehran students reflects audience preferences for action and war films in 1983: 45 per cent of them favored "revolutionary" films, 39 per cent comedies, 32 per cent religious films, 32 per cent crime films, and only 10 per cent socially relevant films.

51 "Iranian Film Biz Revisited: Lotsa US Cassettes, Picture Backlog," *Variety* (June 6, 1984), p. 2.

52 "Doshvariha-ye Filmsazi dar Sali keh Gozasht," *Mahnameh-ye Sinema'i-ye Film*, no. 23 (Farvardin 1364/1985), pp. 5–7.

53 "Marahel-e Mokhtalef-e Nezarat bar . . .," pp. 35–6.

54 For a list of these films, see Jamal Omid, *Farhang-e Filmha-ye Sinema'i-ye Iran, From 1351 ta 1366*, vol. 2 (Tehran, 1987), pp. 696–713.

55 "Sansur az Do Negah," *Mahnameh-ye Sinema'i-ye Film*, no. 76 (Ordibehesht 1368/1989), pp. 10–11.

56 "Green Light to Screenwriters," *Mahnameh-ye Sinema'i-ye Film*, no. 66 (Mordar 1367/1988), p. 1, English section.

57 "Sinema-ye Iran 1358–1363," *Mahnameh-ye Sinemay'ieh Film*, no. 18 (Aban 1363/1984), pp. 293–4.

58 "Poshtvaneh-ye Ta'min-e Ejtema'i va Herfeh'i-ye Dast Andarkaran-e Sinema," *Mahnameh-ye Sinema'i-ye Film*, no. 35 (Farvardin 1345/1986), pp. 6–8.

59 "Vam-e banki Bara-ye Filmsazan," *Mahnameh-ye Sinema'i-ye Film*, no. 52 (Mordad 1366/1987), p. 18. Also: "Rahi Besu-ye Esteqlal-e Eqtesadi-ye Filmsazan," *Mahnameh-ye Sinema'i-ye Film*, no. 60 (Bahman 1366/1987), pp. 5–8.

60 "Goruhbandi-ye Filmha-ye Irani va Sinemaha dar Sal-e Jari," *Mahnameh-ye Sinema'i-ye Film*, no. 63 (Ordibehesht 1367/1988), pp. 12–13. Also: "Iranian Films Rated According to Merit," *Mahnameh-ye Sinemay'ieh Film*, no. 49 (Ordibehesht 1366/1987), p. 1 English section.

61 "New Policies for a Year of Challenge," *Mahnameh-ye Sinema'i-ye Film*, no. 77 (Khordar 1368/1989), p. 1, English section.

62 "Moruri bar Vizhegiha-ye Moshtarak-e Filmah-ye Irani-ye Emsal," *Mahnameh-ye Sinema'i-ye Film*, no. 68 (Mordad 1368/1989), pp. 12–13.

63 "Boniad-e Mostaz'afan Miliardha Dolar beh Bankha Bedehkar ast," *Iran Times* (December 9, 1983); "Boniad-e Mostaz'afan 45 Miliard Rial Bedehi Darad," *Iran Times* (February 24, 1984), p. 5.

64 "Az Ravayat va Qesas-e Qor'an Film-e Sinema'i Sakhteh Mishavad," *Iran Times* (July 29, 1983), p. 5.

65 "Zarar-e Mostaz'afan az Kar-e Sinemaha," *Iran Times* (May 18, 1984), p. 13.

66 "Videotapes of Iranian Films for Export," *Mahnameh-ye Sinema'i-ye Film*, no. 49 (Ordibehesht 1366/1987), p. 1, English section.

67 From a leaflet titled "Construction Crusade-1," put out in early 1980s by the Muslim Student Association in the US and Canada. For more information on the ideology and operations of the Crusade, see the periodical *Jahad*, published in Tehran by the Crusade.

68 Markaz-e Amar-e Iran, *Salnameh-ye Amari-ye 1362* (Vezarat-e Barnameh va Budjeh, Tehran, 1363/1984), p. 723.

69 Hamid Nafici, *Iran Media Index* (Greenwood Press, Westport, CT, 1984), pp. 190–220.

70 Naficy, "The Development of an Islamic Cinema," p. 459.

71 Iraj Karimi, "In Nakoja-Abad Kojast?" *Mahnameh-ye Sinema'i-ye Film*, no. 72 (Day 1367/1988), pp. 52–4.

72 *Variety* (August 16, 1989).

73 "Sarmaqaleh," *Faslnameh-ye Honar*, no. 3 (Spring–Summer 1983), p. 16.

74 "Basij-e Emkanat-e Jang dar Khedmat-e Jang," *Mahnameh-ye Sinema'i-ye Film*, no. 37 (Khordar 1365/1986), pp. 6–7.

75 "How the War was Reflected on Screen," *Mahnameh-ye Sinema'i-ye Film*, no. 72 (Day 1367/1988), p. 1, English section.

76 "Sinema-ye Iran va Hafteh-ye Jang," *Mahnameh-ye Sinemay'ieh Film*, no. 5 (Shahrivar 1362/1983), pp. 4–5. For similar analysis three years later, see: "Durbin dar Jebheh va Posht-e Jebheh," *Mahnameh-ye Sinema'i-ye Film*, no. 41 (Mehre 1365/1986), pp. 6–7.

77 "Marahel-e Mokhtalef-e nezarat bar Sakht va Namayesh-e Film," pp. 40–9.

78 "Goftegu ba Homa Rusta, Bazigar-e Film," *Mahnameh-ye Sinema'i-ye Film*, no. 58 (Day 1366/1987), p. 59.

79 Mas'ud Purmohammad, "Ebteda Sangha-ye Kuchak," *Mahnameh-ye Sinema'i-ye Film*, no. 64 (Khordad 1366/1987), p. 8.

80 "Honarpishegan-e Zan az Film Hazf Shodehand," *Kayhan* (London) (September 26, 1985), p. 11.

81 Based on my lengthy interviews with a prominent Iranian actress who wishes to remain anonymous.

82 "Andar Ahvalat-e Filmi Keh Mojavvez-e Shar'i Nadasht," *Foqoladeh* (Los Angeles) (Mehr 1364/1985), p. 16.

83 "Zan dar Donia-ye Honar Hashiyeh Neshin ast," *Zan-e Ruz* (12/18/ 1362: 1983), p. 33.

84 "Aramesh dar Hozur-e Hemingway," *Mahnameh-ye Sinema'i-ye Film*, no. 60 (Bahman 1366/1987), p. 59.

85 For example, in *Noqteh Za'f* (*The Weakpoint*, 1983) directed by Mohammad Reza A'alami, the relationship between a political activist and the security agent who captures him displays strong but deeply ambiguous and incommensurate sexual undercurrents: we see two men treated as though one of them (the captive) were a woman. The two engage in activities that are shown typically in boy-meets-girl-falls-in-love formula films. They go to a park and play soccer with the kids, kicking the ball back and forth to each other like two lovers, and at the beach they sit side by side and gaze at the horizon as a wild horse gallops by and an extradiegetic romantic music seals the scene in its romantic moment. During the course of the film, a role reversal occurs with the captive assuming the masculine position.

86 "Mohemtarin Mas'aleh Bara-ye Man 'Ertebat' ast," *Mahnameh-ye Sinema'i-ye Film*, no. 67 (Shahrivar 1367/1988), pp. 51–3.

87 The figures for 1985 are for the first nine months of the year. See "Movafaqiyatha-ye Eqtesadi va Natayej-e Kaifi."

88 *Natayej-e Amargiri az Hazineh va Daramad-e Khanevarha-ye Shahri Sal-e 1362* (Markaz-e Amar-e Iran, Tehran, 1363/1984), chart 3.7.

89 Naficy, "The Development of an Islamic Cinema," pp. 461–2.

90 Author's interview with Barbod Taheri, September 1985, Los Angeles.

91 "Sinema-ye Pass az Enqelab, dar Aghaz-e Dahe-ye Dovvom," *Mahnameh-ye Sinema'i-ye Film*, no. 75 (Noruz 1368/1989), p. 73.

92 "Khameneh'i ba Sinema Mokhalef ast va Rafsanjani ba an Movafeq," *Kayhan* (London) (5/30/1985), p. 2.
93 "Ma Agar Sinema ra az Ja-ye Khodash Kharej Konim Digar Sinema Nakhahim Dasht," *Kayhan Hava'i* (10/24/1984), p. 15.
94 "Nazar-e Emam Khomeini dar Bareh-ye Filmha, Serialha, Ahangha, va Pakhsh-e Barnamehha-ye Varzeshi E'lam Shod," *Kayhan Hava'i* (12/30/1987), p. 3.
95 Interview with the author, Tehran, August 1991.
96 Teshome H. Gabriel, *Third Cinema in the Third World: the Aesthetics of Liberation* (Ann Arbour, Michigan, UMI Research Press, 1982) p. 100.

9

POPULISM AND CORPORATISM IN POST-REVOLUTIONARY IRANIAN POLITICAL CULTURE

Manochehr Dorraj

INTRODUCTION

As interesting as the study of culturally determined human behavior might be in illuminating differences responsible for diverse political conducts, the study of commonalties, the broad cross-cultural social dynamics that give rise to the specific meanings and interpretations of culture at different historical junctures is lacking in much of the literature on political culture. Utilizing the concepts of populism and corporatism, particularly prevalent among the scholars of European and Latin American politics, the present chapter examines their applicability for understanding the metamorphosis of the dominant Iranian political culture in the post-revolutionary era.

The attempt here, however, is not to present political culture as a mechanical manifestation of such "deeper realities" as class or economic base. Rather, the objective is to expound on the broader components of socially determined political behavior that cuts across cultural barriers. Other developing societies that have experienced rapid dependent economic development, authoritarian rule and foreign domination also display the same populist and corporatist tendencies. The challenge is to explain what specific form this populist syndrome takes under Iranian political culture.

For the purposes of the present study, populism is very briefly and broadly defined as an ideology that glorifies the common people and advocates the supremacy of the laity over the elite. Taking its inspiration from the indigenous traditions and values, populist ideology denounces foreign economic and cultural domination.[1] Corporatism is recognized as a populist strategy that reconciles class differences and incorporates the

214

nation into an organic whole. Corporatist strategy encompasses integration of both realms of economic and cultural life. While negating both Marxism and capitalism, corporatism purports to present a third path of political development. The corporatist state is delegated with the moral mission of purging the corrupt elements, providing social welfare and guiding the people toward salvation. Laying claim to "authenticity," it champions cultural nationalism and uses traditional political symbolism and religious values for mass mobilization. Populism and corporatism are defined here as two organically linked ideologies, one reinforcing the other.[2]

The idea of creating an organic egalitarian society in which class and social antagonism have been replaced by a community of believers united around the banner of Islam found a large following among the clerics, the lay intellectuals and a sector of the popular masses during the 1960s and 1970s. The intellectual origins and development of this populist–corporatist interpretation of Islam deserves closer scrutiny.

THE IMPACT OF THE POPULIST METAMORPHOSIS OF THE PRE-REVOLUTIONARY ERA

The post-revolutionary political culture of Iran had its immediate roots in the neo-Islamic political culture of the 1960s and 1970s.[3] While deeply rooted in the past, the Iranian political culture in the post-World War Two period had to come to terms with the rapidly shifting winds of global political change and their impact on Iran. The decades immediately following World War Two witnessed the radicalizing impact of such events as the Egyptian revolution, followed by the Algerian, Cuban, Vietnamese and Palestinian revolutions and movements. Revolutions are potent producers of ideology and the eruption of these Third World revolutions culminated in popularization of Third Worldist ideologies. The impact of this ideological current on the Iranian intelligentsia was immense. Due to a widespread sentiment of national humiliation that marked the period after the 1953 restoration *coup d'état*,[4] the appeal of this populist Third Worldism was far reaching and it influenced some of the traditional sectors of the Iranian society, including the *ulama*.

As the process of industrialization and urbanization of the Iranian society was accelerated in the post-1950 era, alienation and anomie became widespread. This, coupled with the increasing migration of peasants to the cities due to the Shah's ill-fated land reform program, induced a concentration of large groups of uprooted and alienated individuals in the urban centers. The rapid increase of the urban population of Iran between 1956 and 1976 and the spread of literacy provided Shi'ite traditionalism with a new vitality. This period witnessed a tremendous growth in Islamic literature, associations and political activities. The number of these religious associations in Tehran alone is reported to have exceeded 12,300.[5] Both lay intellectuals, a sector of the middle class that had tenaciously maintained traditional Islamic values, and the new migrants figured prominently in these Islamic associations and their political activities. The bureaucratization and centralization of power, which in the 1960s and 1970s constituted an integral part of state building, went hand in hand with the declining power of the common man and the breaking of communal bonds. While the middle-class intelligentsia resented the political absolutism of the autocracy, the bazaar witnessed an increasing emergence of economic policies that threatened its livelihood and discriminated in favor of the new industrial sector. Hence, the influx of petro-dollars and the economic boom of 1973 were followed by the economic bust of 1975 which ushered in tremendous disillusion and resentment.[6]

The impact of these social changes on the political culture of the 1960s and 1970s was profound indeed. The political articulation of these new realities found their manifestations in a neologism, a synthesis of populism and religion. Several clerics, such as Ayatollahs Khomeini, Taleqani, Motahhari and Beheshti, were among active advocates of a populist interpretation of Shi'ite traditionalism. Lay intellectuals such as Ali Shariati and Mehdi Bazargan, advocates of Islamic modernism, were particularly influential among the radicalized youth, some of whom founded the organization of *Mojahedeen-e Khalq*, an urban-based Islamic guerrilla group. Among the latter, the populist impact of Shariati's political thought was the most distinct. Under the radicalizing impact of such international events as the Algerian, Cuban and Vietnamese revolutions on the one hand and the ideological challenge of the domestic

Marxist organizations such as Tudeh Party and the *Fedaiyan-e Khalq* on the other, gradually a total, self-conscious and highly politicized interpretation of Islam emerged among both the traditionalists and the modernists. The fact that the secular intelligentsia also experienced an intense populist metamorphosis in this period further contributed to the development of Islamic populism. A major catalyst, however, was the charismatic authority of Ayatollah Ruhollah Khomeini that was deeply rooted in his populist interpretation of Shi'ism.

The populist roots of Ayatollah Khomeini's charisma

As an orphan who had lost his father at the age of one and his mother early in his intellectual development, Khomeini began to identify with the deprived and the oppressed. Khomeini's interest in *erfan* (mystical philosophy) as a student of theology in Qom, also indicates an aversion to accumulation of wealth and material pursuit. There was a certain ascetic element present in his persona as well as his simple lifestyle. As a theologian in the holy city of Qom, Khomeini distinguished himself by presenting his students with a highly politicized rendition of the faith. Khomeini's interpretation of Islam increasingly meant a commitment to social and political causes. Several of his former students, who after the Revolution of 1979 became the leaders of the Islamic Republic, recall his enduring political impact. Many of them were inspired by Khomeini's conviction that the clergy must be actively engaged in liberating the poor and the oppressed.[7] Calling the Shah "a servant of the dollar" and condemning the "corrupt" lifestyle of the ruling elite, he was consistently outspoken in defense of the downtrodden. In Khomeini's declarations and speeches, the Shah was depicted as a lackey of foreign powers who had been ordered by his masters to undermine the spiritual integrity of Islam and ultimately to destroy it altogether.[8]

Since Islam was the protector of the poor and the oppressed, Khomeini would explain, an attack on Islam was an assault on the rights of the downtrodden. To his followers, Khomeini personified both compassion and authenticity. In addition, his religious credential as *Marja-e Taqlid* (the source of emulation) and a Grand Ayatollah bestowed upon him the aura of a sage, a savior with a message of deliverance and salvation. The epithet of *Imam-e Mostaz'afeen* (the leader of the dispossessed), given to him by his devotees, was a potent symbol evoking the popular image of the return of the Mahdi, the twelvth Imam, to restore justice. The appeal of Khomeini's simple lifestyle was matched by the appeal of his simple language. He possessed an uncanny ability to communicate with ordinary people and relate to their consciousness. His high spiritual standing was complemented by the allure of his political stature as an uncompromising figure of political struggle against the Pahlavis for more than three decades.

In 1979 Khomeini seized power on the basis of a populist agenda. He came to power promising to cleanse the society of the vestiges of the corrupt autocracy and Western influence and to restore the right of the oppressed. Khomeini asserted that the meek and the dispossessed who had given blood, and martyrs for the revolution were its true heirs. Dividing the society into two fundamental classes, *mostaz'afeen* (the dispossessed) and *mostakbareen* (the nefarious oppressors),[9] he admonished the leaders of the Islamic Republic that "those who have been deprived throughout history, under the Islamic Republic must no longer suffer deprivation."[10] In the post-revolutionary period, Khomeini's charismatic authority was both the source of inspiration and legitimization of the political system. For the pious Shi'ites, Khomeini represented a cultural link with their past amidst the turbulent and uncertain world of the present. If the policies of the Islamic Republic were marked by political inconsistencies and abrupt fluctuations, Khomeini exuded confidence and personified certitude. His implacable spiritual and political credentials lent him an aura of invincibility, evoking a synthesis of fear and awe, adoration and love. In the popular image, the orphan had now become a grand patriarch, the foremost protector of the deprived and the disinherited. This bestowed legitimacy on the new and fragile revolutionary institutions, whose primary recruits were drawn from the ranks of the lower classes.

Perhaps no less significant was the institutional basis of Khomeini's charisma and populist appeal. Through his absolute powers of appointment and dismissal, Khomeini put his confidants, former students and associates in all key positions of power. They informed him of major developments in the country at large and within the government. While the Friday-prayer leaders and Imam's representatives in provinces informed him of the popular mood and sentiments, his former students and associates reported to him on the intricacies of intergovernmental affairs and power politics. Thus he was in a position not only to feel the political pulse of the populace, but also to coordinate the policy response accordingly, a practice at which the clergy historically have been extremely adept due to their close ties with the laity.

The all-encompassing and total character of Khomeini's neologism was buttressed by such institutional outlets as neighborhood committees (*komifehs*), popular militia (*pasdaran* and *basijis*), a network of mosques (*masjeds*) and Friday prayer leaders (*Imam Jom'ehs*). The hierarchical and patrimonial structure of power was based on the charismatic supremacy of a jurisconsult (*Faqih*), a Council of Guardians (*Shuray-e Negahban*), revolutionary courts (later incorporated in a ministry of justice) with revolutionary guards as its executive arms, and the foundation for the dispossessed (*Bonyad-e Mostaz'afeen*) as its financial repository. These institutions have proven to be effective instruments for wielding power and control.[11]

This network of power was complemented with a very skillful method of exerting power and influence. Elevating himself above political factionalism and the mundane administrative tasks of the state, yet reserving for himself the role of ultimate judge and arbiter in matters of political dispute, allowed Khomeini to intervene in politics selectively. Thus, he threw his weight behind this or that faction or leader depending on the issue or the individual involved. This style effectively shielded him from the vulnerabilities associated with mundane policy-making and maintained his moral authority.

The lack of political ritual in Iranian history and the pre-eminence of religious rituals in cultural life as a paradigm for social action have been noted by some scholars. This sacred symbolism and primacy of rituals that involve devotional acts such as the commemoration of Imam Ali or his martyred son, Hossein, play an instrumental role in social integration of the individual and strengthen the community.[12] An equally important component of Khomeini's charisma can be traced to his adept utilization of Shi'ite mythologies and legends to mobilize the masses and rally their support around Islamic causes. For example, aware of the devotional attachment of Shi'ites to their first Imam, Ali, Khomeini asserted: "*Hazrat-e Ali* sacrificed everything he had for Islam. We must follow the paradigmatic example of a perfect man like Imam Ali. In virtue and knowledge, in kindness to the disinherited and the needy, in bravery and war, in all dimensions, we must follow Imam Ali."[13] Hence, the example of martyrdom of Imam Hossein was utilized to mobilize hundreds of thousands of Shi'ite zealots in the war against Iraq. Armed with the messianic and egalitarian message of Shi'ism that promised a classless unitarian society and a reign of justice, Khomeni's use of political symbolism evoked emotive images and symbols that had deep roots in popular culture. Thus, as personification of cultural authenticity, Khomeini's brand of revolutionary traditionalism that was deeply imbued with populist rhetoric found wide appeal among the lower echelons of the Iranian society.

A POPULIST REVOLUTION

The key to the victory of the Revolution of 1979 was its broad popular base. The tenacious, spontaneous and polyclass character of the anti-Shah movement, permeating major urban centers, made its suppression a difficult task indeed. The mass power conferred a sense of invincibility, elevating the level of political commitment and bringing hopes of victory amidst a hopeless condition. While the revolutionary forces came from multi-class backgrounds, the urban poor and migrant peasants also played a very prominent role. In a sense, this overwhelming participation of the lower echelons of the society in the revolutionary process was a realization of populist ideology that power stems from "the people." Having realized that the revolutionary leaders of all persuasions carried their banner and purported to champion their cause, the urban poor had an ambivalent sense of self-confidence sustained by strong cynicism. While they were imbued with feelings of moral superiority that the revolution bestowed upon them, the disinherited (*mostaz'afeen*), extolled as the new masters of the society, were not yet convinced of the reality of the new populist rhetoric that dominated the post-revolutionary political discourse. A dialogue between a secular intellectual, Nader Ebrahimi, and one of the residents of a shanty town in south Tehran (Fatemeh) captures the essence of the new pervasive populist mood. Responding to some intellectuals who had gone to the slums of south Tehran to clean up the dirty alleys and streets, Fatemeh asserts: "My neighborhood is clean. This is the place the oppressed live and they are the best and the purest of all humankind."[14]

Throughout the revolution the slogan that "behind every treasure lies a criminal" became widely popular. To denounce the royal family's lavish lifestyle, its palaces, private resorts and luxuries were shown to the public. As the royal family and the financial elite tied to them were depicted as venal, decadent and corrupt, the downtrodden (*mahrumin* and *mazlumin*) were portrayed as the repository of innocence possessing genuine human values. If unbridled pursuit of material wealth had rendered the elite heartless lackeys of capital, the suffering of the oppressed had humanised them. This conferred a new self-confidence among the poor:

> Isn't it true that your writings were appealing and you had a big audience because you wrote about our wretchedness? Isn't it true that in your political parties you spoke about our historical suffering? And isn't it true that when your brave militant political prisoners were tried in military tribunals you used our pain and suffering to justify your actions and absolve yourselves? Yes, you used us to gain reputation, to become "national heroes," to become proud and popular. You owe us for all your glories. But today we are in the periphery of the Revolution.[15]

While they still remain on the periphery, measures on their behalf have been forthcoming since the revolution. The Islamic Revolution allowed the excluded social access and participation. It incorporated the declining traditional social groups (the *ulama* and the *bazaaris*), some of the upwardly mobile social groups (a sector of the alienated lay intellectuals supportive of the regime), as well as the downtrodden of the city and the countryside. Many younger militant clerical leaders of the revolution came from rural and provincial backgrounds.[16] Hence, some of the reforms implemented on behalf of the lower classes are notable. One assessment of the regime's social policy summarizes them as follows:

> A housing foundation was created to provide housing for

the poor, particularly in urban areas. The Ministry of Planning and Budget was directed to allocate national resources more equitably throughout the provinces. The Reconstruction Crusade (now a ministry) was established to provide rural areas with electricity, water, feeder roads, schools, health clinics and housing among other social and infrastructural services. Legislation was passed to reduce the gap among wage rates, resulting in a 60 per cent boost to workers' wages. A policy of price support in the form of subsidies for basic need items was instituted to protect the poorer groups from the rampant inflation that had followed the economic decline during the Revolution.[17]

Indeed a closer examination of the social policies of the Islamic Republic reveals certain ideological tensions in the populist state. While in the early years of the revolution the new regime was preoccupied with an ideological crusade, gradually it opted for a more pragmatic political course. Presently, two distinct trends can be discerned in the realm of social policy: one populist and another moderate.

Social policy

The general tenor of economic policies of the Islamic Republic before Rafsanjani's presidency was based on self reliance, small-scale production, encouragement of the agricultural sector and domestic industry, and a tight control of foreign investment. After the revolution many capital-intensive projects were replaced by labor-intensive ones. In an attempt to reverse the massive migration to the cities and bridge the wide gap between the city and the countryside, the construction of rural areas was given priority over many urban projects. The consumption patterns after the revolution shifted in favor of rural households. In urban areas, "the 40 per cent of households with the lowest expenditure have experienced an improvement in their share of total expenditure." Hence, the top "20 per cent of households bore the brunt of the decline in private consumption,"[18] the governmental policy to deal with inflation was discriminatory on behalf of the poor. While many luxury consumer items dear to the upper and middle classes have disappeared from the market, or if available, were heavily taxed, the food subsidy program and the distribution system were designed to benefit the lower income groups.[19] While steps have been taken to improve the economic conditions of the poor, the salaried employees of the governmental bureaucracy and the technocrats have experienced an erosion of their purchasing power and salaries.[20] The emergence of an austerity program during the war years that witnessed widespread rationing of food, gasoline and other major necessities treated the lower class constituency of the regime, especially the family of "martyrs," preferentially.

After the revolution the government nationalized a large sector of the major industries, banks, insurance companies, construction and large-scale agriculture. Foreign trade also came under the partial monopoly of the government. However, realizing that extensive nationalization implied that now the government was responsible to pay the staggering debts and deal with labor unrest, as early as 1982 some of the leaders of the Islamic Republic began to reconsider the policy and encouraged investment in the private sector.[21] The battle between state control and economic liberalization tendencies has raged on unceasingly since 1979. After the outbreak of war with Iraq, the new regime also established the foundation for economic mobilization (*Bonyad-e Basiij-e Eqtesadi*) that created a wholesale and retail center and took over the domestic distribution of major consumer goods. Another institution especially active in the rural areas was *Jehad-e Sazandegi* (crusade for construction). The latter was established on the orders of Ayatollah Khomeini in 1979 to rebuild the underdeveloped and neglected sectors of the economy. *Jehad-e Sazandegi* has been active in building roads and bridges, digging wells and providing tractors at a subsidized rate. According to its own statistics, during the year 1979–80, the organization built 1,934 houses, 1,997 schools, 48 mosques, 1,464 public baths, and 80 hospitals, dug over 2,000 wells, distributed over 4 million books and held more than 3,000 literacy classes.[22]

Despite these and other reforms on behalf of the lower classes, the actual achievements in reducing the gap between the rich and the poor a decade after the revolution remain meager indeed. A 1989 report filed from a seminar on economic reconstruction in Tehran cited the assessment of Hojjatoleslam Gholam-Reza Mesbahi as the following: "On the eve of the eleventh year of our revolution, we still possess an economy that is dependent on oil, the unemployment rate and inflation remain high, the migration of peasants to the cities continues at an alarming rate, and social justice is yet to be realized in our society."[23] In fact the devastating economic impact of the war of attrition and a plummeting oil income has led to the general decline of the standard of living and has adversely affected the lower classes, further pauperizing them. Dr Azimi, the head of education sector in the Ministry of Planning and Budget reports that "the level of production in 1989 equaled that of 1972–73. This means we have stagnated sixteen years."[24] This statistic assumes more significance when we consider that the population has increased by more than 12 million since then. Losses in the production sectors have absorbed the funds that the government needs to invest in other fields. Despite the government's original plan to maintain agricultural self-sufficiency, the agri-business sector has been severely damaged and its production has declined. The drop in production is partially due to the massive peasant flight from the Iranian countryside to the major cities.

Some of the estimates indicate 40 per cent of the urban population growth between 1977 and 1983 was due to peasant migration. Since then, the number is projected to have reached 6 million or more.[25] Due to the backwardness of the agricultural sector, i.e. its primitive technological tools and methods of production, its capacity to absorb further capital investment is very limited. Compared to 1986, the government's assistance to peasants witnessed a decline in 1987. Distribution of fertilizers and mechanization of agriculture have also experienced a decline since 1987. Therefore, reliance on traditional methods of production, capital investment without technical change and price policies that cannot keep up with the cost of production have rendered the goal of agricultural self-sufficiency an unattainable one in the near future.[26]

The industrial development and reconstruction of the country are among serious challenges that the regime faces. Iranian industries are dependent on international markets for about 65 per cent of their imports. To revive the industry to the pre-revolutionary level will cost some $6.5 billion per year in foreign exchange. The government's need for foreign exchange in the fiscal year 1989–90 was projected to be $12–15 billion.

Yet Iranian oil income which accounts for 90 per cent of foreign exchange amounted to $13 billion, out of which only $6.5 billion is available for reconstruction.[27] This renders the task of reconstruction a formidable one indeed, if the government was to rely solely on domestic resources.

Unemployment is another major economic burden facing the regime, a problem that has been compounded by the demobilization of *basijis*, originally mobilized for the war against Iraq. Unemployment is estimated to exceed 4 million. Taking into account open and hidden unemployment in the countryside, we reach a far higher figure. In April of 1986, the plan and Budget Minister stated that hidden unemployment and underemployment accounted for 39 per cent of the economically active population. The current figures are similar to those of 1986. The unemployed and their families that number 12 million live in dire poverty.[28]

According to Mr Mir-Ali Negarandeh, an ex-member of parliament, "presently, an amount that exceeds six times the general budget of the government is concentrated in the hands of three thousand families in the private sector."[29] In response to these developments and pressures from the lower classes, the populist tendency within the *Majles* has launched a campaign against "economic terrorists" calling for their liquidation.[30] When sound economic policies that address the fundamental structural roots of "profiteering" are not forthcoming, the populist rhetoric intensifies. A member of parliament poses the following question: "In a situation in which the dispossessed bear the main brunt of hardship and stand before it like a mountain, shouldn't the economic terrorists be hung?."[31] This is a thorny issue for the Rafsanjani government. While the regime does not seek to alienate its traditional ally, the bazaar, it is under pressure to do something for m*ostaz'afeen* under whose name the revolution was launched.

The major debate between the two tendencies concerning development strategies revolves around the tempo, the target, as well as the role of foreign capital and investment in this process. The "open door" or the moderate tendency as enunciated by Mr Rafsanjani in his five year program, favors the strategy of rapid growth to improve the social condition of the people who have sacrificed in the past decade and whose patience may be running out. Only through such a policy can the government respond adequately to the need of 65 per cent of the population who are below the poverty line. They welcome foreign investment and favor less governmental control on the private sector. The populist tendency, led by radical clerics such as Khoiniha and Mohtashami, on the other hand, favors a slower pace and the use of domestic resources and investment in indigenous industries to provide social services for those on the bottom of the social stratum. Instead of supporting the private sector, the government must strengthen the cooperatives. Open door policy, they argue, would increase social inequality and Iran's dependence on foreign capital.[32] The recurring tension between the two tendencies indicates that the outcome of ideological and political struggle between the populist and moderate factions has not yet been resolved. However, there are signs that in the post-Khomeini era the populists are on the defensive. For example, the 1992 parliamentary victory of Rafsanjani's supporters, the relaxation of barriers to foreign investment, and the increasing reliance on technocrats and private sector investors are among the major indicators.

So far, the clergy has proved to be quite adept in inner elite conflict management. The consensus formation, coalition building and factional compromise that were legacies of Khomeini's leadership have been passed on to his two former students, Mr Khamenei and Mr Rafsanjani, the present leaders of Iran. The populist and moderate tendencies have reached a *de facto* compromise. Whereas the state predominates in major heavy industries, the private sector holds sway in other sectors.

The strategy preferred by Mr Rafsanjani is to create a mixed economy framework to guide the coexisting public, private and cooperative sectors. In this scheme, the public sector will dominate the major industries, mines, banking systems, exports, some social services and all infrastructures, while the private sector will dominate the small-scale productive activities. The Iranian government would receive loans from major Western banks, oil companies and industries organized in a consortium and repay them by selling oil to oil companies within the consortium. Iran hopes to use this proposal submitted to the German Minister of Foreign Trade in 1988 as a model to deal with foreign investment.[33]

Both the populist and the moderate tendencies have now

reached the conclusion that the highly ideological politics of the past have not produced the desired outcome. Lacking Khomeini's charisma, the Iranian leaders agree that in order to survive they must opt for a more moderate political course. Therefore, in selecting his new cabinet members in 1989, Rafsanjani bypassed the former Prime Minister, Mir-Hossein Moussavi, and the former Interior Minister, Ali-Akbar Mohtashami, who were identified with radical populist politics. The majority of the new twenty-two cabinet members come from the ranks of moderate technocrats, some of whom are Western-educated. There is also a consensus emerging that economic reconstruction requires political stability and security which in turn necessitates political liberalization. Even former hard-line Prime Minister Mir-Hossein Moussavi, now apolitical consultant to Rafsanjani, has stated that "We cannot succeed in economic reconstruction unless we allow freedom of thought and criticism."[34] Likewise, Zanjani, the deputy minister, asserted that "without a precise and scientific analysis of changes in the global political and economic structure we cannot reach a sound strategy for our own development."[35] These developments indicate that there is a clear turn away from highly ideological politics in favor of a more pragmatic political course in the post-Khomeini era. Given the highly ideological nature of the Islamic Revolution, however, ideology continues to assume a significant role not only as a guide for action but, more importantly, in legitimizing the political process and the ends it seeks.

The ideology

The building of a populist–corporatist state was enhanced by a rich tradition of the religious symbols and rituals with communal connotations. Historically, Shi'ite rituals have been "mass-based and mass-oriented."[36] The devotional rituals of Shi'ism such as commemoration of the martyrdom of Imam Hossein in the ceremonies of *Ashura* and *Tasu'a*, are designed to integrate the individual in the society. By bringing the people together, these rituals strengthen their sense of social solidarity and religious identity. Other rituals, such as *sofreh* (serving food in the name of a particular Shi'ite saint), have a distinct function in social welfare: "the food is to be shared with the poor and thus it is a social leveling device to preserve the welfare of the society rather than a means of saving souls."[37] Such traditions provided the Muslim revolutionaries with a reservoir of popular religious and political symbols unavailable to secular groups.

Under Ayatollah Khomeini the populist–corporatist character of the state was marked by a total, self-conscious, exclusive and holistic ideology enunciated by a charismatic leader and an active campaign of mass mobilization. This neologism aspired to intervene and Islamicize major aspects of social and private life. As Ayatollah Khomeini once asserted: "There is not a single topic in human life for which Islam has not provided instruction and established norms."[38] This total character of the ideological creed of the new regime, in which religion and politics were synthesized to the proclivities of Iranian culture, proved to be a potent force in mass mobilization. The repeated purges of "corrupt elements" from bureaucracy and the launching of a cultural revolution on campuses in order to cleanse the educational institutions of the vestiges of Western cultural influences were designed to mold this holistic idea of polity: to create an authentic, righteous Islamic *umma* on the march toward unity with God (*Kamal*).

The neologism of the Islamic Republic synthesized Shi'ite ascetism, forbearance and emphasis on social justice, on the one hand, and an elitist concept of leadership (the rule of jurisconsult) and authoritarian rule, on the other. The new populist state embodied the rule of virtue and wrath. The regime's motto "neither East, nor West" rendered it opposed to both communism and liberalism. The slogan served a two-pronged purpose. While, internationally, it was meant to put Iran firmly in the Third World non-aligned camp, domestically it was intended to discredit the opponents, including the leftist Tudeh Party and Fedaiyan and the liberal National Front and Bazargan's Iran's Freedom Movement.

As the only Shi'ite state and the leader of the only Islamic Revolution in the twentieth century, the regime's self-perception as the guardian of authentic Islam makes it incumbent to spread the message of revolutionary Islam and launch an ideological crusade. The relationship between ideological and pragmatic politics, however, is a complex and delicate one. Generally, there is an inverse relationship between ideological politics and the success of the regime in delivering its promised program of social reform and progress. The more the regime is able to produce tangible results and progress in social and economic realms, the less it beats the drums of ideology. When such success is meager, the emphasis on ideology and propaganda increases. During the austerity program of the war years, when food items were in short supply, there was an incessant campaign reminding the people that Imam Ali and Imam Hossein bore more hardship and suffered harsher conditions for the cause of Islam. Since the end of the war and as the revolution has run its course, the ideological crusade has yielded to more pragmatic politics.

Before its dissolution in 1987, the Islamic Republican Party which acted as the ideological mouthpiece of the regime also functioned as the instrument of centralization and monopolization of power. This, however, did not connote that power was a monolithic phenomenon exerted downward in post-revolutionary Iran. There has always been an element of spontaneity and mass initiative present in the political process. While the regime, especially during the early years of the revolution, maintained its constituency politically enticed at a fever pitch, ready to crowd the streets and chant slogans, it is also the case that it was influenced by them in its choice of policy. The leaders of the Islamic Republic have displayed a remarkable capacity to understand the mass sentiment and to manipulate it for their political ends. This has enabled them to stay afloat and navigate the turbulent waters of political change. Seen in this light, the depiction of the fundamentalists in much of the popular Western media as unyielding fanatics is basically simplistic and one-sided. Behind the harsh rhetoric of the fundamentalists always persisted a reservoir of pragmatic deeds. The ideological crusade was circumscribed by the compelling dictates of the politics of survival.

After the death of Ayatollah Khomeini and the concomitant declining political significance of the *faqih* (jurisconsult) and the strengthening of the office of President under Rafsanjani, the autonomy of the executive branch has increased. The element of spontaneity, mass mobilization and street power is gradually being replaced by increasing bureaucratization and rationalization of power. The more qualified technocrats are creeping back and the ideologues, finding themselves increasingly out of style, are trying to hold on to their positions of leadership in governmental institutions. The power struggle between these two groups will not only determine the course of public policy but would have an immediate impact on the new interpretation of Islamic ideology as well.

CONCLUSION

If revolutions begin the era of open and active entrance of the popular masses into the political arena, then ideologies will seize the day that celebrate the mass power and provide the organizational outlet for its realization. The emergence of neo-Islamic populism before and throughout the Iranian Revolution allowed the clergy to come to terms with the realities of a radicalized mass movement. Hence, the synthesis of populism and religion rendered Shi'ism revitalized and a potent political ideology. This neologism, in turn, enhanced the goal of building a strong corporatist state. Much of the success or failure of the present regime is dependent upon holding the tenuous forces that mold the present populist coalition together. Lacking Khomeini's charismatic authority, the new leaders must provide tangible benefits to their constituencies.

The Iranian failure to defeat the Iraqis in the war of attrition proved that faith alone does not guarantee the achievement of political goals. To ensure its survival and political viability the new regime has heeded the fact that it must maintain its comparative edge in modernization and technological development and to do so successfully it must break out of its political isolation. The new policy is to encourage modernization without compromising the protection of traditional Shi'ite culture and institutions. Clearly, the leaders of the Islamic Republic perceive the past cultural heritage as the source of Iran's strength and identity. They also contend that the Islamic character of the Iranian Revolution is a unique attribute in the history of modern revolutions that they intend to maintain at all costs.

Populist regimes historically have been transitional ones. In post-Khomeini Iran, while the radical populist tendency is on the defensive and more moderate forces are holding sway, populist politics persist as an enduring characteristic of the Islamic Republic. While populist policies may be fading, populist symbolism is not. While they may differ on matters of domestic and foreign policy, both tendencies, albeit to different degrees, continue to use populist symbolism and rhetoric to advance their political agenda. There are several reasons for this. First, the populist predisposition of Shi'ite Islam, the guiding ideology of the regime which impacted the present leaders of Iran in their formative years, is still present in their thought and action. Second, the populist legacy of Ayatollah Khomeini still looms large. Third, the promise of reform and progress that were made to the social forces that were energized by the Revolution of 1979, especially the urban poor, are yet to be realized. As long as this constituency has not been politically demoralized or pacified, populist politics will continue to persist as an integral part of post-revolutionary Iranian political culture.

NOTES

1 For discussions of populism, see: Margaret Canovan, *Populism* (Harcourt Brace Jovanovich, New York, 1981); Michael L. Conniff *Latin American Populism in Comparative Perspective* (University of New Mexico Press, Albuquerque, 1982). For a discussion of corporatism see James M. Malloy (ed.), *Authoritarianism and Corporatism in Latin America* (University of Pittsburgh Press, Pittsburgh, 1977). A number of European social theorists have also contributed to the debate on corporatism. Most prominent among them are Durkheim and Tonnies.

2 Ronald C. Newton, "Natural Corporatism and the Passing of Populism in Spanish America" in *Promise of Development: Theories of Change in Latin America*, Peter F. Klaren and Thomas J. Bossert (eds), (Westview Press, Boulder, CO 1986), pp. 219–33.

3 Manochehr Dorraj, *From Zarathustra to Khomeini: Populism and Dissent in Iran* (Rienner Publishers, Boulder, CO 1990), chs 8–12.

4 In 1953, Mossadeq, the nationalist premier was overthrown by mutual collaboration of British and US intelligence and the Shah was brought back to power.

5 Said Amir-Arjomand, *The Turban For The Crown: The Islamic Revolution in Iran* (Oxford University Press, Oxford, 1988), pp. 91–100. See also Hussein Bashiriyeh, *The State and Revolution in Iran (1962–1982)* (St Martin's Press, New York, 1984), pp. 67–8.

6 See Robert Graham, *Iran: Illusion of Power* (St Martin's Press, New York, 1979), pp. 18–21.

7 Shaul Bakhash, *The Reign of the Ayatollahs* (Basic Books, New York, 1984), p. 21.

8 *Ibid.*, p. 36.

9 *Dar Jostejooy-e Rah az Kalam-e Imam: Mostaz'afeen va Mostakbareen* (In

231

Search of the Path, from Imam's Words: the Dispossessed and the Nefarious Oppressors) (Amir Kabir Book Publishing, Tehran, 1982).
10 *Joumhury-e Eslami*, April 29, 1983.
11 Mohsen Milani, *The Making of Iran's Islamic Revolution: From Monarchy to Islamic Revolution* (Westview Press, Boulder, CO 1988), p. 248.
12 For a discussion of the role of rituals in Iranian politics see Ali Reza Sheikholeslami, "From Religious Accommodation to Religious Revolution: the Transformation of Shi'ism in Iran" in Ali Banuazizi and Myron Weiner (eds), *The State, Religion and Ethnic Politics* (Syracuse University Press, New York, 1986), pp. 227–55. On symbolic use of politics see Charles Elder and Roger Cobb, *The Political Uses of Symbols* (Longman, New York, 1983). See also Murray Edelman, *The Symbolic Uses of Politics* (University of Illinois Press, Urbana, 1964).
13 *Joumhury-e Islami*, Thursday, April 18, 1983.
14 Nader Ebrahimi, *Enqelab-e Ma BehMa cheh dad? Nameh-e Fatemeh, Javab-e Nameh-e Fatemeh.* (What Our Revolution Has Given Us? Fatemeh's Letter, A Response To Fatemeh's Letter), (Negar Publishers, Tehran, 1979), p. 35.
15 *Ibid.*,pp. 35–36.
16 Michael M. J. Fischer, Iran: *From Religious Dispute to Revolution* (Harvard University Press, Cambridge, MA 1980), pp. 61–103.
17 Hooshang Amirahmadi and Manosher Parvin (eds), *Post-revolutionary Iran* (Westview Press, Boulder, CO 1988), p. 237.
18 Setareh Karimi, "Economic Policies and Structural Changes since the Revolution" in Nikkie Keddie and Eric Hooglund (eds), *The Iranian Revolution and the Islamic Republic* (Syracuse University Press, New York, 1986), p. 35.
19 *Ibid.*, p. 36.
20 *Ibid.*, p. 35. Since 1989, the government has initiated policies to change this. This includes allowing a larger role for technocrats and increasing their salaries.
21 Bakhash, *op. cit.*, pp. 178–84.
22 Central Office of Statistics, Iran, *Dar Ayeneh-e Amar*, 1981 as cited by C. Bernard and Z. Khalilzad, *The Government of God: Iran's Islamic Republic* (Columbia University Press, New York, 1984), p. 128.
23 Mahin Milani, "Zaroorat-e Demokracy Baray-e Bazsazy va Towssa'ey-e Eqtesadi" (The Necessity of Democracy for Economic Growth and Reconstruction) a report from the seminar on Economic Reconstruction in *Adineh*, no. 38, November 1989, p. 40.
24 *Adineh, op. cit.*, p. 40.
25 Mehrdad Haqayeqi, "Agrarian Reform Problems in Post-revolutionary Iran," *Middle Eastern Studies*, vol. 26, no. 1 (1990), p. 45.
26 *Ibid.*, pp. 46–8.
27 Hooshang Amirahmadi, "Economic Reconstruction of Iran: Costing the War Damage," *Third World Quarterly*, vol. 12, no. 1 (1990), p. 33.
28 A. Kashian, "Can the Iranian Economy be Saved?" in *Comparative Economic Studies*, vol. 1 (1990), pp. 33–66.

29 *Kayhan*, April 12, 1990, p. 18.
30 *Ibid.*
31 *Kayhan*, April 3, 1990, p. 1.
32 Amirahmadi, *op. cit.*, p. 34. See also Richard Cottam, "Inside Revolutionary Iran," *The Middle East Journal*, vol. 43, no. 2 (1989), pp. 182–3.
33 Amirahmadi, *op. cit.*, pp. 38–9.
34 *Adineh, op. cit.*, p. 41.
35 *Ibid.*
36 Sheikholeslami, *op. cit.*, p. 230.
37 *Ibid.*, p. 299.
38 Hamid Algar (trans.) *Islam and Revolution* (Miza Press, Berkeley, CA 1982), p. 80.

10

POWER POLITICS AND POLITICAL CULTURE

US–Iran relations

Thomas M. Ricks

In early April 1980, the United States officially ended diplomatic relations with Iran; the Iranian embassy on Massachusetts Avenue in Washington, DC, was closed and the Iranian diplomatic personnel departed. Two and a half weeks later, eight US Sea Stallion RH–53D helicopters left the aircraft carrier *Nimitz* lying off the Iranian south-eastern coast and headed toward Iranian airspace to begin a "rescue mission" of the US personnel held hostage in Tehran. A hundred years of diplomatic relations came to an abrupt end, and, for the first time, a US military force had invaded Iran. Now, a decade later, the embassy remains closed and US–Iran relations fluctuate from white-hot hostility to open diplomatic disdain.

In 1970, no knowing commentator suggested, or even thought such a rupture in US–Iran relations possible. Even in 1978, in the midst of massive street demonstrations against the Shah and his US-assisted regime, few observers argued that US–Iran relations were to end by 1980, or that US military forces were to invade Iran. Nonetheless, the diplomatic relations did end and a military expedition did occur.

A series of events based on differing ideologies and political cultures within Iran and the United States hastened the severance of a century of strong relations between the two allies. Iranian aspirations for political and economic independence, and a commitment to political self-awakening, ran counter to the US policies of access to Iranian resources and containment of any radical realignment of Iran's political system. Armed with the Quran and convinced of the justice of a national movement for liberation, Iranians in their millions marched through the towns and cities in open defiance of the US-trained and armed Iranian military forces. Awed by the massiveness of the 1977–9 demonstrations and strikes, international observers began to note the seriousness of the Iranian Revolution.

Following the street demonstrations and revolutionary upheaval in 1977–9 Iran, some commentators pointed to the 1979 final collapse of the Pahlavi monarchy as the watershed in the friendship between the US and Iran. Others marked the beginning of problems in US–Iran relations with the CIA-assisted coup in August 1953 while some pointed to World War Two.[1] Since so few of the specialists anticipated the events of the 1960s and 1970s as the beginning of the revolutionary upheaval, many Americans found the Iran of 1977–9 to be both surprising and incomprehensible. The speed of the disintegration of the Shah's 400,000 US-trained armed forces in 1978 and the massive demonstrations in Iran in 1978–9 caught nearly every specialist and scholar off guard. The American public were flabbergasted and viewed the collapse of the Shah with a mixture of amusement and uncertainty.

The Shah's January 1979 flight from Tehran and the emergence of the provisional government of Iran raised questions in the minds of the American public who preferred that "things get back to normal." The October 1979 admission of the Shah to a New York cancer center and the November 4, 1979 takeover of the US Embassy in Tehran, followed by the collapse of the provisional government, startled Americans even more. The Iran "problem" suddenly appeared more complex and more dangerous than previously thought. US officials at the State Department and the White House seemed to have "lost control" of Iran, a trusted client and lifelong friend. If Iran "fell," then, the American media and public asked, "who was next?" The "Iran Crisis – America Held Hostage" was becoming a long-term problem that angered the American public as deeply as it excited Iranians. Once a close friend and ally of the United States, Iran of 1979 had become the "bandit nation" in the Middle East and an "outlaw" in the world community whose leaders were Muslim, whose ideology was Islamic fundamentalism and whose politics was "terrorism."[2]

Iranians, on the other hand, in the villages, towns or cities differed in analyzing the collapse of US–Iran relations; a difference that depended on their class, ideology and politics. The "Great Satan" label was publicly fixed on the US during the hostage crisis of 1979–81, but Iranian antipathy towards intervention into Iranian affairs *even by an ally* was clear in the 1920s.[3] Focusing on self-reliance and independence from foreign rule, Iranian political culture was gradually transformed from the 1920s to the massive street demonstrations of the 1970s. The January 1979 departure of the Shah from Iran and the November 1979 hostage taking were the fruits of decades of nearly continuous clashes with European, and then US, intervention into Iranian economic, social, political and cultural affairs.

US policies toward the monarchy, in the meantime, changed little from the 1920s to the 1970s. The profound change had been the implementation of the policies. Interested in supporting the monarchy against the popular Constitutional Movement, US policies in the pre-World War One period mirrored the policies of Britain and Russia, showing little inclination towards independent action. By the 1920s, US oil companies and financial firms attempted without success "to carve out" a place for US investment. However, with World War Two, US political and diplomatic maneuvers in Iran reflected US increased concerns in safeguarding investments in the Persian Gulf region particularly ARAMCO's Saudi Arabian oilfields and in controlling the population following the collapse of Reza Shah. Britain's post-World War Two powerlessness in "influencing" Iranian affairs was also of grave concern for Washington officials.

No longer interested in mirroring British and Soviet policies in post-World War Two Iran, US policies were re-evaluated and refocused towards Iran's strategic geo-military and economic position on the borders of the Soviet Union and the rich oilfields of the Persian Gulf. The "Cold War" confrontations between Soviet and US global interests, as well as US intervention in the nationalization of Iranian oil, followed from the reassessment of World War One US policies. The reassessment focused more than ever on the containment of the USSR, access to Iranian and Persian Gulf oil, and the promotion of a "stable" government in Tehran.

Indeed, the World War Two military and economic missions laid the foundations for implementing the revised US policies in

Iran.[4] The need for new tactics arose as much from the increased confrontational nature of the Iranian political culture as from the changes in global power politics. Following the CIA-assisted 1953 coup, the Shah and US foreign policy had become one and the same. By 1977, Iranians were ready to confront both the Pahlavi king and the United States.

This chapter will argue that US policy towards Iran remained remarkably consistent in supporting the monarchy from 1909 to 1979. The dictatorial rule under the Pahlavi kings, Reza Shah (1926–41) and Mohammad Reza Shah (1941–79) gradually necessitated changes in the US tactics in supporting the monarchy. Over the same period of time, however, the Iranian people had increasingly changed their views about the monarchy, the role of foreign powers and themselves. Indeed, it was the emergence of an authentic Iranian political culture first in the 1910s and 1920s, and then in the 1950s through to the 1970s, that "demonized" and cursed the United States long before the terms "Great Satan" or "Death to America" made US evening news headlines.

For the majority of Iranians, then, 1977–79 was a period of national triumph and personal joy; triumph in overthrowing the "invincible" Shah, and joy in realizing old aspirations and new self-confidence.[5] The expressions of hatred both toward the Shah and toward the US arose from the collective Iranian memory of the 1953 CIA-assisted coup and subsequent interventions into Iran's politics, society and economy. Iranians were anti-US in the sense of opposing the widespread and aggressive Americanization of Iran.[6]

Iranians were not anti-American; that is, opposed to the people of the US. The street slogans did not say "Death to Americans" or "Death to American Ideals, the Constitution and Bill of Rights," or "Down with American Middle Class," or "Death to American Workers and Students." Rather, the slogans of "Death to the Shah" and "Death to Carter" focused on persons who represented best the political problems of the past seven decades. President Carter represented all those former US presidents who unconditionally supported a corrupt and venal Pahlavi aristocracy. President Carter represented the CIA, ARMISH–MAAG and USAID that intervened in its internal affairs. President Carter represented the Congressional approval for weapon systems far too expensive even for oilrich Iran. Iranians did not believe that such presidents, agents, advisors or congressmen were the "real representatives" of American idealism, or the successors of the Howard Baskervilles or the Rev. Jordans of the American Presbyterian missions.

The history of friendly US relations with the Shah, the Pahlavi court and the elites was well-known to Americans through *Time* magazine articles and CBS or ABC interviews with the Shah. However, the history of hostile US relations towards the Iranian people was well hidden from the American public who did not work or live in Iran. The popular issues of political, cultural and economic independence, the Iranian struggle for control over its history, and the right to experiment with social and economic growth never entered into the nightly newscasts nor appeared in the US government's briefings. The sense of outrage and deep anger that many Americans levelled against Iran and Iranians said more about the poverty of American understanding than it did about the depth of Iranian anguish and trauma. The depth of that struggle and the intensity of Iranian feelings continues to be understated and misunderstood by most Americans including those in official positions.[7] In explaining the dichotomous relations of the US with the Shah on the one hand, and with the general population on the other, one must remember that Iran had a special function in the eyes of the US policy-makers. Ever since the initial comments of President Franklin D. Roosevelt to his top aide in the midst of the 1943 Tehran Conference concerning the "Iranian experiment", US military, economic and political advisers have played a dominant role in the US–Iranian governmental relations equation.[8] Indeed, the names of H. Norman Schwarzkopf (Gendarmeric Mission Headquarters – GENMISH – 1942), or Clarence S. Ridley (Army Mission Headquarters – ARMISH – 1947), Dr Arthur C. Millspaugh (US financial adviser, 1942–4), Max Weston Thornburg (oil executive, US State Department adviser and overseas consultant executive, 1944–9) or Torkild Rieber (oil company executive, World Bank petroleum adviser and General Zahedi adviser, 1951–5) dot the pages of Iran's "development plans" and contemporary Iranian history without the proper credit given to their continuous tinkering with the economic, social and political institutions of Iran.[9]

Unknown to the Iranian people, Iran had been designated a major showcase country for US foreign policy and international relations (between 1942–79). On the other hand, unknown to many US officials or citizens, many Iranians were deeply committed to national independence and cultural freedom. World War Two and the parliament's April 1951 Nationalization Bill struck once more a responsive cord among an even greater number of Iranians. Nearly every outside power including the Soviet Union underestimated the importance of the 1951 legislative bill. While the US saw it primarily as an attack on US and European "global interests," the Bill was concrete evidence for Iranians that *they could change their conditions and achieve their national aspirations on their own*. The Nationalization Bill of 1951 demonstrated the power of street politics to the population.

The purpose of this chapter is to show the steady erosion of the image of the US as a supporter of the Iranian majority and its aspirations for self-determination, and the eventual collapse of pro-US support among Iranian people. The 1910s' "beatification" of the United States and its citizens stands in sharp contrast to the 1980s' "demonization" of US policies and the widespread suspicion of US intentions. For Iranians, the benevolent US image was replaced over time by the image of a malevolent US for three reasons: (1) a century of unflagging support for the monarchy in the teeth of growing popular hostility to Pahlavi venality; (2) a deep suspicion of and, at times, an hostility to Iranian political culture; and (3) a century-long commitment to US "strategic global interests," increasingly in opposition to the Iranian majority's interests. Such policies and interventions by the US contributed to the formation of an anti-US political culture in Iran.

The first noticeable changes in US–Iran relations were in 1907–9 when US personnel in Tabriz and Tehran were instructed to support the monarchy rather than the constitutionalists in the battle for "equal justice under law". The second noticeable change occurred in 1951–3 when the US decided once more to support the monarchy rather than the nationalists in the battle for "Iran for Iranians."[10] By 1962, Mohammad Reza Pahlavi had defeated the National Front and Tudeh Party, purged the parliament and military, and launched the Land Reform Bill. The Shah's February 1963 "White

Revolution" climaxed the 1953–63 US–Shah reforms. However, the June 1963 uprising and subsequent guerrilla movements bloodied the "White Revolution" and indicated that the US-assisted reforms and the Iranian people were on a collision course. The third noticeable change occurred during the 1977–9 Revolution culminating in the seizure of the US Embassy in November 1979. The early relationship between the two governments and peoples, however, started quietly enough.

CONSTITUTIONALISM, TABRIZ AND THE BASKERVILLE AFFAIR, 1907–9

In 1883, the first American resident arrived in Tehran with little more instruction than to abide by the existing protocol, present his credentials and support the Qajar government.[11] In the last decades of the nineteenth century, the resident became increasingly interested in trade activities between the US and Iran, particularly trade in fruits and cash crops. No attempt was made to interfere in the British–Russian rivalry or to assist Iran in any modernization program.

A change came in 1907 at the outset of the Constitutional Movement. The American resident in Tehran requested that a consul be stationed in the north-west province of Azerbaijan in the city of Tabriz in order to insure improved information about the directions of the Constitutional Movement, the involvement of the Azeri emigrés from the oilfields and town of Baku, and the well-being of the rather large American Presbyterian missionary community in Tabriz and Urmieh.[12] The request indicated a new concern for the politics of the country and the role of Americans in Iran.

In the spring of 1907, William Doty arrived in Tabriz as the first American Consul to that city. At that time, Tabriz was run by two very different governments. On the one hand, the Qajar king in Tehran had appointed a governor-general [beglerbegi] to coordinate revenue collection, and to maintain law and order. On the other hand, a popular committee or anjoman comprised of merchants, shopkeepers and professionals had assumed command of the local militia, asserted control over the revenue-collection process and handed out judicial decisions wherever appropriate.

Mr Doty's arrival did little to affect the internal struggle between the king-appointed governor-general and the people-appointed *anjoman*. The dichotomy did cause problems for Doty when he found it necessary to address one or the other on official business. In June 1907, Doty was reprimanded by the Tehran resident and Washington's Department of State for taking a personal matter directly to the *anjoman* and not to the governor-general. Doty had gone to the *anjoman* to free the consulate's servant, Ali, who had been beaten and then arrested by the *anjoman* guards for apparently cutting into a bread line, and insulting a woman and Islam.[13] The governor-general could do little to ameliorate the situation whereas the *anjoman* was directly in charge of local affairs. Doty asked the *anjoman* to apologize for the attack and the arrest which the *anjoman* refused to do so. Soon after, Ali was released without apology.

Doty was to find a greater problem with the American missionaries in Tabriz and Urmieh than with the *anjoman*. In that same year, a young Princeton graduate named Howard C. Baskerville had arrived in Tabriz as a specially employed teacher for the Boys' Memorial School operated by American Presbyterian Missions under the leadership of Rev. Samuel G. Wilson. Baskerville's arrival in the midst of the Constitutional Movement proved to be momentous for him, the Presbyterian missionaries and for the American consul. Indeed, Baskerville's subsequent actions and death at the hands of the Shah's troops greatly complicated affairs not only for Doty but also for the entire Presbyterian community in Tabriz and in Urmieh.[14]

The events of the Constitutional Period continued to disrupt the function of the School, however. In June 1908, Mohammad Shah Qajar ordered the bombing of the parliament building while the delegates were in session. From the Fall of 1908 to January 1909, the city of Tabriz came under siege by the Shah's army. As the months passed, fewer grains or fruits entered the city while the mail and telegraph lines were regularly intercepted. By February 1909, Tabriz was suffering near-starvation and the population began to despair.[15]

Baskerville was very much impressed by the historical events unfolding both within Tabriz and in Iran. From February to March, Baskerville and Arthur Moore, a British journalist, began to help drill the foot soldiers of Sattar Khan, the commander of the Tabriz nationalist forces. Soon, Baskerville realized that he could not continue his teaching duties at the

Boys' Memorial School and participate in the Constitutionalist struggle at the time. On March 30, 1909, he sat down and wrote two letters resigning from his teaching position citing the need to assist the revolutionary forces of Sattar Khan in breaking the siege of the city. One letter went to Rev. Wilson, his superior, and the other to Mr William Doty, the US consul. Wilson wrote the same day to discourage Baskerville from his decision, noting the physical dangers involved, while Doty telegraphed the US embassy in Tehran.[16]

Baskerville replied to Wilson's entreaties with a firm answer the following day, repeating his intentions in joining and assisting the forces of Sattar Khan. Three days later, Doty rode out to the military parade grounds in search of Baskerville, found him and urged him personally to reconsider his decision or, at least, surrender his passport. To the amusement of Sattar Khan and the other officers, Baskerville politely refused to cooperate and asked Doty to be on his way.[17]

By April 1909, Doty's telegrams to Tehran and to Washington, DC, concerning Baskerville were angry comments on the young American's behavior and solicitious for advice as to how to handle the errant citizen. One event was particularly galling to Doty. He related to Washington how Baskerville had asked and then used Doty's encyclopedias and other books from the consul library. Only in late March did Doty realize that Baskerville was getting information from the consul library on how to improve the infantry charges, to make bombs and to use field artillery more effectively.[18]

In the early hours of April 20, 1909, Baskerville and a handful of his Memorial School students made their way to the city limits, seeking a way through the siege lines. The Shah's troops spied the small column and opened fire, fatally wounding Baskerville in the chest. He died ten minutes later in the arms of one of his former students.

The evening wake over the next two days in the Presbyterian chapel was revealing. Several hundred people came to pay their respects to the missionaries and to Baskerville. On the third day, the funeral cortege of several thousand Tabrizis including members of the *anjoman*, the military offices, Sattar Khan, Tabriz dignitaries and revolutionary guards marched from the Memorial School through Tabriz to the Mission grounds where Baskerville was buried. The leaders of the Tabriz *anjoman*, the military leaders including Sattar Khan, heads of the Tabriz guilds and societies, and the students from the Memorial School were present. Fiery speeches about liberty, revolution and constitutionalism were made, songs broke out among the workers and students, and solemn addresses were made by Sattar Khan and Rev. Samuel Wilson.

The April 20, 1909, death of Baskerville exacerbated the already-existing division within the American missionaries; some supported the Constitution and the rights of the National Assembly while others supported the Shah and the rights of the landed nobility. Missionary letters hinted that the rift never completely healed between those missionaries in the "professions" of medicine and education versus those in evangelical work; the former favored the *anjoman* and increased local independent rule while the latter supported the *monarchy* and the existing patronage of the landlords.[19]

In 1958, some Iranians decided to organize a fiftieth anniversary of Baskerville's death. When the US consul from Tabriz requested information on Baskerville from Princeton, little assistance was, strangely enough, forthcoming. The US ambassador, however, did attend the April 20, 1959, memorial ceremony in Tabriz and the Boys' Memorial School was renamed the Howard C. Baskerville School.[20]

OIL, POWER POLITICS AND POLITICAL CULTURE, 1951-3

The 1951-3 period was a turning point in US–Iran relations. Prior to the 1951 nationalization of the Abadan oilfields and the emergence of the Mossadeq nationalist government, the United States was viewed as a reliable post-colonial ally by the Shah and landed nobility, and as a powerful influence in the Pahlavi court by the intermediate and lower classes. Indeed, the United States' credibility rested on a hundred years of missionary medical and educational work, particularly the memory of Howard C. Baskerville's sacrifice and the work of Rev. Jordan at Tehran's Alborz College. The introduction of the 1942 military and financial advisory teams was viewed as war-time activities by the Iranians and did little to tarnish the image of a fair-minded and powerful friend. The CIA-assisted coup of August 1953, however, altered drastically the image of the US in the minds and hearts of the majority of Iranian people. The 1909 death of Baskerville and the activities of the Tabriz consul supported the popular belief that US foreign policy did not represent the views of US citizens. The 1953 CIA-assisted coup convinced the intermediate Iranian classes that the US was indeed hostile to Iranian nationalist aspirations, and that not all Americans were Baskervilles. Indeed, the coup was Iran's second twentieth-century awakening to the problems of power politics with "superpowers."[21]

At the outset of the nationalization "crisis" in 1948–51, Britain and the Iranian parliament began to discuss the oil concession. The US took a "neutral" position and, in time, both sides turned to the US to resolve the conflict. For the US, access to the oil of the region and containment of the USSR from the region were the twin pillars of US foreign policy. The "pillars" rested upon the 1947 decisions of the Truman administration to expand US access to the oil-producing regions of the Middle East and to contain at all cost any possible Soviet attempts to influence or to move into the Middle East.[22] The addition of Iran to the 1947 Truman doctrine reaffirmed the US intentions to "protect" Iran as well as to "invest" in Iran.

By 1951, however, the negotiations between the Mossadeq Committee and the Anglo-Iranian Oil Company were not going well. At the end of April 1951, the Nationalization Bill had been unanimously approved by the Iranian parliament and Mossadeq was Iran's "man of the hour." US Embassy officials expressed grave concerns to Washington and suggested that a high-level "neutral" American negotiator be sought to assist in avoiding the collision course. Mr Averell Harriman was the man whom Washington asked to go to Tehran in July 1951 and negotiate a settlement.

The Harriman period proved critical in determining the direction of US policy. There were three policies that the US might have supported in 1951: (1) Mossadeq's policy of "negative equilibrium"; (2) Britain's policy of compensation; or (3) a policy of increased US economic and political involvement in Iran's affairs, and a shaping of a "new Iran." In 1951, Mossadeq's policy only favored Iran while Britain's "concessions" and policies were unacceptable to the nationalist position, to Mossadeq and to the nationalist parliament. While US policy-makers in 1951 ostensibly hesitated to support intervention, US policy in 1952 favored increased involvement in order to offset any Soviet intrusion and to "stabilize" the monarchy. By 1953, three events had hurried US policy towards increased economic and military intervention into Iranian affairs: (1) the failure of the Harriman mission and breakdown of the oil negotiations; (2) the replacement of Ambassador Henry Grady with Ambassador Loy Henderson; and (3) the ending of British diplomatic ties with Iran.

Mossadeq and the parliament were entirely opposed to the oil concession and intent on a confrontation with Britain. Between July and September 1951, Harriman attempted to restore negotiable positions for both sides but failed. In the midst of Britain's 1951 boycott of Iran oil, freezing of all Iranian sterling bloc assets, the arrival of the "biggest British flotilla" in the Persian Gulf since World War Two and a lawsuit against Iran's nationalization in the International Court at the Hague, Mossadeq traveled to the Hague, visited Washington, and sought out world allies in Europe and Asia. During Ambassador Loy Henderson's tenure beginning in September of 1951, the US began to abandon the pretenses of "neutrality" and, by November 1952, had turned to ways of removing Mossadeq.[23] By June 1953, the US had devised "Operation Ajax" in consultation with Britain. In August 1953, several of the key US intelligence teams were in Tehran to begin the coup operation.

The success of the political–psychological CIA team's efforts on August 19 in the aftermath of the unsuccessful August 16 military option is well-known. However, the subsequent heated arguments between certain CIA officials and Ambassador Henderson concerning the various measures to be taken following the August CIA-assisted coup are not as well-known.[24]

Essentially, several CIA officials argued for leniency in purging the parliament and military in the hope of preserving some semblance of the nationalist leadership within the government. The argument rested on the belief that with the removal of Mossadeq and his closest colleagues, neither the popular support for a deposed Mossadeq nor the historical aspirations for self-determination among Iranians posed any foreseeable threat to the US or to the monarchy. Ambassador Henderson's position was that all semblance of monarchical opposition must be clearly removed particularly from the parliament and from the military before the US can invest in Iran either by way of the oil companies or increased military-security assistance. In keeping with other State Department officials, the ambassador felt that in the long run, nationalism and especially Mossadeq's avowed "neutralism" ran counter to US economic and military interests.[25]

Certain CIA officials, on the other hand, saw only greater problems in any extensive repression of the nationalist movement. Indeed, the officials argued, the US will only "beatify" the opposition to the Shah and lay the foundations for greater problems in the future if the planned purges of the parliament and military were enacted.[26] The ambassador's argument was accepted by Washington and the CIA officials were sent to other areas of the Middle East.

The post-1953 coup debate in Tehran and in Washington is very instructive. With the benefit of hindsight, it is clearer today than in 1953 that the "limited option" of restricting the purges was the wiser course of action. In the context of the 1950s, the aftermath of the Korean War, the heating up of the "Cold War" and McCarthyism, it is understandable how the decision was reached to carry out extensive purges by way of beginning the "US era" in Iran, so deeply felt were the anti-Communist sentiments in upper US diplomatic circles. Between 1953 and 1955, General Fazlollah Zahedi, upon whom the CIA relied so heavily in carrying out the coup, assumed full political and military control of Iran. He placed a number of cities under continuous curfew, reorganized the military, carried out extensive purges of the parliament and military, and laid the foundations for the 1957 State Information and Security Organization, or SAVAK.

During the same period, in September 1954, four major US oil companies and a number of smaller concerns signed an agreement with Britain and the restored monarchy. The 1954 agreement reorganized Mossadeq's National Iranian Oil Company allowing the return of Britain as British Petroleum and the entrance of a number of US oil corportions into the Abadan oilfields. The agreement was a conclusion to the oil initiatives of the 1920s and the beginnings of the "US era" in Iran.[27]

Mossadeq and the National Front were the immediate casualties of the 1953 coup and the 1954 oil agreement. In the long run, however, many of the leading members of the Iranian population, including many writers, educators, military officers and bureaucrats, were the victims of the coup, Henderson's decision and Zahedi's practices. Either classified as "nationalist" or as "socialist," the Iranians most active during the 1942–53 period were arrested in hundreds, tried, sentenced and, in a number of cases, executed. However, the Zahedi "iron hand policy" during 1953–55 did little to alter Iran's political culture. Indeed, like the 1930s and the period of Reza Shah's dictatorship, the Zahedi period forced groups to realign themselves and to redefine their tactics to achieve the goals of self-reliance and independence. The more radical concept of revolution began to be heard and discussed seriously. The monarchy had to be overthrown and, along with it, US power politics.

For the Iranian population and for the US policy makers, the decision was a reaffirmation of the earlier Baskerville case – in choosing between support for the Shah or support for the parliament (*Majles*), Washington chose the Shah. The qualitative differences in US–Iran relations in 1909 and in 1953 were the introduction of two new factors in US power politics: (1) a vigorous anti-communist campaign (containment of the Soviet Union and radical forces within Iran); and (2) oil politics (access to the oilfields of Iran and the Persian Gulf). Neither issue was present in 1909 while both questions were squarely before US policy makers in 1953. While the US decision to support the Shah in 1909 was essentially a political decision, the US policies of 1953–5 were essentially economic and military ones.

For the activist Iranians, the 1950s was a time of reorganizing themselves in face of the dramatic intervention by the US into nearly every phase of Iranian life. Iran's political culture had adjusted to the setbacks of World War One and then to the parliamentary revival of World War Two. Following the 1953 coup and the Zahedi "interregnum," the dissident Iranian political culture as reflected both in Iranian literature and arts, and in Iranian political movements, began to focus on: (1) the need to overthrow the monarchy; (2) a thorough assessment of the strengths and weaknesses of US policies towards Iran and the Third World; and (3) reassessment of political activism in Iran. Underground or "little" journals began to appear during the late 1950s while the Iranian students in Europe and in the United States reorganized their associations and cultural clubs.

Evidence of rural activism among the peasantry and new urban underground groups appeared in local and national newspaper reports. The creation of SAVAK in 1957, the reorganization of the US military advisers groups into one unit, or ARMISH-MAAG (Army Mission Headquarters–Military Assistance Advisory Group) in 1958, and the 1959 mutual assistance treaty between the US and Iran were each in part a response to the new directions of the Iranian opposition and the changes in dissident Iranian political culture.

Before addressing the present US–Islamic Republic relations, however, it is necessary to examine the critical years of 1979 to 1981; that is, the years from the final collapse of the Shah to the final establishment of the Islamic Republic. In doing so, a third phase in the development of Iranian political culture will be seen.

IRAN'S REVOLUTION: FROM MONARCHY TO ISLAMIC REPUBLIC, 1979–81

For the third time in the twentieth century, Iranians moved to the streets to demonstrate their intentions to have an independent Iranian government. The Shah's relations with the Iranian population collapsed and disintegrated in the aftermath of monthly, then weekly and daily, and finally, hourly opposition to the Shah, his family and court, and to the Henderson decision of 1953. General Huyser himself was asked in January 1979 to direct military responses to the gathering political maelstrom outside the walls of the supreme commander's headquarters in the middle of Tehran.[28]

On January 16, 1979, Mohammed Reza Shah Pahlavi and his family left Iran, and, with that departure, the monarchy ended. On February 1, 1979, Ayatollah Khomeini arrived in Iran to begin the Islamic Republic. *Shah raft, Imam amad* or "The Shah Went, the Imam Came" were words on nearly every Iranian street walls. The US policy makers and the White House responded in contradictory ways to the emergence of the Islamic Republic; first, there was muffled approval, but then loud dismay.

For two years prior to 1979, Iranians had increasingly demonstrated skill and determination to push the politics of the mosque and street into the Pahlavi throne-room and onto US

Ambassador Sullivan's desk. No image better captured the triumph of two years of demonstrations and confrontations than the Shah's international meanderings. The January 16, 1979, departure of the Shah from Tehran began an odyssey of misery and humiliation for the Pahlavis. Accustomed to decades of nobility status and royal hospitality in world capitals, the Pahlavis hopped from country to country begging for permanent asylum. The State Department vacillated from affirming and then denying permission to the Shah to enter the United States. Part of the indecision was based on the continuous reports from the US Embassy in Tehran of attempts to seize its personnel and buildings on tree-lined *Takht-e Jamshid* Boulevard in exchange for the return of the Shah.

The Shah's US corporate friends, however, were determined to have their way and end the Pahlavi ostracism. The Shah had become the center of a political and economic tug-of-war unprecedented in US–Iran relations. The State Department diplomats cautioned against any favoritism towards the Shah due to Iran's memory of 1953, while the powerful friends of the Shah in US corporate banking and industry demanded an immediate end to the monarch's humiliating peregrinations. The Carter White House advisers, normally indecisive in previous critical junctions in US–Shah relations, came down on the side of the monarch's corporate supporters and friends.[29] The Shah was to be allowed entry into the US for "humanitarian reasons". By September 1979, the unresolved question was not if but when the Shah would arrive in New York.

In January 1979, therefore, the White House ordered General Huyser, Deputy Commander of NATO forces in Europe, to go to Iran and attempt to accomplish three missions: (1) assess the military and strategic strengths and weaknesses of Iran; (2) preserve the military command at all costs by getting their support for Bakhtiyar and preventing any attempts to carry out a coup; and (3) assess the changing economic and political situation with particular interest in the oilfields.[30]

The Huyser Mission generally succeeded in accomplishing all three objectives including the prevention of a military coup.[31] By February 1979, the US position was "to wait and see" the new directions of Iran's emerging leaders. Following the February 9–11, 1979, clashes between the Air Force cadets and the

Imperial Guards, Shahpour Bakhtiyar fled to Paris with US assistance and the Provisional Government of Iran (PGOI), under Mehdi Bazargan as Prime Minister and Ibrahim Yazdi as Foreign Minister, got under way. By April, Iranians had voted for the establishment of an Islamic Republic, a new flag was devised, and plans were begun to adopt a new constitution. From all appearances, the mass-based Iranian Revolution was moving ahead with little delay.

From February to November 1979, the dual rule of the Islamic Revolutionary Council and the Nationalist Provisional Government was increasingly becoming the single-party rule of the Council. The repeated requests to the US Embassy by Bazargan and Yazdi for a resolution of US–Iran loan agreements and arms purchases confused some US officials who felt that the Provisional Government might be better off trying to run the country rather than closing bank accounts and buying arms.[32] Upon reflection, however, it was clear that Bazargan and Yazdi were attempting to recover their "lost" financial and military clout allowing them to keep the Council at bay.

The Revolutionary Council, on the other hand, set about to increase its own power base through expanding its control over local committees, or komitehs, through organized street gangs or hezbollahis, and the establishment of a national militia or pasdaran. The increasing success of the Council throttled the Bazargan–Yazdi government while Ayatollah Khomeini's continued public intervention in national affairs, such as his denunciation of a number of leftist newspapers and organizations in August 1979, and his advocacy of an anti-Kurdish campaign in September 1979, added to the PGOI's woes. Indeed, the combination of Khomeini's verbal "correctives" and the Revolutionary Council's ground-level activism tied both hands of the Provisional Government thereby leaving the PGOI open to charges of "vacillation", "indecisiveness" and even dealings with the CIA; the latter charges were later proven to be accurate.[33]

By November 1989, therefore, increasing popular demands for clear governmental directives, or "revolutionary action" and an end to the PGOI's vacillations came as no surprise. The "political deck" was stacked against the liberal, nationalist coalition of Bazargan and Yazdi. It was becoming increasingly clear to many observers that the PGOI was doomed to failure. Following the recommendations of the Huyser Mission, the official position of the US was to support the PGOI while its actual position was "to wait and see" which direction the internal political struggles took: a direction towards liberal, secular constitutionalism or a direction towards conservative, religious chauvinism. The US did not have to wait long for an answer.

In late October 1979, Henry Precht, the State Department Director of the Iran Desk, arrived in the evening to deliver the bad news to Bazargan and Yazdi. The US had decided to allow the Shah to enter the United States for humanitarian reasons; his health was failing and the US was offering him expert medical care that he could not receive during his stay in Mexico. Precht asked that the PGOI provide adequate protection to all US embassy personnel in the event of a hostage-taking attempt.[34]

Bazargan and Yazdi could not believe their ears. Not only did they have continued difficulties from the Council and Khomeini but now they faced a potentially dangerous national crisis through an action by their strongest ally. Both men questioned Precht thoroughly on the reasons for the Shah's admittance into the US and the request for embassy protection. They both assured Precht that the PGOI was no longer in control of the streets or the local committees. Indeed, they refused to give Precht any assurance that the US embassy would be safe from a hostile attack.[35] Having given the PGOI the message, Precht returned to the United States and the November 4–6 events unfolded as if on schedule – the Shah arrived in the US in October, the US embassy was taken on November 4 and the provisional government of Iran collapsed on November 6.

For the next 444 days, US–Iran relations centered primarily on the "hostage crisis." The attention of the media was intense and ABC launched a special evening program ("Nightline") to cover the event.[36] The State Department maintained constant contact with the families of the hostages, brought them occasionally to Washington, DC, for briefings, offered psychological assistance and arranged their press conferences.[37] No Greater Love, a Washington-based, private and non-profit organization, sponsored special events for the families, and the United Methodist Church organized letter exchanges between the hostages and their loved ones in the US.

The widespread reaction to the hostage-taking, Iranian "terrorism" and the US responses was unprecedented in contemporary US history. At no time since the bombing of Pearl Harbor had the American public responded so quickly or so intensely to an international crisis. Indeed, commentators drew parallels between December 7, 1941, and November 4, 1979, including the suggestions for massive roundups of Iranian citizens for incarceration in the former Japanese–American detention camps, the bodily attacks on Iranian–Americans, the stoning of Iranian homes, slashing of their automobile tires and occasionally hinted deportation orders for all peoples of Iranian background. Some even suggested a US hostage-taking raid on Iran. The atmosphere of nearly blind hatred for anything Islamic or Iranian began to approach the levels of the anti-Japanese campaign of the early 1940s.

Therefore, after five months of unsuccessful negotiations for the release of the hostages, the Carter administration decided to send a tactical commando force to Tehran "to rescue our American prisoners." The public reaction was quite positive. The military option for the US was frequently discussed, although the State Department consistently cautioned against such actions, preferring diplomatic solutions to the political problem of hostage-taking. However, when the news of the April 22, 1980 disaster of burning helicopters and a transport in "Desert One" became known to Americans, President Carter's public support dropped rapidly. The President's hopes for another election were buried in Iran's *Dasht-e Kavir* as the hostage crisis continued.

US relations with Iran ceased on April 7, 1980. Privately, however, US emissaries including intelligence agents were in contact with the newly-elected President Bani-Sadr and the American-educated Foreign Minister, Sadeq Qotbzadeh. From April to November, the US maintained contact with various representatives of the Islamic Republic through intermediaries. By November, due to the September 20, 1980, Iraqi invasion of Khuzestan Province and to mounting public discontent over unresolved problems of poverty, homelessness and unemployment, Ayatollah Khomeini approved further discussions with the Algerians on a possible exchange of hostages for Iranian foreign reserves in Britain and the United States. By January 1981, most of the differences of perspective had been worked out. Within minutes of President Reagan's inauguration, the fifty-three US hostages were on their way out of Iranian airspace. Carter had paid for "his sins" and Iran had hopes of regaining most of its frozen assets and undelivered arms. In the end, the economic and political, not the military, card proved to be the key to the hostage resolution.

Iran's problems did not end with the hostage issue. Domestically, increasing dismay with the Islamic Republic's inabilities to resolve fundamental human rights issues created several incidents of destabilization and anti-Khomeini demonstrations. From March to June, 1981, the Mojahedeen-e Khalq movement of 15–30-year-olds from Iran's lower and middle classes increasingly appealed to the urban public to demonstrate against the Republic and against Khomeini.[38] Again, the US position proved to be accurate in waiting to see who would emerge as Iran's long-term leaders. Sensing that the collapse of the Mehdi Bazargan–Ibrahim Yazdi government was not the last time that a liberal coalition would founder on the shores of Khomeini's Islamic Republic, the US decision to bide its time following the nearly unanimous election of Bani-Sadr proved wise. By June 1981, the US hostages had been returned, Iran's money and purchased arms were still in US hands and Khomeini had successfully cleared the political arena of all opposition. The US looked forward to some political stability within Iran while waiting for the increasingly volatile Iraq–Iran War to run its course.

From 1981 to 1989, US–Iran relations focused on four issues: (1) Iran's continued efforts to end the "Pahlavi period" by way of returning all Iranian foreign assets and purchased arms to Iran; (2) Iran's determination to seek a dominant role within the region particularly as a model to other Islamic states; (3) the US interest in containing radical movements within Middle East countries while continuing to gain access to Persian Gulf oil; and (4) the US interest in arming and aiding militarily any country willing to promote US economic and political interests in opposition to the interests of the USSR.

The ideological commitment of Iran's leadership to Islamic politics as well as to capitalist development placed the US in a curious position of opposing Iran's foreign policies but supporting its domestic programs. The former position required the US to maintain a high profile in opposing "Iranian terrorism" and the spread of popular Islamic militia, or *hezbollahis*, throughout the Middle East. While knowing Iraq's role in the origins of the Iraq–Iran war as well as Iraqi attacks on Gulf shipping including the USS Stark, the US nonetheless supported Iraq and opposed Iran in the land and sea wars of the Zagros Mountains and Persian Gulf. The latter position found the US supporting Iran's land reform attempts, the industrialization projects and the vicious suppression of the Left including the Mojahedeen-backed National Resistance Council and its conventional military forces.

The power politics in US–Iran relations rested upon Iran's abilities to maintain economic and political stability while supporting its allies within the region and beyond. Iranian determination to "teach other nations a lesson" appeared to be unquenchable, particularly towards Saudi Arabia, Jordan and Iraq. Iranian official interest in the Palestinian issue remained opportunistic although popular Iranian interest in the "Palestinian Question" is genuine and supportive. Finally, Iran truly sought to become more intimately involved in the Islamic Arab, African and Asian world than ever before, pursuing closer ties with regimes such as Syria, Libya, Yemen and Algeria, or Pakistan, Malaysia and Indonesia.

From 1981 to 1989, the US sought to contain the Islamic Revolution by a number of methods; by supporting Iraq in the Iran–Iraq war, by confronting Iran in the United Nations with evidence of human rights violations, by delaying the transfer of funds and purchased arms, and by characterizing all regional Iranian activities as "terrorist". On the other hand, the US realized that Iran remains potentially radical and revolutionary. Iran had overthrown the Shah and successfully challenged the US–NATO presence throughout the Middle East. Iran remained, therefore, both a potential ally in resolving regional conflicts and disputes (Syria's presence in Lebanon and *hezbollahi* hostage-taking) and a potential enemy in destabilizing the closest allies of the US (Jordan and Saudi Arabia).

CONCLUSION

The century-long relations between the US and Iran had begun with the image of a benevolent and "friendly" US, but had ended with the image of a malevolent and "satanic" power. The former image is the image that most Americans have of themselves and of US foreign policies which they are convinced are sensitive, fair-minded and informed. For Iranians, however, the latter image is most appropriate since US policies, they argue, are fundamentally insensitive, impartial and grossly uninformed. The application of "the Great Satan" label to the United States is most painful for Americans who cannot believe that their government or citizenry deserves such a despicable sobriquet. Iranians, on the other hand, find the label most appropriate in that Iran has found past US policies to be generally deceitful, deceptive and self-centered.

The historical development of Iranian political culture and the resulting ideological commitments to self-determination over the past eighty years from 1905 to 1989 has consistently confronted US interests and power politics. Indeed, the Iranian Revolution of 1977–9 represents the most radical phase in the development of Iran's political culture, both in partial fulfillment of populist aspirations for political independence and in its defense of Iran's Islamic heritage. At the root of the century-long confrontation with the US power politics are three factors: (1) the Iranian demand for *self-control* and *self-definition* which both rejects the "new Iran" image that the US had attempted to create and is a statement of self-reliance that confounds any need for the US; (2) the Iranian desire to be independent nationally coincides with the desire to be independent internationally whereby Iran may be *either* East *or* West, *both* East and West, or *neither* East nor West whether the US likes it or not; and (3) the Iranian conviction that as a "struggling Islamic people," Iran has an obligation to participate in regional and international Islamic affairs including the defense of Islam, Islamic ideals and peoples.

For some US policy makers, all three points remain the greatest obstacles to improved US–Iran relations. For others, while Iran remains potentially explosive, it is also potentially a very important ally in the Middle East and in the Islamic World. In pointing out the positive aspects of past US–Iran relations, the latter group argue that patience and time will create the correct atmosphere for improved US–Iran relations. Indeed, the latter group is quick to point out that the US needs Iran today more as an ally than ever before. In either case, Iran and the Islamic Republic will continue to be a critical factor in US–Middle East relations. Whether sensitivity to Iran's radical political culture, fair-handed dealings with Iranian officials, or the development of informed relationships with Iranian people occur, Americans have been deeply hurt by the Iranian Revolution and the image of the "Great Satan." Like Vietnam, Iran is a watershed in US international relations and will remain a very sore reminder of the problems of power politics with other nations.

Notes

1 For the Shah's collapse and its impact on US–Iran relations, see Gholam R. Afkhami, *The Iranian Revolution: Thanatos on a National Scale* (Middle East Institute, Washington DC, 1985); Robert E. Huyser, *Mission to Tehran* (Andre Deutsch, London, 1986); Amin Saikal, *The Rise and Fall of the Shah* (Princeton University Press, Princeton NJ, 1980); Gary Sick, *All Fall Down: America's Tragic Encounter with Iran* (Random House, New York, 1985); and Sepehr Zabih, *Iran's Revolutionary Upheaval: An Interpretative Essay* (Alchemy Books, San Francisco, 1979). For the Mossadeq period, the nationalization of Iranian oil and the August 1953 coup, see Ervand Abrahamian, *Iran Between Two Revolutions* (Princeton University Press, Princeton NJ, 1982); James A. Bill, *The Eagle and the Lion: the Tragedy of American–Iranian Relations* (Yale University Press, New Haven CT, 1988); Richard W. Cottam, *Iran and the United States: A Cold War Case Study* (University of Pittsburgh Press, Pittsburgh PA, 1988); Fred Halliday, *Iran: Dictatorship and Development* (Penguin Press, New York, 1979) Nikki R. Keddie with Yann Richard, *Roots of Revolution: An Interpretative History of Modern Iran* (Yale University Press, New Haven CT, 1981); and R. K. Ramazani, *The United States and Iran: The Patterns of Influence* (Praeger Publishers, New York, 1982).

2 See William A. Dorman and Mansour Farhang, *The US Press and Iran: Foreign Policy and the Journalism of Defence* (University of California Press, Berkeley CA, 1987) for an excellent analysis of the media coverage of the 1977–9 events.

3 In the midst of World War One, the Iranian poet, Mohammad Reza Eshqi (1893–1924), wrote: "See the impudence – there is a tumult raging in the West: One says 'Iran is mine,' the other says 'It's mine' ", quoted from Munibur Rahman, *Post-Revolution Persian Verse* (University of Aligarh Press, Aligarh, India, 1955), p. 67. For Iranian writers and Iran's twentieth-century political culture, see

Thomas M. Ricks, "Iran: Contemporary Persian Literature," *The Literary Review*, vol. 18, no. 1, Special Issue (Fall, 1974) and Thomas M. Ricks (ed.), *Critical Perspectives on Modern Persian Literature* (Three Continents Press, Washington, DC, 1984). In addition, the 1924 murder of Robert Imbrie in Tehran was but one example of Iran's changing political culture and growing hostility to foreign intervention – see Michael P. Zirinsky, "Blood, Power and Hypocrisy: The Murder of Robert Imbrie and American Relations with Pahlavi Iran," *International Journal of Middle East Studies*, vol. 18, no. 3 (August 1986), pp. 275–92.

4 See Thomas M. Ricks, "US Military Missions to Iran: The Political Economy of Military Assistance, 1942-1979," in *US and Liberation in the Gulf*, edited by Leila Meo (Arab–American University Graduates Press, Belmont MA, 1980), pp. 60–90 and Stephen L. McFarland, "Anatomy of an Iranian Political Crowd: The Tehran Bread Riot of December 1942," *International Journal of Middle East Studies*, vol. 17, no. 1 (February 1985), pp. 51–65 where the author concludes that "the United States after December 1942 began to pursue a foreign policy in Iran increasingly independent of Great Britain" (p. 61).

5 See David H. Albert, ed., *Tell the American People*, (Movement for a New Society, Philadelphia, 1980) and the issues of *RIPEH/Review of Iranian Political Economy & History*, vols 3 and 4 (1979–80).

6 See Jalal Al-e Ahmad, *Gharbzadegi [Westamination]*, (n.p., Tehran, 1961) which addresses the processes and results of the "moderniza-tion" or, to use Al-e Ahmad's term, "Westamination" of Iran. Al-e Ahmad likens the process of modernization to an apparently healthy wheat kernel that is nonetheless hollowed out and empty inside as a result of the contracted disease. See Brad Larson, "The 'Westoxication' of Iran: Depictions and Reactions of Behrangi, Al-e Ahmad and Shariati", *International Journal of Middle East Studies*, vol. 15, no. 1 (February, 1983), pp. 1–23.

7 See Bill, *Eagle*, p. 314 where the author appropriately notes that "The tragedy of America and Iran is that each side – the large numbers of Iranians committed to the Islamic Republic and most patriotic Americans – has failed to understand the other's point of view. Meanwhile, the governments of both countries develop their foreign policy in an atmosphere of paranoia, hatred, ignorance, and emotion."

8 Following the 1943 Tehran Conference, President Roosevelt had remarked to Major General Patrick J. Hurley that "I was rather thrilled with the idea of using Iran as an example of what we could do by an unselfish American policy." Dr Millspaugh, Director of the US Financial Mission to Iran, supported the President's "vision" when he observed that "Iran, because of its situation, its problems and its friendly feeling toward the United States, is (or can be made) something in the nature of a clinic – an experiment station – for the President's post-war policies – his aim to develop and stabilize backward areas." Both statements are quoted in T. H. Vail Motter, *The Middle East Theatre: The Persian Corridor and Aid to Russia*

(US Army in World War Two Series, Washington DC, 1952), p. 445.

9 Ricks, "US Military Missions to Iran," in *US and Liberation*. A number of other specialists have analyzed the effects of US "tinkering" with Iranian society, economy and politics – see the Iranian specialists, Bill, *Eagle* and Cottam, *Iran*, or the international relations specialist, Halliday, *Iran*, Barry Rubin, *Paved With Good Intentions* (Oxford University Press, New York, 1980) and Sick, *All Fall Down*.

10 See Habib Ladjevardi, "The Origins of US Support for an Autocratic Iran," *International Journal of Middle East Studies*, vol. 15, no. 2 (May 1983), pp. 225–39 who argues that October 1946 was a turning point in US–Iran relations whereas Mark J. Gasiorowski, "The 1953 *Coup d'Etat* in Iran," *International Journal of Middle East Studies*, vol. 19, no. 3 (August 1987), pp. 261–86 argues that it was not until 1951 that "US involvement in Iran had increased considerably" (p. 267).

11 See Benson Lee Grayson, *United States–Iranian Relations*, (University Press of America, Washington DC, 1981), pp. 13–5.

12 The murder of the American Presbyterian missionary, Rev. Benjamin W. Labaree near the West Azerbaijan town of Salmas north of Urmieh on March 9, 1904, underscored the vulnerability of American citizens to vengeful attacks and the need for the State Department to be closer to that large community of Americans and the troubled border region of Western Iran. The Labaree case was finally resolved in 1908. See United States, National Archives and Records Administration (hereafter US, NARA) Department of State, "Telegram from Pearson to Hay, Tehran March 13, 1904," *Papers Relating to the Foreign Relations of the United States* (Washington, DC, 1904), p. 657.

13 US, NARA, Department of State, *Numerical and Minor Files, 1906–10*, Microcopy 862, Roll 482, Case No. 5931/13, William F. Doty to the Assistant Secretary of State/Tabriz, June 13, 1907 (received July 5, 1907).

14 The following account is based on research carried out at the Presbyterian Historical Society (Philadelphia, PA), at the National Archives (Washington, DC) and at Princeton University's Seeley Mudd Library, Alumni Archives (Princeton, NJ).

15 See Ismail Amir-Khizi, *Qiyam-e Azarbayjan va Sattar Khan [The Azarbayjan Uprising and Sattar Khan]*, (Tabriz, 1960), and Edward G. Browne, *The Persian Revolution* (Cambridge University Press, Cambridge, 1912).

16 Presbyterian Historical Society (hereafter PHS), *Persia Letters: West Persia Missions, 1909*, vol. 204, Howard C. Baskerville to Rev. Samuel Wilson/Tabriz, March 30 and April 1, 1909.

17 US, NARA, Department of State, *Numerical and Minor Files*, Microcopy 862, Roll 483, Case No. 5931/377, Resident Jackson to Assistant Secretary of State/Tehran, April 3, 1909.

18 *Ibid.*, Case No. 5931/379, Robert Speer to Assistant Secretary of

State, New York, April 7, 1909 and H. Wilson to Robert Speer, Washington DC, April 9, 1909.

19 PHS, *West Persia Mission*, vol. 204, no. 69, Rev. John N. Wright to Robert Speer, Tabriz to New York, April 22, 1909.

20 Princeton University, Seely Mudd Library and Alumni Archives on the "Baskerville File" of 1958-9 correspondence between Princeton's public relations office, the Near Eastern Studies Department and the US Consul Harold G. Josif/Tabriz regarding the April 20, 1959, ceremonies. See S. R. Shafagh, *Howard Baskerville: The Story of An American Who Died in the Cause of Iranian Freedom and Independence*, (n.p., n.d.), 27 pp.

21 The first "awakening" is traditionally the period from 1890 to 1907 when Iranian merchants, clergy and intelligentsia began organized opposition to the monarchy and foreign interventions. The period began with the national boycott of tobacco in 1890-2 and ended with the 1907 Anglo-Russian Treaty; the latter partitioned Iran between Russian northern "sphere of influence" and the British southeastern "sphere of influence." British participation in the division of Iran was acutely felt by merchants, clergy and intelligentsia who counted heavily on Britain's support to counterbalance Russian hegemony over Iran. The second "awakening" occurred with US intervention against Mossadeq and support for the Shah.

22 See United States, Department of State, *Foreign Relations of the United States, 1951, Vol. V: The Near East and Africa*, (Government Printing Office, Washington DC, 1982) for information on US petroleum policy in the Near and Middle East, pp. 1-342.

23 See Gasiorowski, "1953 *Coup d'Etat'*, p. 276 on Ambassador Henderson's opposition to a coup.

24 See Robert G. Hemerl, "U.S. Policy, the Nationalization of Iranian Oil and the Overthrow of the Mossadegh Government," unpublished MS, (American University, 1982), pp. 144-50. The present author conducted a series of interviews in Washington DC with the former CIA agent Howard "Rocky" Stone in the Fall of 1981 and the Spring of 1982 concerning the "heated arguments" and the subsequent events following the coup. Also see Jonathan Kwitny, *Endless Enemies: the Making of an Unfriendly World* (Congdon & Weed, New York, 1984) pp. 174-7 for Stone's comments on the coup.

25 In May 1951, the Assistant Secretary for Near Eastern, South Asian and African Affairs, George C. McGhee, testified before an executive session of the House Committee on Foreign Affairs that Iran in 1951 "may turn more and more to, not association with Russia . . . but a type of neutralism which means we cannot count on Iran as a cog in the system of collective security that we are attempting to build." United States, House of Representatives, Committee on Foreign Affairs, *The Middle East, Africa and Inter-American Affairs*, Selected Executive hearings of the Committee,

1951–6, vol. 16 (Government Printing Office, Washington DC, 1980), p. 53.

26 See Cottam, *Iran*, pp. 261–3 where he states that the "case can be made therefore that the decision to overturn Mussaddiq was a truly historic one" and that "US policy did change Iran's history and in fundamental ways."

27 See L. P. Elwell-Sutton, *Persian Oil: A Study in Power Politics* (Laurence & Wishart, London, 1965) for an excellent brief history of US interests in the Iranian oilfields from the 1920s to the 1950s.

28 Huyser, *Mission*, p. 225.

29 See Mark Hulbert, *Interlock: the Untold Story of American Banks, Oil Interests, the Shah, Money, Debts and the Astounding Connections Between Them* (Richarson & Snyder, New York, 1982) for information on the banking world's concerns with Iran, the Shah and the Iranian Revolution, particularly the concerns of David Rockefeller and Chase Manhattan. See also William Shawcross's *The Shah's Last Ride: the Fate of an Ally* (Simon & Schuster, New York, 1988), pp. 151 and 240 on the role of Richard Nixon, David Rockefeller and Henry Kissinger in persuading the White House to their position.

30 Huyser, *Mission*, pp. 88, 133 and 287. See Sepehr Zabih, *The Military and the Iranian Revolution* (Routledge & Kegan Paul, 1988) for the Iranian generals' views of the Huyser Mission.

31 In the midst of the February 11, 1979 collapse of Shahpour Bakhtiyar's shadow government, Zbigniew Brzezinski, National Security Adviser to President Carter, Charles Duncan, Undersecretary for Defense, and General David Jones, Chairman, Joint Chiefs of Staff spoke to General Huyser about the possibilities of staging a military coup against the Khomeini–Bazargan coalition. Huyser replied that he would do so only if he could have unlimited funds, 10,000 of the best US troops, ten to twelve handpicked US generals and undivided national support. The idea was dropped. See Huyser, *Mission*, p. 283.

32 Personal interview with John Graves, US Information Agency Director for Iran, 1979–82 and the highest ranking US official among the fifty-three hostages held at the embassy. The interviews were conducted between 1982 and 1983 in Reston, Virginia.

33 For reasons other than Khomeini's attacks, Mehdi Bazargan, Ibrahim Yazdi and Iran's Ambassador to Sweden, Amir-Entezam, held a number of meetings with CIA agents between August and October, 1979. The meetings were "documented" later by the students who took the US embassy. Bill, *Iran*, pp. 290–2.

34 On September 24, 1979, US embassy telegram from Bruce Laingen, US chargé-d'affaires, to Secretary of State Vance/Tehran to Washington DC in which Laingen argued that the US must not contemplate allowing the Shah to enter the United States at "this time," but rather some time in the Spring of 1980 due to the possibilities of a hostage-taking attempt. Laingen's argument rested on his observations of the local committees and the failure of the PGOI to control the streets. Laingen advised Washington

that "humanitarian reasons" be cited as the justification for any admittance of the Shah to the US. For further information on Laingen's correspondence with Washington regarding the possibilities of hostage-taking, see Hulbert, *Interlock*, pp. 141–3.

35 Personal interview with Mehdi Bazargan and Ibrahim Yazdi on January 5, 1980, in Tehran, Iran.

36 ABC apparently had been waiting several months to find "the right event" to focus on in order to launch the *Nightline* program. The Tehran hostage-taking was a perfect fit, according to a top ABC news commentator. Personal interview in Washington DC, April 1980.

37 Personal interviews with a number of the families in the Washington DC area, particularly with the Graves family between January and December, 1980.

38 Suroosh Irfani, *Revolutionary Islam in Iran: Popular Liberation or Religious Dictatorship* (Zed Press, London, 1983), pp. 222–3.

INDEX

262